THE SUMMIT AND BEYOND

FIRST ROADHOUSE ON STEWART ISLAND, 1900

PLATE I

THE SUMMIT
AND BEYOND

By

MARGARET CLARK SHAND
and
ORA M. SHAND

ILLUSTRATED WITH PHOTOGRAPHS

THE CAXTON PRINTERS, LTD.
CALDWELL, IDAHO
1959

Printed, lithographed, and bound in the United States of America by
The CAXTON PRINTERS, Ltd.
Caldwell, Idaho
88768

When Ora Shand asked me to write the dedication for this book, I immediately thought of my deep feeling of love for "Auntie" Shand, as she was known in San Diego. I listened almost daily to "The Little Mother of the North" tell of her many experiences during her thirty-eight years in the Yukon. We laughed, we cried over many a cup of tea. I consider it one of the high lights of my life and a great honor to have known Peggy Shand intimately.

This book brings back to life the most vivid and strong character I have ever met!

PEGGY WHYTE

The Lure of the Yukon

Oh, it's calling, calling, calling,
To the very heart o' me,
Crying, whispering, pleading:
"Come back where you used to be,
To the land of great, far spaces,
Where the Northern Lights still play
Across the sky in winter;
Where the air is sweet all day.
The stars are close about you
In the velvet of the sky;
Here the Great White Stillness
To your soul comes whisp'ring nigh.
Oh, the Peace of that great Silence
Steals all the pain away,
Leaves contentment and gladness
At the end of a weary day.
Its peace is God's own message
To the heart that is sad with care;
In that vast and wonderous Silence
Is the lure of the Yukon fair."
Oh, it's calling, calling, calling,
To the very heart of me,
Crying, whispering, pleading:
"Come back where you used to be."

O. M. S.

Introduction

How many times I have heard her say, "I wish I could live my life all over again, every day of it . . . the joys and the sorrows, all of it. I have loved my life. I'd live it all over if I could."

"Even the hardships in the North?" I would ask.

"I never had any hardships in the North," she would answer, in a very positive manner, and she would repeat, "I never had any hardships in all my life."

The woman whose story is revealed in this book actually believed this: Life was to be lived to the fullest each day, just as it came along, and she always found more than enough to compensate for the experiences which others would most certainly have felt were unendurable hardships.

This astonishing little woman was nearing the close of a long and exciting life when she philosophized in this way—she was never to become old in heart. She had given me, through the years, what I considered the material for a life story of inspirational value and genuine human interest—a story of true and enduring love and one which I believe to have real historical merit as well, since it is both broad in scope and authentic, and has captured the real feeling of the North.

Her life has been lived—the most dramatic and fruitful part of it—way up in the North, in that part of the world which had been made famous by gold, the Klondike district of Yukon Territory, northwest Canada, and even though the time is half a century and more ago, she gives to her narrative the freshness of yesterday.

Her name was Margaret Clark Shand, a good Scotch name, and she has been known for years by word of mouth by everyone who has lived in, or traveled through, the Klondike region. Her career there began in 1897 when the gold rush was just getting under way and she and her husband Davy packed in over the Chilkoot Pass in search of their fortune.

Women were not, in any case, too frequently seen on the trail in those days, and the "Peggy" Shand of that era astonished everyone she met with her courage, her endurance, her resourcefulness, her spirit, her kind heart, and—to crown it all—her genuine flair for living and for doing.

She *never* had a hardship — or so she said — but nevertheless she ran the gamut of all human experience in that cold, wild, distant land, and after proving her mettle she remained for more than thirty years to become one of its successes, and eventually one of its legends. In her later years she became known as the "Little Mother of the North."

Life had taken her a long, long way from the quiet little rural home in Scotland where she was reared—and her book would not be complete without telling the whole story.

My purpose in this introduction is to recount how Peggy Shand's story of her life came to be written, and how it happened to be my privilege to write it.

She was well along in life when the writing began,

and she had to recreate her long career for us anew, year by year—and what an experience it was for me when I began to see and to feel the pulsing reality of that strong and courageous young woman as she first went up into the Yukon, and then to follow her as she moved on step by step to the more solid ground on which she finally stood. It was an experience to go with her through her triumphs and her sorrows, and, eventually, to share in her final conquest over the ravages of time and tide. My great concern was to have all this come through in the story just as realistically and vividly as it had been in life, undimmed by the years. Fortunately I was not limited to her recollections alone, for I had support from others who had known her and lived through those days with her.

The Peggy Shand of the gold-rush period would have been a challenging character to any writer. She did not fit into any ready pattern, certainly not the familiar one for popular gold-rush stories. She was never at any time a beauty. In fact she might have been called rather plain. Small and brunette, she wore her brown hair drawn into a large knot at the back of her head. She generally had a characteristic Scotch reserve among people she did not know, but she also had a very spirited and witty side. Her attraction came from something within rather than from anything on the surface.

Once, in discussing Peggy with their mother, her brother Jack summed it up, after taking her to her first ball, by saying, "Mother, our Peggy was a credit to us on the ballroom floor. Though she is small, she had many partners. Some of the most respected men soon filled her dance program. She was always dancing while girls with greater beauty were wallflowers. I don't understand it, unless it is her smiling face and happy laugh."

She was always simple and direct in speech and manner, never losing the strong Scotch accent. At times she was deeply philosophical. With an equally characteristic Scotch thrift, she was also exceedingly generous.

When it came to her rugged life on the trail, not every man would have had her nerve and her verve —the North seemed to challenge her as nothing else had ever done. And not every woman would have felt the compassion she had for the sick, the poor, and the beaten whom she was forever to encounter throughout her life there.

Peggy Shand always had an unbounded confidence in herself and in life; she knew no fear and had a will and a determination of steel. Fear was simply a call to action, and once, when confronted by a band of hostile Indians, she boldly stepped out before them and gave them—the Highland fling. For that performance they wanted to take her into the tribe, and they christened her "Little White Bird."

This paradoxical little Peggy was the one I had come to know so well as I began the book. . . .

But now to go back and tell how it happened. My husband Graham Shand was her husband's nephew, and Uncle Davy had been his favorite uncle. We then lived in Southern California, and they had been in the North for many years before we were able to locate them. Graham's father had died and family ties seem to have been broken. At last the information came from relatives in Scotland that Uncle Davy and Aunt Peggy were living on Stewart Island in the Yukon, operating a widely known roadhouse, or hotel. Graham wrote at once, but it was months before a letter came from Peggy telling of Uncle Davy's death a few years previous, of her loneliness without him, and of her indecision about the future.

The correspondence continued, but with long waits between letters. This was in the spring of 1929, and even at that date the airplane had not yet speeded up the mails as it has since.

I have before me one of Peggy's time-yellowed letters, and she writes:

> Well, the mail got in last night. . . . I was up this morning, we had breakfast at four-thirty A.M. The mail man has to get away on the river as long as the ice is hard, this is the last mail over the ice. . . . I may not get a chance to mail a letter again till the end of May.

She was writing on April 16.

For years they had run the roadhouse which they had built and rebuilt at the confluence of the Yukon and Stewart rivers, a point of great activity during the gold-rush years, and during those busy, exciting times they had been very happy. The boats on the river stopped and people were constantly coming and going; dog sleds arrived in winter with men from the trails. They were full of wild tales of gold and often laden with the real stuff itself.

Davy had been snow-blinded for a time, and he was ill in the later years, but together they had built and maintained this interesting little hostelry. But now fewer and fewer people came this way, except in summer as the new trickle of tourists began. The mighty Yukon, during the breakup each spring, cut away more and more of the bank where the hotel stood, and it was only a matter of time before Peggy's home and business would go into the river. Already the building had once been destroyed by fire and twice washed away by floods.

Gradually we learned more and more about Peggy's career in the North. We knew that whatever came and wherever she went in the Yukon, she would be loved and protected, but this did not satisfy us. She would insist in each letter, "Dear folks, don't worry about me, I'll be all right."

We had a large home and there was a guest cottage which opened out into a pleasant garden. This seemed just the right place for her. I had recently lost my own mother and I wanted her to come and live with us, and at my suggestion my husband went to Skagway to meet her. She arrived in San Diego on June 12, 1929, and lived with us for fourteen years.

It was not long before all our friends and neighbors loved her and called her "Auntie." I shall continue to speak of her as Peggy in this introduction since the story itself does not deal with her San Diego years.

She was "Auntie" to us, but as the people in any gathering would seek her out and surround her, we realized that she would always be the same Peggy within—nothing had changed and she remained what she always was, except that time had moved on. She would still be the center of attraction.

As we saw her there in our home, when she was

already a woman going into her eighties, we realized
that she had an unusual magnetism stemming from
nothing that she did or no effort that she put forth,
but from some quite spontaneous inner source. Even
as a young girl Peggy was always welcome in any
group because she had a way of taking things in hand
and making a good time out of it. She still had this
quality when she came to us—except that her long
experience with people and situations had given her
a firmer touch, which made some of our friends feel
that she resembled Queen Victoria in certain ways.
"Strong and queenly, but plain," as one friend put it.

The same friend said, "The charm of Peggy vibrated even through her still beautiful hands. They
were magnetic, their touch so full of feeling and
comfort. They expressed her soul. They were generous hands, well-covered, firm and solid, hands of
a much younger person; the fingers, in spite of years
of hard work, had remained long and tapering, an
indication of sensitivity and refinement.

"She would pat your arm and say, 'Everything will
be all right, lass,' and you knew by her touch that
she understood your problem. You could never forget that touch and the feeling of comfort it gave."

And yet there was more. There was a certain
lighthearted, pixie sort of quality, which we saw
from time to time, and which always reminded us
of the stories we had heard of her youth.

At first she would sometimes have rather a dour,
Scotch face, but as she spoke her face would light
up into the most beautiful smile. She had a wonderful way of telling a story, and a remarkable memory
for things that went back even to childhood. From

the first I was fascinated with her tales of the Yukon, and she enjoyed repeating them. After a time I began writing them down as she told them. When her dear friend, Belle Brennon, who had been with her in the North and was also now living in California, would come on one of her long, pleasant visits, we all had happy times and more storytelling. Then I would read them what I had written and they would interrupt to explain more clearly or to fill in what I had left out. After a while I had established the continuity of the story and had gone through her entire life. I had what I wanted, a book, and I decided to let Peggy tell it herself in the first person, just as she had told it to me. When it was finished, Peggy and Belle were pleased with it.

One day Peggy said to Belle in my absence, "There is something strange about her, that niece of mine. . . . She seems to know things without my telling her."

To me she said, "Every word of it is true, lass, every word, but how did you always know so well how I felt? It is just as if you were right there beside me. Yes, it is all true! I could not have done better if I had written it down myself. But I don't see how you always knew so well."

She did not realize how often she had told me.

While I was working on the book, my husband had said, "If you intend to write of Aunt Peggy's life in the Yukon to her relatives in Scotland, you had better go up there and see the country you are writing about and meet her old friends."

Meanwhile, I had engaged in extensive study to insure the accuracy of the details, geographic and otherwise, and sent to Canada for maps and information of all sorts. I corresponded with many who had known Peggy, and had detailed letters from Mr. and Mrs. George Black, both of whom had served as members of Parliament for the Yukon. Mrs. Black, writing from the House of Commons at Ottawa, said in part:

All Yukoners knew and respected and loved Mrs. Shand. . . . We old-timers have missed her greatly. The last time I remember her was one glorious fall day when her husband was sitting outside confined to his chair and she was taking care of her guests with such consideration, and giving her husband kind care, that I shall never forget it . . . she was truly a remarkable woman and many people would like to hear her story of the gold-rush era.

Mrs. Black herself had gone over the Chilkoot Pass in those early days. She knew what Peggy's life had been like.

I later went to the Yukon as my husband had suggested, going by steamer to Skagway and then by rail over the White Pass to the headwaters of the Yukon at Whitehorse. There I began the journey toward Stewart Island and Dawson on the *Casca*. When Captain McKay saw my name on the passenger list he immediately looked me up and told me how happy it made him to hear firsthand news of his old friend, Mrs. Shand, and of her comfortable life in California. He took a special interest in showing me the outstanding points along the mighty river and repeated many of the gold-rush tales that Peggy had told us.

When we reached Dawson word went around that Mrs. Shand's niece was in town, and I was besieged

by her old friends, all eager to know about her. The
old miners gathered about me in numbers, asking
how she liked California and if she was happy away
from the Yukon. Every one of these men had some
kind act of hers to relate which had been very important to him, or some incident revealing her courage and bravery during the early days. There was
always a great love and respect for this little woman
and an appreciation of her kindness and helpful
understanding. They spoke of her as the "Little
Mother of the North." They told me how they
would come into her kitchen to find comfort and
drive away despair. The lonely men would return
from working their gold claims and sit on her wood
box and watch her cook. They called her "Mother"
to themselves and sometimes to each other. But the
gay little Peggy did not think of herself as a mother
to anyone. She lived her life impersonally, leaving
herself out of it and living only to express life as
she found it. A gay laugh was her medicine. The
laugh cut away the gloom that surrounded the lonely
soul that longed for home, for friends, for loved ones.
She would send the men away all new, feeling the
grandeur of the mountains, the peace of the sleeping
river, the healing power of the Great White Stillness.
She lifted from many hearts the ache of loneliness
and discouragement, and helped them to know peace.
It was not what she said, not anything she did, but
just the great understanding within her heart which
radiated as a warmth, something lonely men could
feel and come away refreshed.

Many a sick person had felt the healing power of
her gentle hands. She gave of herself freely after

long hours of work—cooking, working in the garden or, in winter, tending fires, or any labor that came to her. She was never too busy to care for anyone in need of her help.

It was the same with the dance-hall girls who came to her in loneliness and illness—she was always ready to help drive away gloom, always prepared to say a kind word. Now, as the men crowded about me, each wanted to tell of some great kindness of the "Little Mother of the North."

On our return trip Captain McKay stopped the *Casca* at Stewart Island and took me ashore to the little burying ground under the tall pine trees. I was pleased to see the nice fence that Captain McKay and another captain on the river had put around Uncle Davy's grave as a surprise to Peggy—she had told me about it and it had pleased her to have them show her Davy such respect.

I was taken through the hotel on Stewart Island —by now it was perilously near the bank of the river—and I went out into Uncle Davy's garden. Captain McKay and I tramped all over the island together, and I could now understand more fully what this home had meant to Peggy through those exciting years. She had been active and happy, but now it had all changed, and I was glad she was safe and comfortable with us in warm and friendly San Diego, in the "Garden of the Singing Wind" which was now her home.

I came back filled with enthusiasm for the wonderful country I had seen and pleased with the friends I had met. Peggy was interested in it all, but she remarked:

"You did not see the real country at its best. No one has any idea of its grandeur until he becomes a sourdough. He must 'go in with the ducks' and stay from the freeze-up to the breakup, spend the winter in a cabin on the river alone and be a part of it to realize the soul of the *Great White Silence*."

I could see that it was hers for always, and this was her peace.

At various times members of three different families came all the way from the North to California to see how the Little Mother was keeping (as the Scotch say), and it was very revealing of the love and interest that never ceased. They came, each one separately, to look us over and see what kind of home we had given her. The first were Dr. and Mrs. Nunn. Mrs. Nunn was the daughter of Mrs. Wilson, who had lived in Dawson and had been one of Peggy's best friends.

The second visitors were Mr. and Mrs. McDonald. Mr. McDonald was the brother of Jack McDonald, who had been a close friend to Peggy and Davy ever since they had arrived in the Yukon. He was younger than she, had never married, and it was not until a year after Davy's death that he had written to Peggy that she was the only woman he had ever loved. He asked her to marry him, but he had died of pneumonia before he could come for her answer.

We were all in the living room and Peggy was telling how much she would always love the Yukon. Mr. McDonald said, "Now I must tell you why we came all this way to see you. Before Jack died he told us he had built a nice home on his farm for you and hoped you would come and share it with him. Everything was planned for your comfort.

"We have come to offer you this home. Jack would want it this way. There is a beautiful farm and a fine home and they are yours as long as you live. Will you come back with us?"

He held out his hands to her. Peggy turned pale, her hands trembled, and after a long time, it seemed, she rose and went to him. My husband and I did not know what would happen. With great dignity but in a shaking voice, she said:

"You are very kind to offer me Jack's home and I do appreciate it, but I canna' go. I do thank you, but I will stay here with my nephew Grahamie and his wife. They are kind to me and I am happy here. This is my home."

Graham and I gave a sigh of relief and tears came to my eyes. We were glad she was contented with us.

The third one who came to see if all was well with his dear friend was Johnnie Lawrence, the young man Peggy had helped raise as a wee lad. He, too, came with love in his heart. If she would ever need a home and protection, Johnnie was there to give it.

In 1950, before putting the final touches on the book, my husband and I went to Scotland and met members of her family and saw where Peggy had spent her childhood and her early years. Everything was just as she had described it, still, and I want the book to go back there to her friends and relatives to tell them how she had lived in the Yukon. I inscribe it with deep love and affection from her niece.

ORA M. SHAND

San Diego, October, 1957.

Table of Contents

List of Illustrations

THE SUMMIT AND BEYOND

My Home in Scotland

I MUST BEGIN to tell this story just as it started in our native Scotland all those many years ago.

My mind goes back to the old mill, my father's mill, and the big wheel spilling, always spilling the water endlessly from our beautiful Arnprior Glen, with the five dams that held it back and let it come gurgling over the mossy stones. It had all been there, just as it was, for ages. The green moss at the mill had not been disturbed for generations, clinging to the ancient stones and hanging like a green blanket over the spillway and coloring the water a smoky brown, like the tea that Mother poured into Father's cup.

It was like a world apart, and it was a heavenly world for children. No one told us this, but somehow we knew it. We lived in a comfortable old stone house near the mill, and it was surrounded by hawthorn hedges, all twined with sweet-smelling roses. I will never forget their sweetness in the long twilight hours, when Father would come home from the mill and sit on the wall by the door of the house, resting, and we would climb on his knees and put our arms around his neck. Father was kind and affectionate, more so, we thought, than other fathers we knew. And while he lived and worked in this world of the mill and the dams and the great wheel, he saw far beyond it.

Father and I were very close. Sometimes at night,

when everyone else was quietly inside the house, he would lift me to the wall and show me the stars. At first, for some reason, I was afraid to look—they were too far away and too big. Father would put his warm and protecting arm around me, then, and would say, "Never be afraid of anything, lassie. Look everything in the face. The stars are your guide, lassie; you can never lose the stars—they are like God, always with you."

I can remember so well how he told me this, told it to me again and again, and as the years passed I came to know what he meant, to look things in the face.

I, Margaret Clark, was born at Paisley, just outside Glasgow, but in the time I am telling about we lived at Arnprior, a little to the north, where we had moved when I was about eight. I was born in 1851, and it was then about 1860 when these memories begin.

There were Father and Mother, and my brother Jack, and then, too, Davy was often with us. Hardly a summer passed that Davy did not spend most of the time in our home. He was our cousin, and it was a rare time when he came. Jack was quieter and more like Father, but Davy, even as a boy, was always strong and handsome and full of adventure. We had such happy times. We would race over the moor through the heather, fish in the bourne, and guddle the fish in our hands between the stones.

All the time we were also having a wonderful story-book kind of life. Davy was telling us the enchanting tales he had read about faraway lands. He talked unceasingly of travels and castles and a fortune to be made — or found — in some faraway place. But

wild as the dreams might have been, we could scarcely have wished for all the adventure and the fulfillment that life would bring us.

I can see this now because, on looking back, I believe that life moves us on, somehow, along the lines
of our thoughts. We do not always at first see the
shape and the substance, the nature of the places
and the things, but we know the direction in which
we wish to go, even sometimes when we are very,
very young. I think this is one of the advantages
of remembering, and I think that in childhood my
fate must have been pretty well determined, and
that is why I feel I should tell something about it
as it was then and as it was to continue to be. *I* was
always the same; it was only things that changed.

Davy would say he was going to be a sailor and
sail the Seven Seas and see all the world. Sometimes
he would promise to take me with him; then again
he would get cross and tell me I could not go. This
would make me very unhappy, but always before he
left for his own home he would say, "Dinna mind,
lass, I'll take you with me and we will see the whole
wide world together."

On the wall of our home there was a big picture
map showing the people and animals native to the
different countries. Brother Jack and Davy and I
would look and look at it, and I would ask over and
over again about the Eskimos who drove dog teams
and lived in igloos. I remember how I used to say
to them, quite seriously, "Some day I am going to
North America and have a dog team."

Still, I was only a girl and the youngest of the
three, but I could always run faster than the boys—

and get into more mischief. I was a real trial to Mother as I was hardly ever still—not even on Sundays. I can remember well how we would all start off to walk to the kirk on the Sabbath, Father carrying his prayer book and Mother with her lovely Paisley shawl. Jack was so quiet and obedient, but Mother would frequently call to me, "Margaret, it is unbecoming for a lass to be so gay on the Sabbath. Come to me; walk by my side."

Father would smile and rush to my aid. "Ah, Maggie," he would say, "let the lass skip. Her heart it light and that can do no harm on the Sabbath, or any other day."

The humdrum things of life were always, even at that time, a genuine hardship. I wanted things to happen. To sit beside Mother and knit, which was the custom in Scotch homes of that day, each little girl knitting her own woolen stockings, was torture. I used to plead with Mother just to let me go out and sit on the wall and knit. There I could get closer to the world, and when the gypsies came, I could see them. They used to come and camp back of our home at certain times of the year, and in the evenings Father and Mother would take us to see them in their camp.

I loved the excitement and color, the fires where they cooked their food in the big pots, the gay young folk dancing and singing, and the children moving all around.

The old women told fortunes and would come to our house to beg for food. One day, when one of them told Mother's fortune, I begged her to tell mine, too, and put out my little hand. She looked at me a long, long time and said to me, "You will travel far and see strange lands."

Nothing could have excited me more, to know that she understood. But life was not all gypsies and gaiety and color. Summer was full of flowers and fragrance and beauty, and long days exploring the pools and the dams, with the beautiful primroses—yellow primroses that always came in the spring—all around by the water's edge. I can remember the bleakness of the winter out on the moors, the wind and the sleet and the storm, and no life except a few Highland cattle standing about. Often I had to go out into the cold, black night to turn off the water for Father, and I would run back into the house and be so grateful for its warmth and light. There were so many things, so many more things it seems, to make children afraid in those times. People still had the most incredible superstitions. We had real witches and there were many strange characters about, so naturally children were afraid. One in particular was Jimmie Stewart, the hunchback who, it was always said, had slept out in the field in a full moon and by morning was all drawn into queer shapes. Jimmie would sometimes clutch at little girls with his long claws of hands and scare them almost to death.

Some of these people were just poor beggars who would come to the house for food, but others we had a proper right to avoid. One cold winter day when we were alone, the door burst suddenly open and in staggered a shepherd who was obviously quite drunk. Mother ordered him out but he would not leave, so she took his sleeve and pulled him toward the door. He raised his heavy crook and brought it down on her hand with such force that it bent her wedding ring so badly that it had to be cut off her finger.

I watched Mother with great excitement. Even though she was hurt, she snatched the crook from the drunken man, pushed him out the door, and threw his crook after him. I peeped out and saw it bounce off his shoulder. I have always remembered Mother as a brave and fearless woman, and my home was a school that I shall never forget. It was at times a stern school, and yet it was always full of love and kindness—even for strangers and beggars.

In our kitchen there was a straw tick that could be drawn up before the kitchen fireplace. Here many a lonely person slept through the cold night, and when a beggar would come and ask for food, Father would leave the table and carry a part of his meal to the stranger.

"Why do you do that?" Mother would ask. "There is plenty in the kitchen."

"I have no taste for food when another is hungry, Maggie," Father would reply.

When I would go with Father to feed the poor beggars, Mother would say, "Dear child, if the prayers of the beggars are of value, you will never want."

Mother and Father were quiet and reverent people and our home and our life expressed it. I could not describe Father or Mother too well in those days except by telling the things they did and the way they lived. They wanted us to be reverent and good, too, and often it was a source of unhappiness for Mother when I was so rebellious. I rebelled at anything that was solemn and strait-laced. Mother quite often had the minister come to call, and she would always make him tea and give him a scone with gooseberry jam. I remember how he would eat and smack his lips, and then he would invariably call for Jack and myself to say our catechisms. Jack could always get along well but I was always so intent on watching the solemn face of the minister that I couldn't keep my mind on what I was supposed to say. He would give a great, sad sigh and look at Mother as if she were to be pitied for having such a wayward child.

I remember that one time when the minister called I ran and hid under the bed. The minister said, "Where is small Peggy? I want to hear her say her psalm." Mother thought it would be good for the soul if the truth were to come out, and she answered without any hesitation, "Indeed, and she is under the bed hiding."

Growing up means many things. I remember how independent I became as I continued to grow. And how impatient. When I could not be out in the sunshine and doing the things that I loved, I would frequently say, "Oh, I wish something would happen. I am tired of each day just like the one before. I wish something would happen."

One day, when I was feeling especially bored and Mother was away from home, I went through all her pretty dresses, so carefully hung on their pegs and covered with a sheet. I found a beautiful purple merino with black bands sewed on the flounces, and began cutting it into pieces, then tried to sew it into a shape that would fit me. I worked the whole afternoon, but somehow it would not just come right. Mother arrived home and in her horror she asked me over and over, "Why, Peggy, what do you mean, to do such a wicked thing? You have ruined my nice dress. *Why* did you do it?"

"Well, I heard you say you were going to make a dress out of it for me when you were through with it, and so I just thought I would do it for myself."

Of course it had seemed like childish mischief, but it was more than that. I never doubted but that I could do it, and as I grew older I was always to be like this. I thought there was never anything I could not do.

Whenever I could, I would get out of the house and spend the time with the other children I knew. There were many times when I would stay away so long that Mother would be irked and say, "Margaret, you should go back and get your supper where you have been all day."

It was only after I began to be around other girls, however, that I found out many things about myself that I had not known so clearly. Maggie Bucanan, for instance, told me once that if I would keep my mouth pucked up, folks would not realize it was so large. I wasn't actually hurt. What I most wanted to do was to forget about myself and be happy, and to try to make other folks be happy.

I knew in my young little heart that we had too much morbidity to live with as it was. But that was Scotland, much bitter with the sweet. Funerals, it seemed to me, were always made up to be such great events, and for some reason people seemed to go to funerals mostly in the winter and often to catch their death of cold. Once having seen a funeral in our country, one could not forget it. Only men would attend, and rain or shine they would stand for long hours out in the open in their long black coats. The men got their black coats when they were to be married, and then they wore them practically all their lives, to one funeral after another. That is the way my father got his death, out on a lonely moor, with not a house in sight, and they had to stand in the rain and walk all the way, and take their hats off to anyone who passed. I was only twelve when the happy life at the mill thus came to its end. This was when our father died.

We eventually went to live in the city—Stirling, and then Glasgow— and in time a friend of Father's came for brother Jack and put him in his mill to learn the trade that Father had followed. I went for a time to Lady Erskine's School in Carcross, learning the things one needed to know in those days as one was becoming a young lady, but as opportunity would permit, Jack and Davy and I would often be together again. We three belonged to each other in a very special sort of way—although Jack stayed behind when Davy and I left in time to come. In spirit, though, we were together always, and always would be, and I never forgot Davy's childhood promise that one day we would go away together and see the world. In fact, he kept telling me this whenever he came all through the years. It was no longer a childhood promise any more. We were growing up and we knew that we were in love.

At first Davy wanted to be a surgeon, and his parents sent him to Edinburgh College so he could study medicine, but the blood of countless seafaring ancestors made the lure of the sea too strong. After two years he ran away and shipped before the mast in the merchant marine, sailing to India, Australia, South America, and other foreign places. He was becoming a world traveler, and I was jealous of his adventurous life. I wanted to travel as he did and see strange places—Chinese temples, India, and most of all South America, where Davy bought the beautiful opals he brought me. How I loved those opals—I used to spend hours looking into their ever-changing, fiery loveliness, dreaming of the time that I, too, could see the faraway places.

I had nothing to complain about, however, because, for a young girl of my time, I was especially fortunate. We had many dear relatives who would often ask me to come for a visit, and often it was declared to be "a gathering of the clans" and numbers of cousins would all get together at once. I am afraid that I hadn't changed very much as I grew older, and I think they knew that they could count on me to make a good time out of it, somehow. Otherwise I don't think they would have asked me so often.

One summer one of my favorite aunts took me on a trip through the lake country and the Trossachs. We traveled on a tallyho with a horn sounding gaily at the inns where we stopped, and we had a merry time. I also had a trip to beautiful, green Ireland, and somehow the years passed while Davy was still away.

I was a young lady, and Mother thought I should be busy. She decided to have me learn to make dresses and bonnets, and when we moved to Glasgow she found a French lady who would take me as an apprentice and I began to sew and stitch all day. It was something I loathed, but as spring came around again, Davy arrived home on leave and I saw the brighter side again.

We walked down the lane together, stone walls on each side, green grass under foot. The birds were singing in the hedges, the soft damp air was sweet with roses. It was the first time Davy had ever kissed me when we were alone.

"I'm going away again, Peg," he said, "but I'll be back—will you wait for me? Then we'll be married and go to America to live."

He took a tiny box out of his pocket, and in it was a ring set with three diamonds in a row. "This is to mind you of your promise, Peg," Davy said, as he kissed it and slipped it on my finger. As he did so, he looked at my hand and said, thoughtfully, "Peg, dear, you have beautiful hands. They are the hands of a lady and we will always keep them this way. I promise I will never let you do hard work and spoil them."

It was a common occurrence in Scotland for cousins to marry and, in fact, I had never thought seriously of anyone else. Davy was a handsome young man, and all the lassies were smitten with him. He was more sophisticated than the young men they knew, because he had traveled so far and seen so many other ways of life, and his manners impressed them all. He devoted himself to me all the while he was home, and after he left I wore his ring on a little chain about my neck, instead of where he had put it. I kept the opals safely hidden away in their little box. No one else except brother Jack knew about either the ring or the opals, for it was unseemly for girls in those days to speak openly of their lovers— much as it might have tempted one to tell them about Davy.

After he had gone, I felt more assurance and independence. I had to do something to change the monotony of my life. A friend of our family managed a government store where they carried goods from all over the world. He needed someone to help him in the office and I felt this was my chance, but Mother thought differently. In those days it was unseemly for a young lady to work in an office like a man, but with my persistence I won out, and at last I came into contact with the foreign lands about which I had dreamed so much.

Davy's letters continued to come, from one distant place after another. It troubled me at times that he stayed away so long and had no plans for settling down, but in those days things did not always move as fast as they do now. One learned to wait.

There was a banker, among others, who wished to pay me some attention, and one day he asked me to come to his bank and see some of the fabulous crown jewels being held by the bank as security. When I was there he placed a beautiful necklace about my throat and a tiara on my head, and said, "Now, look in the mirror and see how nice you look with a queen's jewels. If you were my wife, you could have jewels as fine as this, and everything your heart desired."

It was no temptation.

Davy was in India for a few years, then he went

to Panama and to South America, where he was out of the merchant marine and working on an engineering project, taking a deep interest in engineering and studying as much as he could. Finally, he wrote from the United States, where his brother John had an importing business. Davy and John went into partnership, something they had long talked about. John had his office in New York while Davy worked the Central States and the Pacific Coast States. They imported silks and fine laces, china, crockery, draperies, and fine carpets and rugs.

At last Davy felt he could settle down and support a wife. His brother John was going to Scotland on business and Davy wanted me to return to the United States with him. I discussed the matter thoroughly with brother Jack, as I always did, and he agreed that it was right for me to go. Mother, from whom I had been inseparable all these years, accepted the decision and began to help prepare the wedding chest. Once the announcement was made, gifts arrived in profusion from relatives and friends, but the greatest surprise of all came from Jack.

He now had a better position. He had finished his apprenticeship and had been given a good place in the office of a large flour mill in Glasgow and there he was to remain for the rest of his life.

On my last day at home, Jack came back for his midday meal as usual and I walked with him almost back to his office. Not a word was spoken about my going, but in a quiet street he took me in his arms and kissed me, and put something into my hand. It was his bankbook, and he said quite simply, "It is all yours, Peg. Take it." He kissed me again, and we parted. No word of good-by passed between us.

It was June, 1889, when John Shand, Davy's brother and I left for the United States. Davy met us in Chicago and we were married on July 5.

John's daughter, Maggie, was my bridesmaid, and there was a small son, Graham, who was quite a joy to me during those long hours while I was waiting for Davy to arrive. Grahamie, as we called him, had quite a part in my life in time to come.

I Come to America

CALIFORNIA was to be our home for the next few years. After attending to his business in the Middle Western States, Davy took me to San Francisco, where he was going to make his headquarters in the future. I was very proud of my husband and entered into this new life with a feeling that at long last things had come out as they should.

We were living in a city which, even then, was one of the most exciting in the whole world. It was an invigorating and absorbing experience. The crisp, cold air made me feel strong and energetic, and even the fog, drifting in at night like a soft gray cloud, was welcome—it all felt just like Scotland at certain times of the year. The activity of the city was exciting and we enjoyed ourselves thoroughly.

Davy, too, was in his element. To be near the sea meant everything to him, and whenever we went out he would find some reason for going down to the water front, where we could watch the vessels sailing in and out through the Golden Gate.

Although we were both short of stature compared to most folk—our new American friends often called us the "wee Scotch couple"—Davy seemed taller than he actually was because of his dignified manner and his early military training. He had a way with him. When he talked, people listened. His distinguished appearance, with his Van Dyke beard and capable-looking hands, often led people to think he might be a doctor—as indeed he might have been. He was very versatile in his interests and abilities and could talk on any subject.

Davy, as I have said, made me very proud. He was *very* successful in the business he had taken up, and he made friends wherever he went. He was also away from home and out on the road a great deal, and would generally leave me alone in the hotel where we were living. At times a great homesickness came upon me, and I spent most of my time writing letters to Mother, brother Jack, my relatives and friends. I must confess that I had not left Scotland and my family without some heartache. I remember my last morning in Glasgow so well. I awoke in the old familiar room, in the big canopied bed in which I had slept most of my life, and I looked about at all the things I knew so well—the high chest of drawers, the low ladder-back chair with its patchwork cushion, the sampler on the wall that I had made when I was seven. This was home, and one half of me wanted to stay while the other half wanted to go. Aren't we all like that, at times? Is anyone strong and courageous and confident all of the time, I wonder? I had been such an independent, impetuous, carefree person all of my life, and yet, as I lay there in my room, I had a strong sense of premonition, and a vague fear that I could not throw off. Would I be equal to it?

I remembered then what my father had always told me, to look things in the face and not be afraid, and I felt, as I commenced to get ready that morning, that God would lead the way, whatever came, and it brought me courage and comfort.

Yet, again and again, the same feeling of apprehension returned, especially after we reached San Francisco and the excitement of our new life had subsided a bit. I thought at first that it was because I was alone so much. One day, I said to myself, "This will not do; I *must* be happy." I began taking long walks, going up one street and then another until I knew my way and felt sure of myself. I have always been explorative by temperament, and I have always wanted to know what was at the end of a street, a river, or a road. Long years later, a friend once said, "Peggy never sees a river without wanting to trace it to its source."

This tendency led me, in San Francisco, to many interesting places. I loved to go into churches and just sit there, quietly resting and getting a change of thought. One day I found myself in the old Mission Dolores, or San Francisco de Asis as it was formerly called. I relived the explorations of the early Spaniards and came to know more about California and how it was settled.

Davy had a different temperament. He was debonair, sophisticated, and at times unpredictable. On Sundays, instead of going to church, he would order a carriage and take me off in grand style for a ride in the country. He seemed to be quite prosperous, and could do whatever he wished.

Then the first of the blows came. My mother was very ill and brother Jack and Davy agreed it was necessary for me to return to Scotland. She passed away, and my voyage back to the United States was sad and lonesome. Davy, realizing this, had prepared a great surprise for me. He took me to a charming little house in Oakland, all furnished and ready, and there we were to live. It was our home.

It was during this time that the truth dawned upon me. Davy was not a well man. His life in South America and a fever that he had contracted there had affected his health and I began to see him fail noticeably before my eyes. He could no longer conceal it behind his debonair manner. He came to the point where he could not endure the long trips and the heavy responsibilities of his business and we had to do something about it.

The doctor suggested that we try living in the country, and we eventually found a nice place about sixty miles from San Francisco and bought a ranch.

It was a different life on the ranch. The work was the easiest part. The hardest was to keep up Davy's spirits. I had often to remind him of the old Scotch words,

> Ye'll ha' misfortune great and small
> But ha' a heart abinn them all.

Davy threw himself into the ranch with all the strength he could muster. The first thing he did was to have the shabby old ranch house torn down and build a new cottage. It had all cost more than we planned, but Davy said, "If this ranch is to be our home, we must have beauty around us." It was so like my husband, for all his adventurousness and hardy spirit, to think of beauty—he had even planted the flowers before the vegetables. Davy could do almost anything with his hands and he knew no obstacles.

But try as we would, at this time, everything on

the ranch seemed to go wrong, except for one thing
—Davy's health improved. Neither of us had lived
on a farm and we knew nothing about ranch life.
It took a great deal of money to get started. What
money we had after buying the ranch and building
the new house just seemed to melt away. We knew
that something had to be done to get us back into
a more active life again. But what? Conditions eventually forced Davy to think of returning to his old
line of business.

"I've always made good money, Peg," he said. "I'll
go to the city for a few days and see about getting
started again. I can soon make it up. We can get
someone to stay with you here on the ranch while I
build my business. Then we will see how it goes
and what we want to do."

Davy went to San Francisco, and at the end of a
warm July day I sat on the steps of the cottage, waiting for him to come up the carriage drive. The
driveway, with its young pine trees, curved pleasant-
ly. Though we had no carriage, Davy had the carriage drive made even before the carpenters had torn
down the old house to build the new one.

Queen, my little sorrel mare, was cropping tender
weeds about the doorstep. She was my pet and companion, following me about like a dog. I learned to
ride by leading her up to the fence and then climbing up and jumping from the fence to her back.
Around and around the feed lot we would go, my
hair coming down and flying about me like a cape.
When Davy saw how well I could ride, he had bought
me a fine sidesaddle with a red velvet seat.

Coming close to me and putting her soft pink nose

into my hand, Queen invited a loving pat. "He won't be long, now," I told her. "I hope he won't be disappointed about his business prospects." I often talked over problems with the little mare for she was company and seemed to understand. Soon she raised her pretty head, pointed her ears, and listened to the pat, pat, of hoofs on the dry, hard road.

A neighbor had promised to meet Davy at the train, and I could see them stopping at the gate. I ran down the carriage drive to meet my husband, and he was just getting out of the buckboard. I couldn't see his face, but I knew by his very shoulders and the way he carried himself that he had some exciting news.

He was laughing and talking, just as he used to do, and when I looked into his face, I knew that something important had happened.

Davy was so excited he took hold of my arm and pulled me up the driveway. He took off his Panama hat, wiped his warm face on his fresh linen handkerchief, and took me in his arms.

"You can't guess in a thousand years all that has happened," he began. "There was never anything like it in all history! Why, the gold rush here in California in '49 wasn't in it with this. Oh, Peg, gir-rul, every place I went, on the street, in the hotels, on the train, every place, all you heard was this wonderful gold strike in the Klondike. All San Francisco is crazy. I had read about it and heard about it, but I had no idea of the magnitude of it."

Davy's eyes were sparkling and he was actually trembling as he talked. I realized faintly that he had forgotten all about the business he had gone to

the city for. He continued, "The Alaska Commercial
Company's ship brought out twenty-five passengers
with $189,000 in gold nuggets, aside from the com-
pany's sack, which the San Francisco Mint valued at
$250,000. The *Portland* arrived at Seattle with gold
weighing a ton. People say a fortune can be picked
up in no time. The papers say that nuggets are reported as big as potatoes. A boy picked up one that
weighed twenty-one pounds and got $5,700 for it.
They say it often runs one hundred dollars to the
pan."

I tried to interrupt him. "Davy, you're exaggerat-
ing," I said.

"No, I'm not, Peg, it's true and more, too. I could
talk all night and not tell you all I've heard. I talked
to one fellow who had just got back from the Yukon.
He was like a madman. He showed me some of the
gold nuggets from his claim. You should have seen
him, his eyes were shining and his breath coming in
gasps. He told me nuggets are as easy to pick up as
shells on the seashore. The banks of the creeks and
rivers are full of gold. You can take a fortune out
in no time.

"This man came back to arrange his affairs, get
more supplies, and then he expects to find a great
fortune when he gets back to the Yukon. He says
every man who goes there is bound to get rich."

I could see Davy already on his way to finding a
fortune. He continued to tell me how Secretary
Gage of the Treasury had been there himself and had
made a statement to the newspapers that any man
with a brave heart and sound body, nerve and cour-

age, would find a field for his enterprise, without capital or an employer.

"This is encouragement for a poor man," Davy said. "I've met Mr. Gage and I know him to be a man of honor and what he says must be true and not an exaggeration. Now that there is a depression here in the States and men out of work, where everything else fails they begin searching through the pockets of old Mother Earth for gold. That's what is happening now."

Davy said that people were selling their homes and putting everything into the adventure. "I wish I had taken you with me," he said, "and you could have heard it as I did. I tell you, gir-rul, if I had the money for my expenses and your passage back to your brother Jack in Scotland, I'd be on my way tomorrow."

I could scarcely believe my ears. I barely knew where the Klondike was, that it was somewhere up in the northwest of Canada, and I certainly had no idea how one got there. Such considerations were unimportant. But that my husband would go without me!

"Remember, when we were children back home, you used to say we would find a fortune," I reminded him. "This may be the time, Davy, but I am going if you do. I can't understand why you would want to go alone, without me. . . ."

I looked into his face searchingly. He couldn't send me off to Scotland and go by himself!

I hadn't the least idea how a woman, a sheltered woman as I had always been, would fare in this wild, cold country, and Davy would try to explain it to me. We argued about it all night, and Davy told me about being in South America, and the wind and the cold in the high Andes, and how the Yukon would be like that in winter.

"Peg," he said, "you would have a happy time with your brother and your friends back home. Just as soon as I get our fortune, I'd come for you, never fear." He kissed me, then he whispered, "We haven't the money to do it anyway, so don't let us fuss about it."

Strangely enough, it was I who kept feeding the fire of adventure, partly because I could not, would not, let him go alone, partly because I found this new thing taking hold within me.

"We could sell the ranch," I suggested. "One of the neighbors is just waiting for the chance to buy it. His wife told me yesterday, and they have the money all ready. She likes our new house."

We eventually agreed to sell the ranch and put our household goods up at auction. With this money, all we would have in the world, we were going to gamble on finding a fortune in the Klondike. But Davy insisted, "Now, Peg, I know you are making a mistake to go. You have no idea what you will have to go through. But if you insist, remember what I say—no matter what happens I have warned you, and you will have to stand by your bargain."

I agreed. But often, as I saw my pretty home slipping away from me, I felt like giving up the idea, but it was too late. At the auction, things went cheaply. Times were hard and the ranchers had little money. It hurt to see my fine linen sheets go for twenty-five cents. My beautiful damask tablecloth and napkins with my monogram woven in them, which came from my uncle's mill in Dunfermline, one of my wedding gifts, also went for near nothing. Then there was the old solid-silver teapot, which always graced Mother's table on special occasions. It was like a friend from home, and when Mother died brother Jack had insisted I bring it with me to America. I saw it go to a farmer's wife who took it carelessly, laughed, and wrapped it in her checkered apron.

The hardest of all was Queen. She was more than a horse; she was my companion and friend. I just couldn't see them lead her away. On her back was my fine sidesaddle with the red velvet seat. I couldn't stand to watch, but went into the house to my bedroom and closed the door.

After the auction was all over and the ranch was sold—for a fraction of what it had cost us—we were getting ready to go to San Francisco and Davy said, "Peg, remember you can keep with you only the clothes you wear and a few personal things you can put in your little brown valise. You must be able to carry it yourself at all times. This isn't like the other trips you have made—you will have to travel very light, and we will not always be able to get at our outfit."

I grasped the fact gradually that we would make most of the trip on foot and somehow pack hundreds of pounds of equipment along with us. Also, that we would have to hurry before winter would be closing in, and there would be no shelter much of the time.

I looked about at my treasures. Mother's Bible,

all marked and worn. I had known it all my life. I couldn't leave it behind, or the old-fashioned jewelry that had belonged to Mother's mother. Then the beautiful opals from Davy. I must take them all, and photographs of Mother, Father, and brother Jack. Davy weakened, but reminded me again and again that I must be able to carry my valise at all times.

Davy applied himself to a thorough study of the geographical situation of the Klondike region and the approach to it, as well as to the nature of the outfit we would need. We were to go by boat up the coast to Skagway in southeast Alaska, or to some other landing to be decided upon later, and then pack into Canada over one of the passes to the head of the Waterways, where Davy said he would buy or build a boat.

In San Francisco we tried to get passage on first one boat and then another. But it was exactly as Davy had said—the crowd was very great, and unless you could bribe someone to sell his ticket for four or five times the cost, there wasn't a chance, even for a single person, let alone two. The waiting was eating into our money and Davy would stay only at a good hotel.

While we were waiting, a tailor in San Francisco made me a dark blue English storm serge suit, heavily lined. It cost a good deal of money, as the tailor had to get extra help to have it finished quickly. For my head I had a hood, fashioned out of a tea cozy my mother had knitted. When we were packing, I had picked it up and thought that it looked like a hood, so I tried it on. It was made of soft knitted wool and covered on the outside with blue velvet.

I trimmed it with a wee bit of ribbon and it looked very nice, I thought, and I was to find it very useful.

I can never remember all the things that were in that outfit of Davy's but I know that when it was all assembled together it weighed eight hundred pounds! Of course there were the tent and the supplies of food and the extra clothing and shoes and boots, and many things that other prospectors had found to be essential. I let Davy do most of the worrying about the outfit but I was concerned about our money—I was worried for fear it might not hold out.

Every boat on the Pacific coast was pushed into service, good or bad, new or old, and fares were jumping higher and higher all the time. Davy kept trying to get on a good seaworthy boat. "We'll not risk our lives on any of those old tubs that might go to pieces as soon as we get out of the harbor," he scoffed. "I know too much about the sea and I have a worthy respect for her. If we can't get a boat here, we'll go to Seattle and try there." This we eventually did.

At last we had our chance on rather a medium-sized boat, the *Seattle III*, a rust-blistered freighter, riding low in the water.

"She's only a sea tramp," Davy said, "but she looks seaworthy as far as I can tell."

CHAPTER THREE

The Gold Rush

IT WAS THE first year of the Gold Rush of 1897 when we — Davy and Peggy Shand — went aboard this clumsy craft. I mind so well how it all looked and the sounds of the water front in Seattle. I remember the shrill blast of the ship's whistle piercing the salty air, the barking of orders, and the farewell shouts that came from those on shore.

Bellowing cattle added to the commotion. Horses and dogs were packed into the forecastle. Long lines of drays tried to make a passage between the spectators in order to unload their supplies in the steamer. We were caught in the stream of excited people going up the gangplank. I mind I almost got my head knocked off as men crowded by me, carrying their packs on their shoulders. There was either a pick or a shovel cracking me on the head, or a coffee-pot snout poking me in the eye. No one was polite. It was "each fellow for himself, the Devil take the hindmost," Davy said.

The wheezing, rattling, hoisting engine finally lifted its load and the heavy boom swung clear to the packed hold of the ship below. The tired crew battened down the hatches and we were ready to cast off. The tall funnel belched clouds of black smoke and the pungent odors drifted shoreward over the spectators. She was loaded top-heavy and had a slight list to starboard. Passengers crowded to the rail to get a last glimpse of friends on shore.

The crowd on shore and those on the boat were wild with excitement. Davy looked over the group on the boat. "Look, Peg," he said, "its like an opera. I expect the overture to start any time. The characters are all here. See that flashily dressed man over there? He's a gambler. I'll bet anything he'll have his prey's grubstake long before we reach Skagway. There's the preacher, and no doubt that dazzling blonde may be a lady of the town. The preacher is in hopes of convincing the gold-mad souls that treasures in heaven are more to be desired than the gold of the Klondike. The other one wants her riches here and now. The farmer and the merchant are there. All they possess is no doubt in the outfits they are sitting on. See that young man, full of adventure, willing to endure any hardship to get his gold? See the old prospector, with his pack on his back? He knows what it is all about and, grim-faced, he means to meet it. The provident and improvident, the fit and unfit—all are together, with one object. The curtain is ready to go up. Gold is the thing.

"It is surely like an opera, Peg." Davy was enjoying himself; he could always see things that no one else could see. "There is sparkling-eyed spellbinder 'Buffalo Bill Cody.' Look, Peg, isn't he a handsome fellow, with his golden hair and flowing goatee? He is one of the main characters on the boat. I mean to make his acquaintance," Davy said, and he did. He and Davy became close friends and spent a good deal of time together. They parted, expecting to meet again sometime. Davy had a way of making friends with outstanding people.

At last the hawsers were cast off and the heavily laden steamer slipped from the dock into the middle of the stream and headed for the open sea. Davy was glad he had a cabin for us, though it had cost a good deal of money. He was angry when we went in and found a big Negro, his wife, and two little children in the other bunk. Nothing could be done about it, though Davy tried. They had paid their money just like we had. Every available space was taken. How they could all crowd into the one bunk was a mystery.

I couldn't see that we made anything by being cross about it. When the little children, with their bright eyes and cute pigtails peeped out and watched me, I smiled at them and they grinned back. What was the difference? Children were children, white or black. I didn't let it worry me and had fun with them; it passed the time. Their mother was pleased to see I liked them, and it worked out all right. I told Davy we were lucky to have a cabin, lucky to get passage on a boat at Seattle. Many of the people were sleeping on deck, with nothing to cover them but the stars.

At last Davy smiled and there was no more trouble in the cabin. The Negroes were pleased that we were kind to them, and they tried to do everything they could to make it easy.

The beauty of the Inside Passage up the coast of British Columbia was lost on many of the gold-mad stampeders. Men sat on their outfits on deck, telling and retelling the tales they had heard about the vast fortunes taken out of the Klondike district.

I heard that the first gold strike took place on

August 16, 1896, at the junction of the El Dorado
and Bonanza in the Klondike. It was George Holt
who shipped out gold from the Klondike in 1880.
One of the men told me this; he was an interesting
old miner. He said, "George Holt was a strong fellow; he knew the Indians and got help from 'em.
I heard he had the first party of white men to go
over the Chilkoot Pass, through those lakes and rivers
down the great Yukon. But before this, prospectors
and miners knew about the gold in the Yukon and
Alaska." I was interested in this old miner, and Davy
and I learned a lot about the country from him.

We heard the men discussing the different routes.
Some said the most popular was White Pass from
Skagway to Lake Bennett. Our old friend, the miner,
was going the Chilkoot Pass from Dyea—he said it
was shorter. Davy had investigated all the different
routes and he agreed with the old miner that the
Chilkoot Pass must be best.

"Peg, we will go that way, pack in over the Chilkoot Pass. I can get some Indian packers to do the
packing, then when we get to Lake Lindeman, at
the head of the Waterways, I'll build a boat if I
can't buy one cheap enough."

It all sounded easy so I didn't worry, just looked
about and enjoyed myself.

"It takes a smart captain to navigate around these
islands and through the treacherous channels of the
Inside Passage," Davy explained. There were no buoys
or other aids to navigation at this time.

"Look! Look!" I cried. "I thought we were going to hit that island. Now, it has slipped by, but
there is another. We must be going in circles."

"Yes," the old miner said, "these islands are like troubles—as soon as one is passed, up comes another to take its place." I had reason to remember the old man's words.

Our first stop was at Haines Mission on Chilkoot Inlet. The lower deck was filled with horses and cattle. Here a number of horses were to be put ashore to be driven over the Dalton Trail to Selkirk. It was horrid to see the poor things forced by vicious blows and prodding to jump into the water and swim ashore.

"Davy, make those wicked men stop!" I screamed.

He drew me away. "After they get ashore, they will be all right. There is plenty of grass and water along the trail, don't worry, gir-rul."

Davy comforted me. It was a long time after this that I heard many of those poor horses died on the trail, but by that time I knew so well how the poor creatures were treated that I felt glad they could die and get out of their misery.

The scenery was beautiful and the interesting days slipped by quickly. Nothing mattered, not even the food, which was limited. There were hunks of meat and unpeeled potatoes boiled in big tubs and dumped on the table in the same manner a farmer would feed his pigs. At first I couldn't eat, but the salt air and the out of doors gave me an appetite and I was able to eat like the others.

After leaving the Queen Charlotte Islands, the small steamer tossed about like a cork, being top-heavy and overcrowded. Many were seasick, but Davy and I did not have this trouble. However, it was unpleasant in such close quarters.

When the boat reached Skagway, the stampeders

separated. The ones going by way of White Pass landed here; those going over Chilkoot Pass were transferred to a big scow. Their outfits were piled in the middle and the owners held on as best they could. The scow, tipping and moving slowly, was propelled by sweeps or oars.

There was no wharf at Dyea in 1897. Vessels were forced to drop anchor; passengers and freight reached shore by canoes or scows. There was a small swampy beach used as a landing place. The scows were beached as far as possible at high tide and, as the tide went out, Indians waded waist-deep in the ice-cold water, carrying the passengers and the outfits on their shoulders to the beach.

It was my first experience with Indians. I didn't like them; they were so dirty and fierce-looking. I watched them carrying the people "piggyback." I felt I could not get that close to anything as dreadful as those Indians.

"Davy, I can't go ashore that way," I whispered, as I held onto his arm.

"Now, Peg, there is nothing else to do. Just hold on tight and you'll get there safely. It is not very far," he assured me as he accepted his turn to go ashore.

I watched him on the back of a wicked-looking Indian, splashing through the cold water. The Indian's dirty black hair hung in strings over his filthy shirt collar. I feared there might be crawlers on that greasy hair. What if they got on Davy! I was glad to see them reach the shore and Davy free of the Indian.

Then it was my turn. I hesitated. Some of the

men helped me "get aboard" as Davy would have expressed it. I was shaken with fear and excitement. The Indian grabbed my legs and pulled them about his waist. He was that greasy and smelly I didn't see how I could stand it. I held my little valise between the Indian's dirty neck and myself. Just then he stumbled and I almost shot over his head. Before I realized it, I threw my arm about him and held on with all my strength, never losing my hold on the precious valise in the other arm. The Indian slushed through the deep water that came up high. I was compelled to hold my feet straight out to keep them from getting wet. The Indian grunted to let me know I was choking him. It seemed a long time before we got to Davy, waiting on the beach.

Davy secured two packers to get our outfit ashore and help pitch the tent on the wet sand of the crowded beach.

I shall never forget the day we landed in Dyea, September 7, 1897. It was my birthday. In the distance I could see the purple mountains, rising up like a gateway. We must climb over them, for beyond lay our new life and fortune!

The little prayer Mother taught us came to me. I seemed to have the premonition I would need it many times in the future: "Oh, God, show me what to do, and give me strength to do it."

Davy had gone to get horses to pack our eight-hundred-pound outfit to the foot of Chilkoot Pass. From here we were to begin the climb up to the Waterways at Lake Lindeman.

I was alone in the tent. I lay on a pile of damp blankets, listening to the noise and confusion outside.

I mind thinking, "Davy won't be long, I hope." I thought of the dirty Indian who carried me ashore. "I wouldn't want to meet that Indian now, while I am alone." When we were children, my brother Jack and I often read about the American Indians scalping white people and I had always feared them.

Someone was fumbling with the fastening of the tent. A big, black, scaly hand came through the opening, pushing back the flap. A horrible head, with stringy black hair and fierce, piercing eyes peered through. The head did not seem to have a body, but to be loosely floating back and forth; the gleaming black eyes rolled about, seeing everything. I was afraid to move. Another head appeared under the first, even more frightful. Close to the ground, as if the owner were crawling, the third head appeared. All three heads swung back and forth, eyes glittering, as though ready to spring at me. I knew they were wicked, bloodthirsty Indians. I wanted to scream, but couldn't make a sound.

Instinctively I put my hand to my heavy, brown hair. All three pair of eyes followed the gesture. Time passed. I awaited their first move—they waited, too. I felt like a mouse with three fierce cats waiting to pounce on me. I couldn't stand the suspense! If they were going to scalp me, they had better start —waiting was agony!

After a bit I began to think—they couldn't do very much to me. The people out on the beach could hear me scream and surely someone would come to my rescue. I couldn't stand the strain any longer. I must do something, so I smiled at them and gave a nervous giggle. Then, as if an invisible string was attached to each head, first one, then another disappeared, and I was alone in the tent.

After I had stopped shaking and knew they were gone, I went outside. There was a pile of outfits, as high as a house, on the sandy beach. Each outfit was supposed to be wrapped in tarpaulin and marked with the owner's name. I felt sorry for the poor man who had the job of sorting them. Yelling and flinging his arms about and using very colorful, descriptive language, he sprang around like a creature at bay, attacked by a band of wolves. Wild men shrieked and swore, demanding their outfits. The poor fellow did his best, swearing and dancing about in answer to the demands. I thought it was a hopeless job and said to myself, "If ever there were a lot of crazy men—there they are. Gold-crazy, and when they get it they'll not be the happier."

When Davy returned, he brought a man and two horses that stood with tired, drooping heads. "Won't be able to take you very far," the man said. "My horses are nearly petered out—don't get enough to eat. Feed costs so much, when you can get it, but you just can't get it. I gave a fellow ten dollars for a bunch of slough grass that he went out and cut with a butcher knife. Been feeding 'em mostly corn meal and rolled oats. That's pretty high for a horse, but they got to eat or they can't work. There are only a few horses here and they're all worked to death. I'll take you up the river bed a ways, then you have to get down and dig like the rest, if you want to get over them." He jerked his thumb toward the snow-capped mountains. "It takes a lot of nerve and a damn strong back to get over.

A lot of folks are giving it up, selling their outfits—getting a plenty for them, too. Only the strong and young can make it." He cast an appraising glance over Davy and me—it got my dander up. I knew he thought we couldn't make it.

"If others could do it, we could," I told myself firmly.

When we were ready to start, the poor, tired horses stumbled along. I felt sorry for them. Davy and the man had packs. I wanted to help, too.

"I'll not let you carry a pack like a squaw," Davy said.

"I'm as strong as you," I told him, "and it will save getting another packer."

I worried about the money—it seemed Davy was always taking another bill from the belt around his waist. Money melted so fast, I wanted to warn him, but I didn't dare. It would only make him cross and do no good.

The men started on. I pulled on my pack that I had insisted on carrying and followed them.

I stopped still—horrified, as I saw a man abusing a sorrel mare. For a moment I thought it was Queen, my Queen! It was plain to me the poor creature never had a pack on her back before. She must have been somebody's pet, for she acted just as Queen would have done, holding her head high and dancing on her slender legs—big eyes filled with bewilderment and fear, nostrils distended and quivering, her high spirits showing in every movement of her beautiful body. It was too much for me! Slipping the straps from my shoulders and letting the pack fall as it might, I screamed, "Wait! Davy, I must go help that poor horse." Crying out, I ran to the man.

"Don't jerk her that way! Don't yell at her! Can't you see you're scaring her to death? Here, let me hold her." I took the strap from him. The poor creature knew I was a friend, and when I talked to her, she quieted down.

"She'll get over that," the man with Davy said. "When I first came up here I thought the horses had it pretty tough, but I got over it. Now, all that matters is to get to the Klondike. When a horse gets worked out and dies on me, I just get me another."

While I was talking to the poor horse and rubbing her nose, the man took the opportunity to pile more on her back. "Don't put any more on her," I told him.

"Well, you see, lady," he said, "I got to get my outfit up to Finnegan's Point. I just sold her to another fellow with the understanding I could use her to get my outfit up there, then I'll bring her back and get my money. Thank you for holding her, lady. She don't savvy this packin'. The man I bought her off of said she was a Kentucky saddle mare. Gosh, he hated to part with her—cried like a baby when he had to sell her. Had been playing cards gamblin' and got cleaned out. Why he ever brought her to this country, God only knows. He said she never worked, never had a whip laid to her, was trained with a lump of sugar. Well, them days are over—got to work now. I must get movin'. So long, lady." He took the bridle from my reluctant hand and I went back to the impatient men.

"Well, Peg," Davy said, "we can't waste any more

of this man's time. If we are to get anyplace, let's
be on our way." Davy was irritated. I pulled my
pack on my back—blinded by tears of sympathy
for the poor horse. I followed the men along the
river bed.

There was a wide valley at Dyea, with a low,
rocky ridge or point between Dyea Valley and Skagway Valley. The Dyea River runs through the valley and is a swift stream most of the year, but in
the fall it is rather low in places. The river bed is
wooded with poplar and several varieties of willows.
Piles of driftwood, ridges of sand and gravel, and
great boulders, which had to be avoided, made travel
difficult.

The river had to be crossed and recrossed many
times. In some places men had made bridges and
charged toll. In other places the river had to be
forded. It was at one of these crossings that I got
into trouble. The man had hoisted me on top of one
of the already overloaded horses. The extra weight
was too much for the poor creature—it stumbled
and fell in midstream. I shot over its head and landed
in the ice-cold water. The big balloon sleeves of my
jacket filled with air and this helped me keep afloat
until the men fished me out.

My teeth were chattering so I could hardly talk.
I was shaking with cold and fright. They made a fire
and helped me dry my clothes. The heavy woolens
were hard to dry. When we were preparing to come
north, Davy insisted I dress very warm.

I was still damp when we started, but the men
were anxious to be on their way. As we stumbled
along the trail, I laughed to myself. It seemed ridicu-

lous the way I was perched atop of that pack like a howdah on an elephant. If anyone were looking, it surely was a funny sight, but no one was looking —everyone had his eyes on the trail. People seemed to trudge along, never looking up at the mountains or noticing anything—always with their eyes on the trail. As I watched them, I made up my mind, no matter what happened, I'd not do that. I would keep my eyes open, look about and see things.

It was like a parade passing—hundreds of people on the march, each and every one in a hurry. No wonder it was called "The Gold Rush."

The man dumped our outfit, took our money, and turned about, hurrying to get on his way. We had come only a few miles but it had taken all day. We pitched our tent and made a fire, for which I was grateful. I was still shivering in my damp clothes.

As I was cleaning up after supper, I thought to save a little bacon grease, left in the skillet, by pouring it into an empty milk can. It bubbled over and ran down on my hand, causing a painful burn. Davy was sorry for me, but annoyed at my clumsiness. While he was dressing my hand, a young man stopped by.

"Gosh, that's too bad," he said. "Here—I have something that will help." He dove into his pack and brought out a bottle of brandy. "I don't need it anyway and it will lighten my load. Even an ounce helps."

He grinned, picked up his pack, and was gone. Davy made me a strong drink and I lay down in the tent. Between the fiery liquor and the weary day, I never slept better in my life.

It is strange how sometimes we have the opportunity to pay back a debt. It was several years, but
I never forgot the boy's kindness. When he came to
our hotel on Stewart Island, he was sick. It was my
time to give him help, but that is a story that can
wait.

In the morning Davy sorted our outfit into two
piles, some things to take with us and another pile
to cache. The man who brought us up the river
bed told us it was safe to cache anyplace along the
trail.

"It wouldn't be healthy for a man to be caught
rifling a cache," he said. "I saw two fellows try that
trick. There weren't any Mounties to attend to them,
but they formed a Trail Committee which is made
up of men along the trail. They held court and gave
the thieves a trial. Some of the men said 'Shoot 'em,'
but others said 'No.' One of the thieves took his own
gun and shot himself before anyone could stop him.
The other was bound to a tree, lashed, and a sign
put on him, 'I am a thief,' and he was turned loose
on the trail.

"A few lessons like that and a fellow knows men
mean business. Laws have to be made to fit a new
country. The safety of the trail must be established,"
he assured us. "Don't worry, make your cache; no
one will dare bother it."

We made our cache and covered it with tarpaulin
which had been marked with our name. We planned
to take as much as we could pack and go as far as
possible, then pitch our tent, rest a bit, and go back
to the cache for another load, shuttling back and
forth.

It was a slow way to get our eight-hundred-pound outfit up to Sheep Camp, but there didn't seem to be any other way to do it. I was not very helpful for a few days. My burned hand always seemed to be in the way; also, I had a bad cold from my splash in the river.

My teeth were chattering and I was shaking with cold the first morning we camped in the river bed, but as I stepped out of the tent, I saw something that made me forget all about myself and any self-pity I might have had. Not far from us, tied to a stake of the tent, was the poor little mare I helped the day before. She was shaking with cold and plainly showing how exhausted and miserable she felt under the heavy pack on her back. I dropped the part of the tent I was holding up, and it covered Davy.

"Oh, look at that poor horse," I cried. I knew that man had never taken her pack off all night. "How horrible! I mean to do something about it." Davy tore angrily at the tent which was enveloping him and scolded me.

"Peg, if you stop to look after every horse you think is abused, we had better give this up and go back. Use some sense! We will never get to Sheep Camp, much less the Klondike." When Davy was in this state of mind there was no use to argue. I had to mind my own business and go along, but I couldn't get my mind off the sad, forlorn little mare.

Farther along, we came to a marsh. Here the mud was deep and sticky. It was hard to find a place to step. I was glad for the rubber boots that came up to my knees. I had wondered if it was wise to have so many pairs of shoes in an outfit, but now I could see Davy was right. No doubt his big buffalo coat would come to good use, too. Davy's boots were too big and rubbed his heels. I had warmed some water, bathed his feet, and had him put on clean socks that morning. It was hard enough to travel with good feet.

Just ahead of us a packer with a big sack of flour on his back got stuck in the mud, held firmly in the sticky ooze, unable to move. He was calling lustily for help. Davy and another kindhearted man went to his rescue. They pulled and pulled, and at last they pulled him out of his boots! The boots held firmly.

The poor fellow hopped about, treading mud in his stocking feet. He damned the mud, the boots, and the flour impartially. I couldn't help a giggle to myself—it was so funny to see the boots sticking in the mud, awaiting their owner. Davy came and looked at me suspiciously. "Yes, laugh, Peg, laugh at the poor devil. You'd get a laugh out of anything," he said, but there was a twinkle in his eye.

We packed back and forth from one cache to another—we grew so tired and weary we would lie down on a pile of driftwood and fall fast asleep.

> It's easy to tell the toiler
> How best to carry his pack
> But no one can rate a burden's weight
> Until it's been on his back.

People streamed by us. Men bent double under the weight of their packs. There were Indian packers, dogs trotting swiftly and easily along the trail, women dressed in overalls, with caps on their heads, looked almost like men, carrying all they could manage. No one paid any attention to us, sleeping beside the trail. Many others just as weary were resting when they could.

The rain commenced in a drizzle and grew heavier. It kept up for weeks, with only one day of sunshine. Through the wet grayness we struggled, packing the outfit from one cache to another and then put up our tent to try to dry out our clothes by a small fire. The clothes were always damp, but we got used to it and seemed to grow stronger as we became more accustomed to the packs on our shoulders.

We reached a place where the trail crossed the river. It was much too deep to ford. An Irishman with his boat wanted to ferry the weary travelers across for a dollar a head. We paid our two dollars and were rather enjoying the rough ride, when the Irishman said to Davy, "You folks better be careful climbing the trail, going up that steep bluff just ahead—so many accidents happen right there. People have heavy packs on their backs and the trail runs along so close to the edge of that stony cliff. Just one misstep and you get overbalanced. You can slide off the trail mighty easy and go down into this deep water. This place don't seem to have any bottom, it's a kind of a whirlpool. Many's the one who's gone down and not come up. I've seen it. I always tell everyone to watch his climbing," the Irishman warned us.

"Peg, be careful or you'll slip. You'll go down and we can never rescue you. Mind, now, take it easy. See how hard it is for this man to manage the boat. The water is swift here."

"I'll be careful, Davy," I promised.

"You'd better," the Irishman said. "Look at that young fellow going along the trail now. He is from Stirling, Scotland, and he said to me, 'That cliff looks as hard to climb as the rock back of Stirling Castle, and me with this one-hundred-pound pack on my back.' I told him he'd better make two trips than to take a chance, but he wouldn't listen. Watch him, he's most to the top."

We watched our countryman with renewed interest, as he slowly climbed up the stony trail, bent almost double under his pack.

"My God! He's slippin'," cried the Irishman. "Look out! He's goin'."

The lad stumbled and started falling, could not stop himself, as his heavy load overbalanced him. Clutching wildly and screaming for help, trying vainly to break his fall, the boy hurled through the air— down—down, from the steep cliff into the swift, swirling water. Right before our eyes we saw him disappear, the heavy pack pulling him under. We watched intently but the body did not come up.

"My God!" Davy breathed.

"Oh, what can we do?" I cried. "Can't we save him?" The Irishman got the boat to the shore and the men climbed out to see what they could do. Men along the trail stopped to try to find him. It was a terrible time! I felt sick. It seemed we had lost a friend. He was from Stirling where our folks lived. No doubt his family knew our people. I wondered if they would ever know their boy's fate. He

was too young to die. Davy and the men worked
faithfully, but they never found that lad. I could
not forget him and for a long time I dreamed about
it. I was so weak I did not see how I could ever climb
that cliff. I could not do it!

Through the bushes on the banks of the river I
could see and hear a man coming with a pack horse.
He had evidently forded the river about two miles
below. He was cursing and abusing the horse in an
outrageous manner. I had learned to turn my head
and not look at many cruel things. The man with
the horse started to climb the steep cliff. Never
have I heard such a cruel, vicious voice in all my
life. In spite of myself, I had to look. To my horror,
it was the poor little sorrel mare that looked like
my Queen. What a change from the lovely, high-
spirited creature I saw at Dyea!

Struggling under the heavy pack, reeling and swaying on her slender legs, head hanging, sensitive ears
loose and flopping, the exhausted animal staggered
desperately from side to side. I was powerless to
move and stood petrified with a great anger surging
through me. The man urged the poor creature on
with a club in his big hairy hand. The cruelty in
his wicked face was shameful to look at.

"You got to make it, Goddam you, you've got to
get this last load up there! Then you can go to
hell—die if you want to," his guttural voice came
over the trail.

I was frozen to the spot. I could not move! Then
all at once I came to life. I threw my pack from
my shoulders, screaming, "Wait, Davy!" Before he
could stop me I ran, fairly flew up the trail. A power

within me gave me strength! I didn't know what I was going to do, but this fierce emotion that shook me was equal to anything. "Let me at him! I would beat him with his own club! I'd kill him!" I sobbed. I was gaining! Breathless, I urged myself on. I was close enough to see his evil face. The stubble of his beard on his hard jaw, the sweat pouring down from under his dirty cap, his powerful shoulders heaving—a loathsome sight!

"I'll get you over," he grunted.

I wondered what he would do before I could reach him. He tossed away his club, shifting his pack, reached into his pocket and pulled out a knife— opened it. It all happened so quickly I could not get to him. The staggering, spent horse, the cruel hand lunging the glittering knife into the horse's flank— all flashed before me!

With a supreme effort, the frantic horse put forth its last ounce of strength. They were almost to the top of the cliff, the place where the Scotch lad started to fall. "Oh Lord, give me the strength to get to him," I panted. The desperate creature could stand no more—she faced the cliff and deliberately jumped!

I knew she killed herself. I don't care what anyone will say—I knew. I was a witness. The horse, of her own will, leaped into space.

The man, taken by surprise, did not have time to grab at the bridle rein and save his precious outfit, which meant gold and riches to his wicked heart. He had to look down and see the horse and its heavy burden disappear in the swift water. His last chance for gold. If he cursed and used vile language before, it was nothing to the way he behaved now.

Horrified, I watched the horse fall through space
and strike the water. A pain struck my stomach
and wrenched it with sudden sickness. I reeled dizzily
and almost fell over the cliff myself. The greatest
anger I had ever known took possession of me. I
knew real hate for the first time in my life! I felt
like murdering the cruel man. At last I turned away.
I was glad the horse was out of its misery, out of
those cruel hands, glad her troubles were over. Glad!
GLAD! GLAD!

I could not look at him. I could think of no pun-
ishment severe enough to be dealt out to him, as
I stumbled down the steep path.

"God, oh, God!" I cried. "Damn him! Damn him
to hell! Make him suffer as he made that horse suffer.
Damn him! Damn him to hell!" I had never cursed
a living creature before, but I meant just that—I
wanted him in hell. It was a good thing I was not
close to that wicked man, I might have given him
a push and sent him over the cliff after the poor
horse. I was so weak I could hardly pick my way
down the trail to Davy.

When Davy asked me about the horse, I told him
what had happened. He gave me some advice about
minding my own business. I snapped back at him,
"Oh, shut up!"

I had never said this before to Davy in all our
lives, even when we were children back home. That
night I couldn't sleep. I kept seeing the Scotch lad
going over the cliff and the poor horse falling through
space. I could not ask God to forgive me for the
curse I put on that man—I knew I meant it! I did
not regret it.

We got a couple of experienced packers to get our outfit up the bluff and on to Happy Camp. We had, in all, crossed and recrossed the Dyea River thirteen times, sometimes fording and sometimes being ferried across. We were nearly three weeks doing it.

From Happy Camp we went on to Sheep Camp.

Approaching Chilkoot Pass

DAVY AND I, like many others, made our headquarters at Sheep Camp. We paid two Indians to pack our eight-hundred-pound outfit up the steep, stony cliff to this point on the trail. We carried our packs and went on ahead. The Indians made a cache among other stampeders at Sheep Camp, which was the busiest, maddest place in the North the first year of the Gold Rush, in 1897. I'll never forget it!

Even Davy was upset by so much noise and confusion. We could hardly move for people packing in and packing out, coming and going, buying and selling, and combining outfits. Men who had never seen one another before became partners without consideration of personalities or temperaments—all that was necessary was that one must have seven hundred dollars in food or five hundred dollars in money.

The police, who knew the dangers of winter in this cold country, saw to it that there was enough to feed the wild people who were gold-crazy and on their way to the Klondike. I found it all very exciting!

Sheep Camp is situated in a canyon that opens into a basinlike valley surrounded by high mountains covered with snow. "A man told me it was the headquarters for the mountain sheep hunters at one time—that is where it gets its name," Davy told me. "It marks the last timber line on this side of the ridge. That gorge through the mountains is called

Chilkoot Pass. It begins at Sheep Camp, then comes Stone House, the Scales and the Summit, thirty-five hundred feet. It's up there, Peg, where the police collect the customs, as it is the boundary line between Canada and Alaska."

Davy always found out about everything. I was interested as he went on to explain a lot he had picked up about this new country.

"Owing to the necessity of policing the trail and rivers, posts were established every thirty or forty miles. It's good management, because it would be almost impossible for a person to enter the country at Skagway without being seen."

Davy and I sat upon our outfit as we rested and talked. There was so much excitement we did not think of sleeping. The twilight was long into the night. No one went to bed, but slept when he could catch a few winks.

"Now, Peg," Davy explained, "the duties of the police are many: preservation of order, collecting of customs duties at Chilkoot Pass and White Pass, the regulation of traffic, and various other services in connection with the government. When we get to Dawson, Peg, at the confluence of the mighty Yukon and Klondike rivers—there is the Mounted Police post that has the supervision of all this new gold country.

"I hear it has not near the lawlessness that Alaska has. The British are a law-abiding people—well, more or less." He smiled as I had to laugh at his loyalty to his homeland.

The pass was already covered with snow. On the steepest part of the trail, between the Scales and the Summit, it was packed hard as stone. Some men had cut out steps and charged toll for their use. A continual line of packers came up the pass like a parade.

The first time Davy and I made the climb we had a terrifying experience. Davy thought we should not carry too heavy a pack until we got a bit used to the exertion of the hard climb. We stopped for breath. It was tough going, even if one did not have a pack on his shoulders. We rested. I looked up at the high mountains of Chilkoot Pass, looming above us. Ahead was a rugged, exhausting climb.

My pack did not seem so heavy when I started— Davy had seen to that. I struggled along, climbing, climbing, and it grew heavier until I felt I had the world on my back. The straps cut and galled my shoulders.

The weight and the climb put a strain on my muscles in a new place. Underfoot was rough going; my feet slid over the rocks. At times I had to crawl, using my hands and feet in a constant effort, lifting and pulling upward. Davy, too, had a hard time— I didn't complain for I was afraid he would tell me I should not have come. He was puffing and blowing worse than I.

It was hard to breathe. My heart pounded in my ears with sickening nausea. A tottering weakness shook my knees. I had to rest often. Davy was glad when I did, for he was almost worn out himself.

People filed by us in a continuous stream of the gold rush. It made me think of an army of ants I used to watch on the ranch. Everyone was carrying all he dared. Only the Indians climbed easily and lightly along the trail.

About two miles from Sheep Camp, at Stone

House, a cutoff from the main trail runs close to the base of the mountain.

"Peggy, see that overhanging wall of ice?" Davy pointed it out to me. "It certainly looks dangerous."

We could see this glacier below us from our position on the upper trail. We were packing along slowly when suddenly there was an ominous rumble. It shook the ground under our feet. There was a terrific explosion, another, and then another, each one louder than the one before—a cracking, splitting sound as if the whole mountain were being torn apart.

"Look, Peg," Davy cried. "Look! It's an avalanche! It's breaking loose."

As we watched we saw a widening wall of water and ice crashing down the mountainside, sweeping everything before it.

"Davy, what shall we do?" I screamed. "We shall be killed. The mountain is going."

"Stand still, Peg," he commanded. "It's on the other side of the trail and below us. See those fellows running for their lives? God! I hope they make it."

They were tearing their packs from their shoulders to run the better. The packs fell in the terrifying, moving, slipping avalanche and were quickly carried out of sight. I felt as if the whole mountain were sliding out from under us. Suddenly it was over as we watched. The mountainside was swept clean. I stood frightened, weak and trembling.

After we had regained enough strength we plodded along until at last we reached the Summit. We were wearying and loosened our packs to rest a bit. Davy

left to see about getting our outfits through the
government customs.

Alone, sitting on my pack, I looked far away at
the distant mountains, purple and majestic — over
these we must climb. They were like a wall guard-
ing a new world beyond. The sight gripped me. I
trembled all over. Nothing in my life had ever
frightened me like those snow-capped peaks. To
struggle over those mountains meant going into a
new land, a new life, like being born again. Just
Davy and I! Were we equal to it? Could we measure
up to this great challenge?

I can never explain the fear that shook the very
heart of me. I wanted to get Davy and hurry down
the mountainside, back to the things I knew, back
home, back to Scotland and brother Jack and security. I was shaking with terror. I covered my
face with my hands. What had we gotten ourselves
into? I dared not look again at those mountains.

After a bit I grew calm. I remembered experiencing this same strange fear when a child. One cold
winter night Father had lifted me up on the old
stone wall and told me to look at the stars in the
heavens.

"No, no," I cried. "I dinna want to look. I 'fraid."
I covered my eyes with my hands and hid my face
on his shoulder.

"Never be afraid of anything, lass," he told me.
"You can never lose the stars, lassie; they are always
in the sky, just as God is always with you. Mind this."

I opened my eyes now and looked at the mountains. My father's voice came back to me, as he
read at family worship: "I will lift up mine eyes

unto the hills from whence cometh my help." Suddenly a great strength and power possessed me. I felt equal to any trial that might come. A golden light shone about and within me. My heart prayed, "Oh, God, show me what to do, and give me strength to do it."

When Davy returned he looked at me twice and said, "Well, Peg, what happened? You don't look like the tired gir-rul I left here. You seem all rested." I couldn't tell Davy about it just then, but I shall never forget this experience on Chilkoot Pass, when I gazed in awe at the summit and beyond.

It soon became necessary to contrive a better way to get the outfits over the steep trail to the summit. A company of men fixed a trolley by running a long rope through a sheave anchored at the summit; one attached to a drum and the other to the loaded sled. The drum was wound by horsepower. It proved a satisfactory contrivance to transport the goods to the summit. For a good price, a person saved himself a lot of hard packing.

To the right of Chilkoot Pass was the Patterson Trail, longer and more gradual. This was used for freighting. Horses, dogs, oxen, tame elk, goats, or anything that could pull a load up to the Waterways, was used for the purpose.

We worked hard to get our outfit up to Crater Lake. Here we made our cache on the mountainside, along with others. It was now October and getting very cold. Traveling over the trail so often, we grew to know those who, like ourselves, were packing in. I talked little to strangers. Davy stopped to chat and hear the news. I stood beside him, listening. The Indian packers grew to know me and called me "Little White Bird." I never knew why this name. One time, when I was resting by myself, an Indian said to me—"Hurry! Hurry! Get outfit cached up lake. Very soon, very cold! Little White Bird and man too late. Every day snow come down more, more, from high mountain—cover trail. Wind howl. Sagna, home of North Wind, live in high mountain. He howl all time." Looking up, he waved his arm toward the snow-capped peaks where the North Wind lived—"Little White Bird no go all snowed in." He shifted his pack, grinned at me, and trotted down the trail.

There were many interesting things happening along the trail; some of them amused me a great deal. I saw a man pay five dollars for a cup of coffee. I thought that if it had been a cup of tea, there might have been some sense in it. I heard two men talking. One said to the other, "I just gave a fellow eight dollars for a pound of tobacco." His partner was shocked.

"You don't mean to tell me you gave all that money for just tobaccy! It must be mighty good tastin'. I never chewed myself, but if it's that good, think I'll get myself some." And he did.

One cold, foggy day, when we were packing up to the Summit, Davy had a cold and was feeling weak. He stumbled and almost fell backwards. A young man who was just behind, caught Davy. They got to talking. We asked him to share our lunch and he accepted. We often met the lad on the trail after this, as he, too, was packing up to Lake Linde-man. Though he was a rough-looking fellow, Davy

took a great fancy to him and it grew into a nice
friendship. He was one of the kindest men we met
along the trail. Always full of fun, we were glad
when we saw him. In later years he visited us on
Stewart Island. He sent us one of the first books
he published. Davy was very proud of it. His name
was Jack London.

One cold morning we were nearing Stone House
when we came upon six dead horses. It was a strange
sight to see them lying in a circle, as if they had
their heads together for comfort in their misery.
They had died from exposure, abuse, and starvation.
In place of the backbreaking loads, the terrible pull
up the mountainside, the weakness from hunger and
the chill of the icy wind, they were mercifully released from their suffering. One of the strange sights
of the trail. We never knew why they died in this
way.

The way the animals were abused on the Patterson and other trails is too horrible to think about.
I often told Davy, "All the gold in the country is
not worth this cruelty."

It became necessary to make greater haste in packing up to Crater Lake over Long Lake to Lake Lindeman. We must get the outfit to the Waterways before the big freeze-up. We heard the old prospectors
and others who knew this northern country talk of
the long, cold winter. We must reach the Klondike
and get fixed as comfortably as possible before the
winter set in.

On the way from Crater Lake a blizzard struck
us. The dark sky opened up and pelted us with
blinding snow that stung like bird shot. The wind

howled and screamed like a banshee. It was terrifying. We could understand why the Indians believed
that storm demons lived in the mountains.

The wind tore about us, tugging at our clothes
and hissing in our ears. The thick, slanting barrage
of snow shut out the light. Even when only a few
feet from one another, the white gloom completely
concealed us.

"Peg, stay clost by," Davy shouted. "Don't get
separated from me. I must find the markings of this
trail. There is an old boat turned upside down; we
slide down into the canyon from there. For God's
sake, don't get lost. You know how you are, always
taking the wrong direction. You might get out on
the lake. Can't tell how far it's frozen out there.
You'd go down into the water—that would be the
end. Stay close by."

"I will, Davy," I promised.

I twisted about to straighten my clothes that were
tugging about me and to adjust my pack. In that
second I lost sight of Davy. Squinting into the blizzard I shouted with all my might:

"Davy! Davy! I don't see you! Answer me,
Davy!" But Davy was trying to find the markings
of the trail. I heard him call to me above the howl
of the storm:

"Come on gir-rul! Keep close and don't be idling."

"But Davy, I can't find you!"

In one hand I carried a bucket in which I had
packed a bit of tea, sugar, dried meat and hardtack,
a candle, and little odds and ends I had learned by
experience to always have with me. In the other

hand was my precious valise. On my shoulders were my blankets.

"Oh, Davy!" I screamed, "I'm lost!"

The blinding storm shrieked and I cried again and again into the face of it: "Davy, oh, Davy, come to me."

Davy, burdened by an eight-by-ten tent, by ridge-pole and blankets, could hardly stand in the terrific wind. While struggling with the gale, I stumbled and fell. As I tried to get to my feet, I touched a slippery surface and knew I was out on the lake. For a moment panic gripped me; I was sick with horror.

"Davy, Davy!" I shouted frantically. The wind seemed to force the words back into my mouth. I thought of the tales I had heard of men frozen to death before they realized what was happening. I struggled to my feet. The snow had sifted into my mittens when I fell, but I knew I must not let go of the bucket of food and the precious valise.

Each step I took might take me nearer to where I would fall off into space, and the black, icy water close over me. I was facing death. I could not die here all alone, drowned in the black water.

"Oh, God, help me find Davy!" I pleaded. Then I heard Davy's frantic voice through the storm: "Peg, Peg, lass! Oh, Peg!"

"Davy, come to me!" I sobbed.

"Why did you do such a daft thing?" he chided when we were together again. "I told you to stay close by! Now I don't know where we are!"

"But everything is all right now, Davy. We are

together again!" I was breathless, but relieved and happy.

"I'm not so sure," answered Davy. "If I could only find that boat, then I'd know we were not headed out on this damned lake!"

"Davy, I know we're going in the wrong direction. We should go the opposite way," I argued.

"That settles it, Peg," Davy scolded. "Come on. This *is* the right way. You are always wrong about the way to go."

We struggled, weary and exhausted, I keeping close to Davy. The wind grew fiercer. At last, just as we thought we could go no further, Davy found the boat. We both felt we had been reprieved from almost certain death.

Crater Lake is the bed of an extinct volcano and its banks are steep. The distance into the canyon from the lake was a hard climb even in pleasant weather, but in a blinding blizzard it was next to impossible to accomplish.

Davy surveyed the situation and then said, "Now I will slide down, and then when I am ready, you must come as I tell you."

I could hardly see him as he worked his way down the steep incline. I waited until I heard his voice and knew he was safe at the bottom.

"Throw me down your things," Davy called. I tossed my valise and Davy caught it.

"Davy, be careful of the bucket," I cautioned. "It's a good thing I tied the cloth over the top so the things won't fall out."

"Now, come on, gir-rul," he ordered. I slid down and landed in a big snowdrift where I lay, spent

and exhausted, unable to pull myself out. Davy
struggled to me.

"Ah, Peg, gir-rul," he grieved. "I never thought
I'd bring you to this when I married ye." He put
his arms about me and tried to pull me to my feet.
After a time we found our belongings and again
got the burdens adjusted to our weary shoulders.
The storm grew worse and the cold more deadly.

"Peg," Davy gasped. "I think we had better put
up our tent. We can't go on; we're too tired."

"No, Davy!" I screamed above the hiss of the
storm. "We couldn't get the tent up in this tearing
wind, and there is no way to make a fire. We'd
freeze without one. We're above the timber line and
no way to find wood to burn. We'd better go on.
Better keep moving. We'll find the trail and get
back to the Summit," I urged. But Davy's strength
was fast deserting him.

"Peg," he moaned, "I can't make it." He sank
down in the snow.

"Oh, Davy, please don't faint!" I pleaded, struggling to his side. "Wake up! Open your eyes!" In
the dim light, through the whirling snow flurries, I
could see him fade from me. A ghastly blue came
over his face. I shook him desperately. "Wake up,
Davy!" I begged. "We can't freeze. Oh, God, help
me save Davy."

But the only answer was the fierce, desolate howling of the wind. Suddenly through me flashed the
same strength I had felt the first time I climbed
Chilkoot Pass. I must save my husband! I didn't
know how, but I knew it could be done!

Peering through the slanting sleet, I could make

out a faint star close to the horizon in the distance. I realized, suddenly, that it wasn't a star. It was a light shining—the light from the open flap of a tent as someone went in. If we could only get to the tent and blessed warmth! I pulled the pack from Davy's back and piled all our things together and stuck the ridgepole in the snow above them so that we could find them later. Then together we dragged ourselves to the tent from which the light had come.

"How is it for getting in, boys?" Davy called out in a trembling voice.

Voices came from the canvas walls: "No chance, no room; all filled up; ten men in here now."

"But we must come in. My wife is nearly frozen," Davy called.

"What! You have a woman with you?" somebody asked.

"Yes, we're lost; we lost the trail on Crater Lake," Davy answered.

The flap was thrown back and Davy and I were welcomed into the shadowy tent, where the flickering light of candles showed a blur of faces in the cloud of steam from wet blankets. A fire was burning in a small Yukon stove, and the air, mingled with the body heat of the men, was heavy and hot.

Kind hands led me to a pile of brush that had been gathered for fuel to keep the little stove roaring. Here we rested and were given a cup of hot tea. I sat on a pile of brush and Davy leaned against my knees. I was happy to have him close, to be out of the storm, to be safe!

A wave of contentment came over me. My heart was filled with peace and happiness. I wanted to

stay awake all night so that I could continue to realize, consciously, that we were safe. I begrudged myself the sleep that now and again closed my tired eyes.

I would nod and awaken suddenly to hear the
storm still shrieking. In my heart was a prayer of
gratitude that Davy and I were away from the terror
of the wind.

The men were telling of adventures in other lands
where gold had been found. Each man had his own
experience to relate—about what had happened in
Africa, Australia, India, China, California. I wished
Davy was not so tired and could tell them of his
adventures in South America, of the engineering job
he had superintended in the high Andes. I wanted
these men to know that Davy, too, had traveled and
had accomplished things before he became sick.

The night passed and when morning came the
storm was still raging with no sign of abatement.
Davy wanted to go out and find our tent so that we
could have a shelter of our own.

"Davy, I can't bear to see you go alone," I insisted.
"I must go with you."

But the men would not let me go out into the
storm. Several of them offered to go. While they
were gone I helped the owner of the tent prepare
hot tea, hardtack and dried meat for the men. Davy
and his companions erected the tent and we moved
in, but our privacy was short-lived. We were no
sooner in than four men came, asking for shelter.
These men were packing merchandise and government supplies for the Mounted Police at Lake Lindeman, and they, too, had lost the trail.

"May we come in out of the storm?" they begged.

"Well, we can't see you freeze," Davy answered.

They all managed to squeeze into our tent. The men were hungry and lost no time in preparing some food. Two of them rustled brush to burn, and the wind-swept tamarack and juniper bushes made a hot fire. One of the men had a little Yukon stove, another a bag of flour. Two of them were packing a hundred-pound firkin of butter apiece. The flour sack was opened by making a round hole in the top. In this hole, pancake batter was made of melted snow and baking powder, using what flour was needed without spoiling the rest. A firkin of butter was opened and a generous slab shaved off for baking and for spreading on the finished pancakes. My tea, sugar, and other useful things came out of the bucket to contribute to a fine meal for the hungry travelers.

I thought, "It's remarkable how little one can manage to get along on and still fare very well."

After eating the good supper, they made their beds in their blankets and then talked long into the night of politics, travel, mining, and of gold being found in the Klondike. One of the men told of his home in California and bragged about the fine bread their Chinese cook could bake. He gave us the details of the baking, even to mixing in a cup of boiled rice, while I listened and followed each step. I had never baked a loaf of bread in my life, but now I felt sure I could do it.

Davy and I crawled into our blankets; I stayed awake to listen as long as I could, but soon I was lost in sleep.

I slept next to the wall of the tent. During the night my heavy braid of brown hair had escaped from under the blanket, and when I tried to get up the next morning, I found that it had become frozen to the ground. I pulled it loose and thought it quite funny. Nothing seemed to matter; I felt strangely happy and ready for anything.

Now we had to find the trail and begin the journey back to Sheep Camp. Although the storm was still raging, we packed our things and started on our way. The wild wind was so strong that frequently we were forced to our knees.

On the way we came upon a band of Indians caching their things under a tarpaulin. They were yelling and screaming, making weird sounds above the hiss and howl of the wind. I was frightened and wished I did not have to pass them. One of the packers told Davy that the Mounted Police were giving them double pay to show the white packers how brave Indians were to bring packs up the mountainside in the blizzard, but the wind was so fierce that even the Indians, who were accustomed to it, could hardly go on. Passing us, they dogtrotted down the steep trail, shouting and screaming above the howl of the wind. The storm and the shrieking of the Indians were terrifying and unearthly in the eerie green light.

Going down the slippery trail I could not keep on my feet. Slipping and rolling, I slid most of the way to the foot of the trail. But I held fast to my little valise.

At last we reached the Summit. The Indians had reported that a white woman was in the storm on the trail, and Major Walsh of the Mounted Police was waiting to meet us and took me to the barracks.

I was brushed free from snow, for I looked like an animated snow man. I was given a hot, juicy steak, the first fresh meat I had had for weeks. Davy went to the tent of a friend, where he arranged for a bed. Later he came to the barracks for me and found me rested and happy, listening to the police tell of their experiences on the trail.

The storm abated, but the white caps of the mountains seemed to close in. The Mounted Police sent out warnings that no more small boats could be used on lakes and rivers on account of the running ice. The big freeze-up was upon the land. Soon the only way to travel would be by the frozen trails on lakes and rivers. This was a great disappointment to Davy and me, for now we would have to stay in Sheep Camp all winter. What would we do for money?

Facing this problem was bad enough, but soon Davy came to me with more bad news. There had been a snowslide on Crater Lake, carrying everything away that was cached on the mountainside. A large cache of goods had been stored there for the winter, and our outfit was among them.

"Now, what will we do?" Davy asked. "The outfit's gone, and there's no hope of getting anything until spring. All we have left are the few things cached here at Sheep Camp. We have no money to live on, because things cost so much, nor have we enough money to go back. What will we do?"

"Davy, dinna ye fret; something will come up. We'll get through somehow," I told him, with a bit more confidence than I really felt.

"But where is the money coming from?" Davy wanted to know.

"Wait a wee," I said.

Later I heard two men talking. One said, "If I had known how to run an engine I could have had a good job. Cavanaugh at Sheep Camp offered to give me work at his wood camp running the engine to cut the lumber, but I didn't know enough about it."

I hurried to find Davy. Davy could make any engine run. He knew all about a job like this; he had done this sort of work in South America. He was pleased to hear of it and hurried at once to get the job. Davy even got a place for me to help Mr. Cavanaugh's sister cook for the men at the lumber camp. I could at least earn my keep and we would be able to save all our money to get a new outfit.

All women are supposed to know how to cook, and a man offered me fifteen dollars a day to make biscuits and pies in his hotel. Davy was insulted. "I will not allow my wife to work as long as I am able to care for her," he said.

I never forgave Davy for spoiling my chance to make all that money. However, I did not know how to make either biscuits or pies at that time, but I was sure I could learn.

Chilkoot Pass

DURING THE WINTER, while Davy was running the sawmill engine, I was helping cook and learning a great deal about cooking, and earning my board besides. Miss Cavanaugh and I had a lot of fun; there was always something to laugh about. There was a young woman sent out by an Eastern newspaper to write up the gold rush, and she liked to enter into our good times. We three set out one afternoon to go to the Summit. As usual, I carried my little valise.

"Why do you always carry that little valise?" the newspaperwoman asked. "You must have diamonds in it."

"Not diamonds," I said, "but opals." I took the lovely stones out and showed them to her.

"Oh, my goodness!" exclaimed both girls. "Don't you know opals are unlucky?" they asked.

"Why don't you get rid of them?" the Eastern woman said. "Sell them, or give them away even."

"Shall I give them to you?" I asked.

"Not me; they're beautiful, but I wouldn't have them. I don't believe in tempting fate, especially in this country. One must be careful of one's luck up here. Everything depends on it. No opals for me."

We talked about it several times. Finally they convinced me the opals had cast their spell over Davy and me. Davy had had poor health ever since he was in South America. Then there was the ranch, and now the snowslide. The more I thought about it the more I was certain the opals had brought bad luck. I went out on the trail alone. I knew I must do something about it. I lifted the opals out of the valise and looked at them. They were full of fire; it was as if they were alive. For a moment I wondered how anything so beautiful could bring bad luck. But if they were responsible for Davy's poor health! Davy had never been sick as a boy; he was always so strong and well. I must not run the risk of anything happening to my husband. I had always loved the opals, but now I closed my mind to the lure of the jewels. At my feet was a hoofprint of a pack horse. It had been made in the soft mud, but now it was frozen into a little well which seemed to me a suitable grave for these omens of evil. So I dropped them into the hole and covered them with stones. The opals were again hidden from sight in the dark earth! I was relieved and felt free of our bad luck and went back to tell Davy.

"That's just like you, Peg, to do a thing like that," Davy said.

I have thought that if I ever went back to that part of the country I could find those opals. I don't believe in bad luck now.

The last of March Davy left his job at the sawmill. He and I went to Dyea to purchase a new outfit. Though this one was not as large as the first, it was more practical. Living in the northern country had given us an understanding of its needs. We made arrangements to have the new outfit sent to Lake Lindeman by a company which was freighting goods to the Waterways.

Some of our first outfit was still cached at Sheep

Camp and had to be packed over the Summit to the lake. We were working at this when the great snowslide of April 3, 1898, took place. This calamity occurred at Stone House, about two miles above Sheep Camp, where there was a cutoff from the regularly traveled trail. It was in this same place that Davy and I had witnessed a snowslide the first time we went over the trail. The Indian packers had warned the people of this danger, telling them that it was especially bad at this time of the year.

The heavy snow from the night before obliterated the trail, causing exceptionally hard going toward the Summit. Most of the white packers had quit and the Indians refused to travel, warning everyone against a possible snowslide. But some did not heed this warning and were caught in the tremendous avalanche of snow which roared down the steep mountain and choked off a long stretch of the trail. Sixty-three men and one woman were buried alive, under snow piled over them to the depth of thirty feet. The following day as we climbed the trail we looked down and saw some of the bodies being removed. Seven were taken out alive, but only three survived.

The sight of the snowslide disaster had upset me, so Davy insisted that I rest in the hotel at Lake Lindeman, a rudely constructed shelter, while he went back to Sheep Camp for another load.

I was resting when I heard a confusion of voices outside. Above the babble arose a woman's voice, crying and swearing. The man who owned the hotel was trying to quiet her.

"Woman," he ordered, "quit that cussing. There

is a lady in here, so shut up!" This only made the woman cry harder and louder.

I ran out in time to see the woman pull a baby out of a dog sled. The child, so rudely awakened, joined its mother in crying. But after the mother had nursed the baby, it quieted down and went to sleep in my arms. The woman, too, seemed to feel better after she had eaten and told her troubles. Her husband had left her at home in the States while he joined the gold rush. She had determined to follow him. It had been a long, hard trip, and the farther she traveled, the angrier she grew. At the end of almost every sentence she swore vengeance, and threatened she would "kill him in cold blood."

The woman rested overnight at Lake Lindeman, and the next morning she started on her way in spite of advice to the contrary. She was a large, strong woman, and her anger gave her power to overcome bodily fatigue. The child appeared healthy in spite of the long trip.

I never learned if this incident ended in comedy or tragedy. I often thought of the poor little baby. In this country nothing was too bizarre to happen. I saw the first chapter of many wild tales, of which I never heard the ending.

Davy was returning back to Lake Lindeman when, on the trail between the Summit and Lake Lindeman, he was overtaken by a terrific storm, the last big storm of the year. The wind screamed and howled as it had done the time we were lost on Crater Lake. On this trip Davy was packing a sack of flour. He could hardly stand, the wind was so strong; he struggled on, step by step. The driving sleet pierced his face

like steel needles. For days now he had been traveling with the glare of the sun on the snow. Suddenly he was struck by a pain in his eyes. He realized
at once what this pain meant. He had seen men
driven crazy by snow-blindness. It made them helpless, panic-stricken.

Fear almost overpowered him. He was shaking so
violently he could hardly make headway in the wind.
It tossed him about and threw him to his knees. He
crawled about on the trail, shielding his aching eyes
in his arm as though trying to ward off the blows
of devils. He *must* get up on his feet and keep going. He fought on and on, doggedly, with grim
stubbornness. At last he realized he could carry the
pack no further. The trail was familiar to him, even
in the thick storm, so he left the sack of flour in a
place where he knew he could find it. The pain in his
eyes grew worse. Would he lose his sight entirely before he could reach me? Frantically he struggled on.

It was somewhat easier traveling without the burden of the pack. Mile after mile he stumbled along.
Lake Lindeman was eight miles from the Summit;
it was hard going, trudging into the teeth of the
blizzard, and racked with the pain of snow-blindness.
The pain in his eyes was constantly growing more
maddening. When he finally stumbled into the little
hotel he could not have gone another yard.

I had a man put up our tent, and we went to our
own two selves. There I made Davy as comfortable
as I could.

"Davy," I told him, "ye will get over your blindness."

I tried to comfort him. But Davy's suffering was

almost more than he could bear. An ulcer was forming at the back of one of his eyes. The pain was so
severe that beads of perspiration stood out on his
forehead. I would hold his head in my arms for hours,
and sometimes Davy slept this way, utterly spent
with pain. Tears would stream down my face as
I watched my husband who had always been so independent and sure of himself. Now I led him by
the hand like a little child.

"Oh, your wonderful healing hands, how could I
stand this pain without these hands!" Davy would
say. "I hated to see you spoil them by helping to
cook for those rough men last winter. God! How I
hated it! You had never done work like that before.
What would your brother Jack think?" Davy fretted.

"Don't worry about my hands. What does it
matter? These hands are glad to work for you," I
told him.

April and part of May passed, and Davy was in
agony most of the time. I did not know what we
were going to do. But never once did we consider
going back to the States, even if there had been
enough money for our passage.

We waited patiently for our second outfit to come
up from Dyea. We had paid to have it packed up
to Lake Lindeman. It must come. I had sent message
after message about it, and had had one in return,
to the effect that the goods had been lost in transit,
but that the outfit would be found and sent on to
us soon. Each day we watched and waited. I thought
of going back to Dyea to find out about it, or make
them pay for the goods. But I dared not leave Davy.
He needed my care. A great fear gripped me.

"What will I do?" I thought desperately. Then there came to me a scene from my childhood. It was a cold day in early spring. The slush of snow was underfoot. I had walked with my father, mother, and brother Jack to church in Arnprior—as no one ever thought of taking the horses out on the Sabbath day. It was three long Scotch miles, and the old stone kirk was even colder than the snow outside. There was no heat, for such comforts were sins, frowned upon by religious folk.

I was cold and I snuggled under my mother's plaid and kept swinging my little feet back and forth to keep them warm. In spite of the cold I felt myself getting sleepy. All at once I heard the minister reading the Ninety-first Psalm. Jack and I had just learned it. I sat up and began saying it to myself.

"He shall cover thee with his feathers, and under His wings shalt thou trust—" On and on went the good man's voice. "For he shall give His angels charge over thee, to keep thee in all thy ways."

" 'Angels charge over thee!' " I thought. "Why, if God sends his angels to take care of me, why do I have to be afraid? I never shall be again, for God keeps his promises. I won't be afraid of anything again."

I thought of the lovely white feathers in the angels' wings. I could cuddle under them just as I could under Mother's plaid. A door seemed to open in my child's mind. Everything was all rosy and gold. For the first time God seemed real and close. His angels meant protection.

I felt this same protection now. I said over and over the Ninety-first Psalm, finishing with the plea:

"Oh, God, show me what to do, and give me the strength to do it."

At last the answer came to me. My mind was made up. I must go back to Dyea and find out about the outfit and get the medicine for Davy's eyes.

A man we knew was camped about a mile from our tent. I went to him and asked him to stay with Davy while I made the trip to Dyea. I offered to pay him well and he agreed to take good care of Davy and to cook his meals. I then told Davy my plan. He thought he could not bear to have me go alone. He was afraid I might get lost, especially since the trail was more or less deserted at this time. He feared for me to go by way of the ice, which might be too melted and rotten. And then there were the bears, just waking from their winter's nap, cross and hungry. Davy was filled with fears—black, horrible, sick fears. He could not protest against my going, however, for what could he do? He was blind and helpless.

The distance from Dyea to Lake Lindeman was twenty-four miles. I prepared for the days I would be away, cooking as much as I could. I made Davy comfortable with our meager supplies and placed blankets over the ridgepole of the tent to keep out the heat of the sun, for it was hot during the day and the daylight lasted through the night.

The man I had hired promised not to leave Davy, but I was not sure I could trust him. As I made my preparations, I prayed over and over, "Oh, God, take care of Davy!"

Never in all my life had I found anything as hard to do as to leave Davy alone in his suffering and blindness. I leaned over him and kissed his thin cheek lightly. I did not want him to know when I left. He pretended to be asleep when I hurried out of the tent and commenced the long trek back to Sheep Camp and Dyea. My knees trembled as I ran along the trail. Over and over again I said my little prayer for Davy's protection.

I had set out at one o'clock at night, because it was colder then and the top ice, which had melted on the lakes and rivers during the day, would be frozen again so that I could travel on it. There were still a few more days before the breakup. Davy had warned me that the ice might not be safe. When I reached Long Lake, which connected Lake Lindeman with Crater Lake, I stopped to heed his warning. The ice looked safe enough, but there was a five- or six-foot stretch of water that separated the shore from the solid ice that bore the trail. I stopped to determine what was best to do.

Just then a man appeared. He, too, stood gazing at the ice.

"Wonder if it will hold," he said, as much to himself as to me. He was a tall young man with a kind face and a pleasant smile.

"My husband warned me not to try it," I said timidly. "He told me to follow the shore."

The man darted a quick glance at me.

"Well, I'll take a chance on the ice if it's at all possible. You know about the bears, don't you?" he asked. "They are just waking up from winter and I don't fancy meeting one now. Oh, I think the ice will hold all right. The part where the trail runs is the strongest of all and the last to go out in the thaw.

I'm going to take a chance. I'll put my sleds together to make a bridge over this water next to shore and get out on the ice."

As I stood watching him I thought about the bears. The man now carried his goods over the uncertain bridge and then called his dogs. They picked their way daintily across the swaying sleds.

"Want to try it?" the man called to me. "If you're going down to Sheep Camp it's the quickest way. And it's safer than the bears." His eyes twinkled at me.

"Do you think I can get across?" I asked hopefully.

"Well, you'll have to take a chance." He smiled good-naturedly. "I'm due at Sheep Camp at a certain time or there's no use in my going, so I'll have to travel fast. If you are coming, come on. You stay about ten feet back of me and if I don't go in, it'll be all right. But if the ice gives, turn back and run like hell!"

Before we started he looked around and grinned. "I've got on borrowed boots," he laughed. "It cost me seven dollars for the loan of them. If I get drowned my friend will be out of luck."

He hurried along the trail. I followed as close as I could, although keeping up with him and his dogs was difficult. The ice was covered with a slush of water which soaked my clothes up to my knees, but I did not have time to think about it.

The rotten ice held and I crossed Long Lake in safety. My companion was far ahead, but he waved his hand and then sped on. Before I could reach the shore, however, I had to wade almost to my waist in icy water. I tried wringing the water from my skirt, but gave up and let it cling, wet and cold, to my legs as I ran along the trail to get warm.

Near the Summit there was an opening in the trail. I was startled as an evil-looking man came toward me. He had brazen black eyes and a drooping black mustache. He had fine new clothes and a heavy gold watchchain swinging from his plaid vest. He carried an overcoat over his arm and seemed out of place on the trail.

"Hello, there!" he greeted me as if he knew me. I mistrusted him at once. I knew no men of his type. Never before in my life had I feared a man. Never before had I been alone and unprotected. He came toward me.

"Where do you come from?" he asked. "Are you lost? Well, it's good I came along and found you all alone. How did you get all wet? Fall in?" he grinned.

He came close, ready to put his hand on me. I shrank back. I was frightened, but I did not dare show it.

"Oh, say now, you're a right good-looking gal. When we get you dressed up, some of the fellows will fall for you all right. I'm waitin' for Nell Martin. She's to be along. She'll give you a job in her dance hall. She's to be here most any time. I been waitin' down there at the Summit for her. Thought I'd take a walk. Good thing I come along and found you."

I looked him firmly in the eye. I would not let him know how he frightened me.

"I must go on," I said. "Let me pass, please."

"Ah, see here." He stepped in front of me. "Don't you want the job? You're not afraid of me?"

My heart was pounding.

Just then, down the trail toward the Summit, there came shouts and cursing. The man stopped leering at me.

"Listen, what's that?" he exclaimed. "Guess someone's comin'. Let's go see." He started toward the trail. "Come on, sister," he called. "Don't get scared —I'll take care of you. Don't try to run away from me."

I looked about. What should I do—try to run? No, I would not let him know I was afraid of him; and besides I could not run fast enough to get away, should he want to stop me. I would stand my ground.

A string of packers came along the trail. A flashy, rawboned woman strode into sight at their head. The man went toward her, grinning.

"Hello, Nell," he called. "I thought you'd never get here. Waited down there at the Summit. Come out here for a little exercise."

The woman looked him up and down with bold, bright eyes. "Why didn't you meet me at Dyea? Afraid of an extra climb?" she jeered. "Well, I got here, but I've had a hell of a time, packing in all this stuff for the girls. Who's your friend?" the woman asked, eyeing me with cold, unfriendly eyes.

"Thought you might have a place for another girl," the man laughed.

"Looks a bit wet and bedraggled," the woman answered indifferently, and went on talking of her trip Outside.

As they talked, I slipped away. Just as soon as I

was out of sight I ran with all my might down the steep trail. At last I reached Sheep Camp and went at once to the Seattle Hotel. Mrs. Card, who ran the hotel, was the sister of Miss Cavanaugh, the woman I had helped in the winter.

"What on earth has happened to your eyes? They look all washed out. I remember them as a dark hazel," Mrs. Card exclaimed.

The glare of the sun on the ice had caused an attack of snow-blindness and now my eyes felt as though a handful of splintered glass had been thrown into them. Mrs. Card treated them, dried my clothes, and made me as comfortable as possible.

The pain in my eyes was severe. I could not sleep, for I kept thinking of blind Davy and how terrible was his suffering. "Oh, God, don't let me become blind now!" I prayed. I cannot fail him. What would become of Davy if I did not get back to him? He had very little food and no medicine or tobacco. My eyes *must* get all right, for in the morning I had to go on.

Morning found my eyes sufficiently improved so that I could go on to Dyea. Here I found that the company which had been entrusted with my outfit was unable to locate it; but they were willing to pay me a part of its value. I could not wait longer to argue about it, for I must get back to my husband; so I accepted what they offered.

I was hurrying back from this errand and decided to look for a shelter for the night, as I felt I must rest before I began the long climb back to the Summit. To my chagrin, I came face to face with that man I had met. I was badly frightened, but made no sign of recognition. I wouldn't let him know I was afraid of him.

"Hello, there, sweetheart," he said flippantly. "I thought I had lost you. Glad to see you again."

I was in front of a small eating house. I walked in and the man followed me. I asked the motherly-looking Irishwoman back of the counter for something to eat, and inquired about finding lodging for the night. As I sat at the table the man seated himself beside me.

"Oh, come on, now," he said coaxingly, pulling at my arm. "I'll take you to a dance tonight. Let's be friends. I bet you can dance, can't you? Why don't you like me? All the girls do. Come on, let's get acquainted."

Worn out by a hard day on the ice and nervous from the attack of snow-blindness and shaking with fear, I could stand no more. The tears were very close.

"You wouldn't dare talk to me like that if my husband were here." I jerked away from him. "You let me alone!" I was so angry I would have struck him if I had had something to do it with.

The big, kindhearted Irishwoman, taking in the situation, came to my rescue and advanced toward the man with an angry gleam in her eye. He took one look at her and got to his feet in a hurry. Facing two angry women was a different matter, especially when one of them was big and strong and used to fighting.

"Now, you low-down trash, get out of here, and pretty fast, too! Don't you let me be a-seeing the likes of you about here again!" the woman said, picking up a chair.

He got out in a hurry.

"Now, don't you worry," said the good woman. "Come, dearie, you'll sleep right here with me and my family." She took me into the room back of the restaurant, and there she made me a bed on an old couch. I was safe, and warmed by the woman's friendship, I was soon asleep.

I awoke in the morning thinking of Davy and the long miles between us. This thought gave wings to my feet. The trail was greatly improved and I was able to travel with much less difficulty than the time Davy and I packed over it.

At last I reached Sheep Camp. I visited our cache and found things I had forgotten we had left there. I had to have help, so I engaged an Indian boy to pack it to the trading post. I determined to trade or sell the things for necessities. I had a rest at Mrs. Card's and then was ready to start.

Sheep Camp was in an uproar. A fire was sweeping up the canyon and the men were preparing to protect the camp. A pall of smoke drifted in on the wind and a sharp, acrid tang was in the air. Suppose the fire cut off my immediate return to Davy?

I had difficulty in persuading the storekeeper, whose mind was on the fire, to listen to me. But my necessity was so great that I lost all my shyness and insisted on his buying what I had to sell.

"But," said the storekeeper, "I can't buy your things. I might be burned out any time. Look at that smoke."

I paid no attention to his refusal. "If you can't give me money, won't you trade me some tea and tobacco for the things? If you get burned out you'll lose what you have in stock now anyway."

He thought that might be good reasoning, and accepted my things in trade for about ten pounds of tobacco and a large carton of tea. I bought Davy some medicine, new underwear, and a bottle of good liquor. I would not let the storekeeper leave until I had finished the trade and made all my purchases. By sheer force of will I made him help me get started, in spite of his interest in the fire. The Indian packer was loaded, and what was left I carried myself. I started on my way regardless of the advice of the excited people. The fire raged on, but I paid no heed to it.

At the Summit I had to declare the merchandise at the customs. Before doing this, however, I went into a place where I could get a cup of coffee. The proprietor asked me what I was taking in, and I told him some tea and tobacco for my sick husband.

"Well, you'll have to pay double duty on that tobacco if they know you've got it," he warned, and looked wise.

"Why should I be paying double duty on that tobacco?" I thought. "Davy needs it as much as he does medicine; and I must get it to him. No one shall stop me. Why let them know about it?"

I could not spare the money to pay double duty, having barely enough to meet our needs and get into the Klondike. I asked the restaurant keeper if I might step into the back room off his kitchen. I was wearing my suit of strong blue serge, and full bloomers underneath my ankle-length skirt and large balloon sleeves. Once before the big sleeves had been of use to me. They had filled with air when I fell off the horse into Dyea River. Slipping off the coat, I filled the large sleeves with small sacks of tobacco. And the bloomers, which had elastic about the knees, were filled with Star and Horseshoe Plug. I was now ten pounds heavier.

When the proprietor of the restaurant did not notice any change in my appearance as I passed him on going out, I felt confident that I could pass the customs officers without attracting undue attention.

I had to climb a long flight of steps to reach the Customs Office, which was built on high stilts to keep it above snow level. I started my ascent. I felt sure the police would notice my heavy load. However, up and up I climbed. What would happen if the rubber bands in my bloomers broke? Would the steps never end? They seemed mountain high. On and on I climbed, nearly stumbling in my fear and haste.

"They will just think me a fat old lady," I comforted myself.

At last I reached the Customs Office. Looking in, I was glad that I had hidden Davy's tobacco; for great stacks of money were piled on shelves, and on the floor in lard cans. Money every place. They didn't need our money. I looked the customs officers squarely in the face as I declared all my visible goods, including the tea. If the customs officers and the Mounties did suspect me of adding ten pounds since they saw me last, they did not voice their suspicions. I got my possessions past them successfully; waddling along, I made it by. The rubber bands held, and the Star and Horseshoe Plugs in the bloomers went down the long flight of steps.

With the aid of the Indian packer I now reached Crater Lake, cached my goods, and paid the Indian. Now that the goods were safe, I could travel the remaining eight miles to Lake Lindeman. The trip would take the rest of the night. The thought of bears kept me close to the shore along the muddy banks of Long Lake. I kept to the trail, sleepy, awearying, urging myself on with the thought of Davy and his happiness in receiving the medicine and tobacco.

I thought to myself: "What would my good mother think of my smuggling in that tobacco?" I remembered the time, when a wee lass, that my mother talked to me about the sin of deceiving. Our family saved the peelings from the vegetables for a neighbor's pigs. He would give my brother and me a penny now and then for bringing them to him. This morning my mother said to me:

"Peggy, you must not take a penny, should the farmer offer it to you. There is not enough—remember."

"I won't, Mother," I said.

But the farmer thought the peelings worth a penny, so he offered it to me. I hesitated, but the money looked so big and fascinating that I could not refuse it.

When I got home I ran and hid the penny in my bed. But I was afraid my mother would find it, so I hid it again. Then it did not seem safe there, so again I put it in what I thought a better place. I

worked at hiding the penny all day, and by night
I was worn out. I could not sleep, but lay looking
out of the window. The big, round, golden moon
looked in, watching me. Tears began to flow and
sobs shook me.

My mother came to my bedside. "What's wrong,
lass? Have you a stomach-ache?" she asked.

"No, Mother," I sobbed.

"Why do you cry?" Mother asked.

"Well, I did take the penny. I couldn't find anyplace to hide it. Here it is. It burns me!" I held
out the hot penny.

My mother sat beside me and told me what a
terrible sin it was to take what does not belong to
one—how wicked to deceive.

I thought of this as I ran along the trail. Well,
Davy must have his tobacco, no matter. This time
I was not sorry, even if it were a sin to deceive.

Suddenly I heard a crashing of brush and a scuf-
fling of padded feet. My heart stood still for a long
moment, and then it nearly tore itself out of my
breast with pounding. There came a snorting sound,
and a brown, hairy body about the size of a large
hog, scurried on ahead of me. Snorting and blowing,
the bear padded along the trail, and then turned off
into the brush. In the voilet light of the morning
I saw him disappear.

I ran and ran, stumbling, falling, and picking myself up again, the thought of Davy spurring me on.
Then at last I saw our tent. I forgot my weariness
as I ran in.

"Davy, oh, Davy, I'm back! And look! This is
your medicine, and here is your tobacco!"

"Oh, Peg, gir-rul, you're back! My God, I thought
—well, when you didn't come back, I thought. . . ."
But he never told me what he thought. Only his
trembling arms about me told me what it had meant
to him to have me back. His tears wet my cheek.

I laughed through my tears. "Davy, this is the
thirteenth time I've crossed that Chilkoot Pass. And
I'll say, 'I'll gan no mere to yon toon!' "

It did not matter now that our second outfit had
not been found and that there was little money.
Nothing mattered; for now Davy could have his pipe
and there was medicine for his eyes. We both laughed
and forgot everything. We were together.

Waterways

DAVY WAS WELL informed about this great northern country before we left California. He had made a study of the lakes and rivers, which are the highways. He knew that in summer the waterways were navigable, and in winter the ice made the trails.

Over and over he told me about the mighty Yukon River. Little did I think, at that time, what this river would mean to me. It sounded very interesting: a river 2,300 miles long, rising in Lake Lindeman, within twenty-five miles of the tidal waters of the Pacific, and flowing, in a northwesterly direction, just crossing the Arctic Circle. Like a great arch, it turns southwest through Alaska to reach the Bering Sea. The Yukon River is formed by the confluence of the Lewes and the Pelly rivers, the Lewes rising in Lake Lindeman.

It was at Lake Lindeman, the beginning of the Waterways, where Davy planned to buy or build a boat. We were to sail the five hundred miles to the Klondike. We, like other gold seekers, found it was not so easy as that. Although Chilkoot Pass had been a tough climb, we had before us the real hazard of our journey.

Davy knew all about boats and how to build them. He looked forward to the experience of the Waterways with perfect confidence that he could build a boat and manage it in any water. All he was told about the treacherous waters only gave him more interest.

There were few boats in 1898, and most of them had to be built. Men who had never made a single raft that could float on a peaceful pond constructed queer, crude crafts in which they hoped to navigate the stormy lakes and shoot the rapids of the Yukon country.

We were camped on the shore of Lake Lindeman. On the opposite side of the lake, the Carey Mill Company was building the largest scow that ever went through the Waterways. They were transporting supplies and machinery to build a sawmill at the mouth of White River.

There were enough provisions to last twelve men eighteen months, food for four horses and many dogs. There was engine equipment for the sawmill, also room for twelve men and their outfits on board. The scow was nearly completed when Mr. Parker, the manager, learned about Davy, and that he had run the engine for the sawmill at Sheep Camp during the winter. Mr. Parker figured if he could get an experienced engineer it would pay him to do so. He came to see Davy.

"I would be very glad to run the engine," Davy told him, "but I am blind. Had snow-blindness and haven't been able to get over it. I would be of no use to you."

"Oh, you'll be all right by the time we get there. People get over snow-blindness," encouraged Mr. Parker. "You can at least direct the men about setting up the machinery, and your wife might help with the cooking. We can make some sort of arrangement," he urged.

I assured him that I'd do all that I could. Davy and I were glad of this opportunity to get into the Klondike. This would solve our problem and give us security for a year. By that time something else would show up, I felt sure.

"I have only cooked for our own two selves," I told Davy, "but I know I can do it. I learned a lot last winter; I'll get along."

I had great confidence in my ability to do anything I wanted to do. Even as a wee lass I had this trait. Once when I was about eight years old, I thought to do some dressmaking for myself. Mother never forgot this incident, and was always telling it until it became family history.

During the trip I succeeded very well with the cooking. The men took great pride in my bread baking and would boast, whenever the opportunity arose, that they had the best bread baker in the Yukon on their scow. I recalled the night we were lost at Crater Lake and the man who shared our tent. He went into great detail about how his Chinese cook made bread. I made my bread step by step just that way, and it turned out fine.

One of the men on the scow liked to cook and was always bragging about his ability. I never allowed him to see I did not know much about cooking, but led him on to tell me how he did things, and then I would say, "That is a good way. Shall we do it like that?" The man was pleased and flattered and helped me a great deal. In fact, I could never have done the cooking without his help.

The engine and machinery were in place and made secure. The provisions were packed away. I watched the animals being put aboard.

"Davy, it's like Noah's Ark. There go the animals two by two."

I was happy that we were not apprehensive about the immediate future. Our troubles were behind us.

The time for starting came. It required hard work —pushing, pulling and shoving to get the clumsy scow on its way. The men worked with all their might. On each side were great sweeps or oars. Two men operated these, one pushing forward and the other pulling backward, and the man with the sweep at the stern steered the scow. When under way, they hoisted the sail.

I stood beside Davy, telling him everything that was happening. I was glad to see his interest and to listen to what he thought they should do about the sail. Davy, having been a sailor, knew a great deal about sails.

All at once a wind struck us and the scow began to plunge along at a rapid rate. I was anxious. The shore slipped swiftly away and the gale gathered strength. I stood close to Davy, watching. He was calm. I was glad that it did not worry him. I would not let him know that I was frightened as the scow raced in the wind.

"Oh, what if we upset," I thought. "I can't swim, and how could I save Davy?"

I could see that the men were uneasy as they came near the shore. All hands on board worked with a will. Strong muscles were needed to keep the scow from crashing against the rocks. Poles were caught beneath submerged stones and torn from the hands that held them as the barge swept swiftly on. However, we managed to navigate this first lake in safety. I was relieved when the sail was taken down and we slowed up a bit.

Lake Lindeman is eleven miles long and one and a half miles wide. It is drained by a small river called One Mile River, seventy-five to one hundred feet in width and a little over a mile in length. It is a repetition of shallow rapids, cascades and boulders, and a network of driftwood. The course of the river is split by huge boulders. We were soon on this small waterway.

Ahead of us a boat had crashed on the rocks. The lone man who was on it managed to scramble upon the rock that had wrecked his boat. Here he stood watching the angry waters tossing away his hopes of reaching the Klondike. He had built his first boat at Lake Lindeman, we learned later. When taking it through One Mile River it was dashed to pieces on the rocks. He had gone back, built a second, and it, too, met a similar fate. Having some money left, he patiently built a third; but One Mile River said: "You cannot pass." Here, about him, whirled the wreck of his last boat. Money gone, discouraged, he drew his gun and shot himself, falling forward into the mad little river.

We saw this tragedy. The accident caused hours of delay. Our men rescued his body from the river. Now they must wait for the Mounted Police to take charge.

Our turn came to go through the same narrow passage. The scow was almost too large. Everything removable had to be portaged by land, and the scow was dragged and pulled and snubbed until finally it managed to crawl through. It was a whole day's job. Fortunately, daylight was twenty-four hours long.

I went ashore, but Davy said he would stay aboard. From the high bank I could look down and watch the men working. I felt lonely and worried, for it was impossible to get back to Davy. There he was alone, the men working all about him. I thought how helpless he was without me. I must never fail him. My proud Davy, blind and helpless! I could not stand the thought.

I heard a man's step. It was Jack, one of the Mac-Donald lads. "Have you been here all day without anything to eat?" he asked, smiling at me.

"I was wondering how I could get back to my husband. He is all alone down there. I did not think of that when I came ashore," I said.

We watched the slow-moving scow.

"Don't worry about it. They'll soon get through; then we'll make speed when we get on Lake Bennett," Jack encouraged me.

He had a kind, gentle way of speaking. I felt comforted and was now sure all would come out well. I had been interested in the MacDonald lads, strong, sturdy Scotchmen, from the first. They were paid passengers on the scow. Jack, the elder, was tall, sandy-haired, with kind blue eyes and an ever-ready sense of humor.

We climbed down to the shore together. Jack's hand on my arm made me feel safe and protected.

When the struggle in One Mile River was over, the men encouraged one another: "Well, if we made

it through there, we can make it to the Klondike.
There surely can't be a worse mile in all the North
than that one mile of trouble."

On Lake Bennett we tied up, dried our clothes,
and rested. The things which had been portaged were
loaded back on the scow again.

I searched my mind for adjectives to describe lovely Lake Bennett to Davy. The blue ice glaciers in
the distance, in relief the red rocks and ridges of
Iron Mountains, and over all a pink light as if it
were seen through a rosy veil.

Davy was feeling better; being on the water helped
him to forget his suffering a bit.

The work seemed almost like play at times; the
men were kind and helpful and showed my Davy
every consideration. Jack was always ready to lend
a hand. We two found many things to laugh about,
and a deep understanding grew up between us.

The scow was open. The grain and other perish-
able things were covered with a canvas. But everything else had only a sky overhead. Jack fixed a
shelter for Davy and covered it with a tarpaulin so
that he could be in a dry place when it rained, or
when the spray flew over things. Here I could crawl
in beside him at night, or to rest a bit when I had
time.

I went about the cooking as though I had cooked
all my life. I learned quickly, and there was plenty
to cook. The stove was fastened securely to the deck.
I was glad of that. When the scow rolled, the cooking utensils jingled about from one side of the stove
to the other, and they sometimes slipped off. There
was a big pile of wood to use, and Jack always tended

the fire. I fried ham and bacon, cooked rice and beans, and dried fruit. I put the bread to rise as soon as I had finished one meal, and it would come up like magic and be ready for the next.

The men told me they had never enjoyed food more. I smiled to myself and thought that the fresh air and water might be helping, but I never suggested this.

The men would come to the stove with their plates, and with cups for coffee. They would take their knives and spoons and find a place to sit on a sack of grain, a box, or anything available. There was a lot of laughing and telling of experiences and jokes. Even Davy would try to join in the fun. It was almost like a picnic.

After a rest, the men were ready to tackle the thirty miles of beautiful Lake Bennett. The sail was hoisted; the men called back and forth. I could hardly get the dishes washed for watching all that was happening. When they got out on the lake, a wind came up, tossing us about. The scow picked up speed. Spray was flying and clouds were rushing over the blue sky, hiding the sun. A disagreeable rain began spitting over everything. I helped Davy to his shelter. The wind whipped about me, tossing my hair into my eyes and tearing things about.

I climbed back to the stove to see about the food, and to find a safer place for the batch of bread that I had put to rise in the big dishpan, with a "gold pan" turned over it. The rain was coming down in sheets and I was getting pretty wet. The wind increased to a storm and waves swept over the scow. The wind caught the canvas over Davy's shelter and pulled at it, while rain whipped in upon him. I made my way to his side and held the canvas in place.

Jack said, "Here, crawl in beside your husband out of this rain."

But I said no, I had to watch the stove and try to save my bread. Besides, I did not want to miss anything.

The scow pitched and tossed. The men yelled at each other, arguing as to whether it was better to drop the sail or take a chance on continuing to make good time. I hoped that they would do the former. I was afraid that the scow would be wrecked and Davy go into the water. Jack tried to comfort me.

"Don't worry," he shouted above the wind. "Don't be afraid. It's letting up a bit."

I screamed back as best I could, through chattering teeth, "Oh, I'm not afraid. But if we go in, will you please save my husband? I can't swim."

"Sure, and I'll save you, too," Jack assured me.

The barge was headed for the shore and the sail was dropped. We could see the beach strewn with big boulders. It took all the men to keep the scow off the rocks and guide it to a safe anchorage in a little cove.

Everything was all right now. I forgot that I was wet and cold. The bread was not spoiled by the rain. There was a rim of water about the edge of the "gold pan" but it did not stop it from rising. At supper the men said it was the best bread I had ever baked. The storm was soon forgotten; I was ready for the next adventure.

It was over four hundred miles from Lake Lindeman to our destination at the mouth of White River.

The men organized the work into day and night shifts so that they could keep moving all the time. There was little difference between day and night. It meant that there must be meals at all hours. But the men were kind and told me that I need not stay up all night. However, I did, in spite of Davy's anger at my working so hard. I felt thankful that we had food to eat and a way to reach the Klondike. I wanted to do all I possibly could. Besides, I was enjoying the excitement. I could catch a few winks of sleep between times. Always, there was the sense of well-being and living for the moment.

Jack and I laughed at everything. It was all so gay. Just as soon as one bit of danger was past, it was forgotten.

"Davy," I called, as I climbed over to him, "if you were only well, I'd like nothing better than this— sleeping with just the sky overhead and the water rippling for music. But you *are* better. The worst is past," I said, as I snuggled up close for a few minutes of rest. "I am so glad that we're here in the North. We'll make the Klondike, and everything will be fine. I'm happy, Davy; are you?"

"Yes, gir-rul, I am," Davy agreed.

But I could not forget his blind eyes. Proud, blind eyes.

We arrived at the end of the outlet to Lake Bennett without mishap. The sail was lowered and we entered a river. The scow floated peacefully along. The men were enthusiastic.

"All troubles are over now; it will be much easier on a river," they said. "The river has it all over a lake."

Just then the scow grounded and ran upon a sand bar! It was a big job to float it again.

At the foot of Lake Tagish was Tagish House, the government post where all on board must go ashore to register. Here I saw two Indians in custody, murderers who had killed a white man. They were to be made an example of, in order to make the Indians understand that white men were not to be molested.

The river at this point was full of sand bars, on some of which we got stuck. Mr. Parker, the manager, who was supposed to do the steering with the big sweeps at the stern of the scow, grew tired of so much criticism.

"We're wasting time trying to find all these sand bars. Why don't you keep downstream?" the men would shout.

At last Mr. Parker shot back: "Now, you fellows who know so much, suppose you take a try."

One man tried his luck, and then another. At first they laughed, then at times grew edgy. Even Davy tried directing the men. I felt sure that he could do it. But he, too, failed. Jack MacDonald was the last to take his turn. When he also struck a bar, his face flushed and he looked unhappy.

"Dinna you mind, lad, you struck the best sand bar in the river," I told him. Then we both laughed. But I stopped when I looked at Davy's sober face. I suddenly realized that Jack and I were always laughing together.

Time after time everything portable had to be packed ashore to float the scow off a bar. The horses and dogs enjoyed it, and so did I. The horses had some green food, and the dogs a good run, but the men were impatient at the loss of time.

Sometimes, when I returned to the scow after having been ashore, and came upon the men suddenly, one man would call out: "Shut up that talk. Here she comes." There was no "cussing" when I was around.

I was glad that it was daylight all the time—even if I didn't get much sleep. Sleep wasn't needed when there was all the outdoors to enjoy. The songs of birds drifted to us from the banks. Feathery white clouds floated softly in the sky above the lovely purple and blue mountains in the distance.

Sometimes the men fished. The graylings seemed eager to bite. The jackfish could be caught as fast as lines were thrown in. It was a real gypsy life; I was happy.

At mealtimes all our troubles were forgotten. The good food was all that interested us. One of the men told me how his mother used to make cookies, said to be the best ever baked, but the men declared that mine were even better! I made piecrust out of bacon drippings, and the filling out of dried peaches or prunes. I made rice puddings. My cooking talent was growing.

The most miserable part of our trip was the five days on muddy Marsh Lake, the banks of which were boggy and covered with reeds. The mosquitoes, like fiendish gray ghosts, made life intolerable for both the men and animals. But for some reason they didn't bother me as they did the men.

One of the men told Indian tales of how the mosquitoes would kill animals in the woods by causing

their eyes to swell shut so that they could not see to
find food, and thus they starved to death.

"Jack, your eyes are almost shut. The mosquitoes
can't find many more bites on you," I said, and
laughed at him. "You won't be able to eat. You'll
be like the bears and dogs."

"Don't you fret; I'll be able to find my mouth
when I smell those pies you make," Jack answered.

I had to keep everything covered when I was cooking. Taking a cover off of a pan would reveal a rim
of dead mosquitoes. It was hard to keep them out
of the food. "Well," I would tell the men, "when
you find a dead mosquito, be glad, for he won't ever
bite you."

Our nerves were frayed when at last we came
into the swift waters of a river three hundred yards
in width, and gradually contracting as it neared
the upper gate of the canyon. Here the stream became a white-capped wave of rolling water. Through
this narrow sheet of corrugated rock the wild waters
rushed in a milk-white foam. The thundering vibra-
tions, intensified by the rock walls which acted as a
sounding board, could be heard at a great distance
—a terrifying sound! The bank was overshadowed
by spruce trees. When the men on the scow heard
the noise of these mighty waters, they thought them
much closer than they really were, as sound carries
farther in the clear air.

They brought the scow to one side of the bank,
and all the men got off to inspect the thundering
rapids, each one thinking that the other had tied
the scow. Davy and I were left alone on board.

While the men were away I watched a man and

a woman on another raft that was tied up close to ours. They were having a heated argument, which later came to blows. The man was trying to bargain with another man who had a larger raft, to which he wanted to tie his frail craft in order to get through the rapids more easily. But the woman cried, and insisted that she would not be tied to any other raft, but would go through on her own. Her husband, at last, used force to beat his ideas into her head.

"I'd rather be dead! I'd rather be dead," the woman screamed, "than be tied up to any raft."

"Oh, go to hell!" the man bellowed.

"Well, you'll both go there if you try to go through in that pile of logs," a man from the shore yelled to them.

While I was watching the fight, I became conscious of the fact that the scow was moving slowly out into the channel.

"My God! Don't you know you're untied!" someone shouted to us from the shore! "Where are your men? You're moving out into the current. You'll get into the rapids of Miles Canyon. That'll be the end of you!"

The thundering of the waters was terrifying. I didn't know what to do.

"Davy! Davy!" I cried to my husband.

Frantically the men on shore were getting a boat ready to come to us. I could see them, but I was afraid they would be too late to save us. At that moment Jack MacDonald appeared, ahead of the other men. Instantly he saw what was happening. Shouting loudly for the others to follow him, but not waiting for them, he leaped into a boat and rowed madly to the rescue.

The men followed in another boat. They got on board the scow and, with all their combined strength, they managed to get the barge turned before it was caught by the current and carried into the angry, whirling waters of thundering Miles Canyon.

Mr. Parker and the other men were excited as they talked about how near the scow came to getting into the canyon, where the river closes in abruptly and races with terrifying strength through the dark, narrow canyons and then over a series of rapids. The canyon and rapids together made five miles of the roughest kind of water. They said how great a loss the valuable cargo would have been.

But Jack MacDonald seemed to think more about Davy and me.

The men had found out that the Mounted Police compelled all boats and barges to employ an experienced pilot through Miles Canyon and the Whitehorse Rapids.

Everything that was movable on the scow was portaged. Davy and I walked around Miles Canyon and Whitehorse Rapids. I was glad for the walk, and when I got a glimpse of Whitehorse Rapids I was grateful that we were not going through them.

At the northern outlet of the canyon the rushing river spreads to its former width, and travels, thundering and whirling, over boulders, bars, and driftwood. It is even more dangerous than Miles Canyon, and is known as the Graveyard, or Whitehorse Rapids. The banks were strewn with wreckage and scattered outfits. Here was the end of many a man's hopes of getting to the Klondike.

We had engaged a capable pilot. The scow came through safely into Lake Lebarge, the largest of the lakes, thirty miles long and five miles wide, and entirely surrounded by mountains.

A big forest fire was burning as we emerged from the river into the lake and I kept watching the fire brands carried across the river by the wind. It seemed as if little imps rode on them to start a fire on the other side. It was a frightful sight, and the smoke got into our eyes and throats.

On Lake Lebarge a wind came up that made the storm on Lake Bennett seem like a mere breeze. The lake was like an ocean, and the strength of the waves tossed the scow about like a toy. It raced and plunged in the wind until the men feared it would go to pieces, and the boom struck me on the head and knocked me out. When I regained consciousness I found myself beside Davy, where Jack MacDonald had carried me to shelter. Even the animals realized that it was more than a mere "blow." The dogs howled and the horses stampeded. And my head ached so badly that I could hardly get my senses back.

Lebarge was the last of the big lakes. We tied up not far from the *Alice May*, which was under construction at the time. She was later given fame by Robert W. Service, who wrote of how

> on the marge of Lake Lebarge
> I cremated Sam McGee.

Davy was now getting partial sight in one eye

and could take care of himself. This made it easier
for me.

Along the rivers the sweeps caused me much
trouble. These were the trees that the river had par-
tially washed out of the bank. They would fall,
leaning over into the water, held only by their roots.
As the scow came along, the sweeps would knock
all before them. One day I had my entire dinner
and my favorite cooking utensils brushed off into
the water.

When we were tied up at different places we exchanged experiences with others who were resting,
too. The men on the scow often bragged about my
cooking to others who did not have a cook on their
barge. My success with bread baking was due to
hearing a man tell how it was done that night we
were lost on Crater Lake and we shared our tent
with the four government packers. This man's description of his Chinese cook's bread had stayed with
me and I recalled it clearly when I needed to use it.

At Big Salmon some Indians came up beside us
in a flat-bottomed boat. "Got any fresh meat?"
the men asked them.

"No," answered the Indians.

"What, no meat?" The men could see part of a
butchered animal in their boat.

"Yes, got meat," contradicted the Indians.

Then began the trade. The men held up a bar of
hard pink soap, then two bars. Indians liked soap.
I doubt if they ever used it! At last the trade was
made. When the men got the meat on board they
smelled it and said, "Why, the damn stuff stinks."
Then they threw it into the water. The Indians

watched. Not to be outdone, they sniffed and sniffed at the pink soap they had traded for. They said, "Damn stuff stinks," and tossed it far out on the bank. But they watched where it fell, so that later they could retrieve it. Indians are smart. They howled and laughed. It was all a fine joke. "White man had strange ways, white man queer."

In the early days one of the largest Indian camps in the Yukon was situated at the mouth of the Little Salmon. There was a trading post and the missionaries had built a church there. Along the bank of the river the round-eyed, dirty Indians looked on in wild curiosity at the passing boats and barges. Indians loved to barter or trade anything they possessed.

When our scow was tied up beside another raft at this place, I was much disturbed about a trade that was taking place on board the raft next to us. A family of Indians were trying to trade a girl of eleven years to the men on the raft for a sack of "white man's flour." Our scow pulled out before the trade was finished. I was shocked and wanted to interfere. But the men assured me that it was quite impossible to civilize the Indians; besides, there were missionaries for that purpose.

About thirty miles below Lebarge, the river is very narrow, crooked, and swift. It is known as "Thirty Mile River." In order to pass through it the greatest navigation skill had to be exercised. More wrecks took place here than in Whitehorse Rapids. Sunken, treacherous rocks and a shallow, rapid current, reaching a speed of ten miles an hour in places, made the scow almost impossible to manage. The whirling waters lashed into foam over the great boulders on which a boat could easily be smashed.

On both sides the banks were sprinkled with the wrecked hopes of many a gold seeker who had safely made it past Miles Canyon and Whitehorse Rapids, only to go to pieces here. Bags of oatmeal and sacks of provisions from some poor fellow's outfit mutely told the tale.

There were boats that were mere boxes—anything that could float. It might have looked comic, had it not been so tragic. The old sourdoughs would say with a wistful grin: "The chechacos must learn":

> Winter Freeze-up,
> Summer Break-up,
> Chechaco first year,
> Then a Sourdough.

About two hundred and twenty-five miles below Whitehorse we met the most exciting part of the route. Here the boats must shoot the Five Finger Rapids, so named because of a row of huge conglomerated boulders which formed a series of small, flowing currents or fingers. Only one of these channels is navigable. Many did not know this. When our scow approached this smooth body of water, there seemed to rise, at the end of it, four natural castles of rock, apparently a long way off. As I watched, they appeared closer and closer, until soon we rushed at them!

Our scow was headed for the channel. We could see the opening before us. I held my breath—would we make it? The rapid current picked us up. No criticism of the pilot this time! All were wanting to help. It was now or never. Other exciting adventures paled beside this moment. Now, there was a strong current. We were tossed first toward one cliff and back again, and then toward the other and back again, while aiming at the opening. We seemed to be climbing a mountain of water, then plunging into a chasm. The scow plunged and fought like a bucking horse. It seemed to fight going through the channel but our pilot held her firm. I couldn't bear to look, so I clasped Davy's hand and shut my eyes, dreading the crash.

We had witnessed the wrecking of a raft that was torn to pieces just before it was our turn to try going through the channel. It was a double-decked raft, filled with cattle and sheep. It began to pick up speed and, in spite of the efforts of the men, a great wall of water carried them helplessly toward the rocks. The current, with powerful fury and irresistible force, dashed the raft upon the jetty points of the great boulders and broke the heavily built craft to pieces. The cattle and sheep were thrown into the surging water. The heavy, sodden pelts of the sheep drowned them; however, some of the cattle were able to swim to shore.

This was a tragedy. I felt sorry for the poor animals. The men were all saved from drowning. We were grateful we got through safely.

Below Five Fingers Rapids is Rink Rapids; then comes "Hell's Gate," a bad piece of water in the early days because the river was narrow in the actual gate, and then it spread out until there was scarcely any channel to navigate. Later the government improved it, and made this stretch of water navigable.

The Lewes is commonly considered a part of the main stream of the Yukon. At the confluence of the Pelley and the Lewes rivers stands old Fort Selkirk, established in 1845. It had always been an important fur-trading post. An abundance of big game —moose, caribou, timber wolves, mink, marten, wolverine, beaver, ermine, and muskrat are found along the rivers.

We were nearing the mouth of White River, which flows from the Nutzotin Mountains along the International Boundary Line. The water is colored a milky white from the Chalk Cliffs through which it flows, and it retains this color for miles as it joins the Yukon.

The Yukon has many islands. On one of them— Sullivan Island, near the mouth of the White River, the sawmill was to be built. Below these islands, more than one hundred miles away, lay Dawson. It was here the lumber, when cut, would be sold.

All on board the scow looked forward to going ashore. I had enjoyed the trip, and the men had been very kind to me.

"They couldn't have treated me better if I'd been Queen Victoria herself," I often told Davy.

The men tied the scow and unloaded everything. Davy and I pitched our tent and made ourselves comfortable. We had been on the water seventeen days.

Sullivan Island

MORNING, AND the men were ready for work. They went about whistling and joking with one another. The air was alive with spring. All about, wild flowers grew in profusion. The birds were busy building their nests and singing gaily. Even the horses were affected, kicking up their heels and snorting. It was good to have so much freedom after the close quarters on the scow.

I crawled out from the blankets and began my simple toilet, drawing the comb through my thick, brown hair and later dashing cold water over my face and arms. Outside the tent I stopped in surprise. All about me was a sweet, haunting fragrance. I had not noticed the bower of wild roses when we pitched our tent in the midst of them.

"Davy," I called, "come here. These are like the roses that grew in the hedges at home. Smell them! The air feels like Scotland, too, fresh and lovely. We shall be happy here."

The men set up my stove under a shelter until they could build a cookshack. Everyone was in the best of humor, laughing and hurrying about.

The days passed in this pleasant atmosphere were very happy. Davy's eyes grew better. The sawmill was built on the island and the island connected by a bridge to the mainland. Davy was able to direct the men in installing the engine and keeping it running. The men built the cookshack, a storehouse, and a place where they could eat and sit about, talking or figuring how much money the lumber would bring in Dawson. They built me a cabin by the river. The mill was soon operating at full capacity, the golden sawdust piling up, and the boards coming out smooth and clean. The first scow of lumber they took to Dawson brought forty thousand dollars.

It was a happy gypsy life under the trees. I learned to manage the cooking very well, and often had time to run down to the river and watch it flow along; its rhythm fascinated me. I was beginning to love it.

Summer waned and autumn came creeping through the woods. Plans were made for the freeze-up and the long winter.

The company intended selling the mill and equipment. The last load of lumber was ready to go to Dawson. Davy was going along. He wanted to see the doctor about his eyes and also purchase winter clothes and a new outfit. I decided to stay on the island until Davy returned. Then we would make further plans.

There had been a good deal of talk all summer about bears, and as Davy was afraid to leave me alone, he hired one of the men to stay at the mill until he returned. The scow was barely out of sight when the man began talking about going home to Seattle. I, being independent, told him not to stay on my account; I was not afraid to be alone. He took me at my word. Signaling the next boat, he secured passage for the Outside.

Now that I was alone, I remembered that the

man had been hired to stay because Davy feared all the bears hadn't hibernated. I recalled hearing the men tell stories of a bear tearing down a cabin and attacking a man. They said it was not safe for one person to stay alone. I began to think about it a good deal, and wondered what I would do if a bear did come. I decided that it might be well to try the gun, to see if I could possibly shoot it. I went into the cabin and took the big black gun from the wall. It required all of my strength to hold it, but I shut my eyes and pulled the trigger. It roared through the quiet woods like a cannon, kicking my shoulder so that I thought it was broken.

"No more of that! I'll wait until the bear appears and then take chances on that gun," I said to myself.

The first night I shut the door of my cabin and piled cordwood against it. I lay listening to the myriad night noises until I fell asleep from very weariness. But days went by and nothing happened. There was only the great stillness of the autumn woods.

Life in the Northland is measured by the freeze-up and the breakup. The freeze-up usually starts during the first half of October. It was October now, and ice formed along the shore, but the swift current broke it loose and whirled it downstream. This went on for weeks before the actual freeze-up began.

Each day the river grew more companionable to me. I liked watching the power it possessed. Small ice cakes whirled and stuck fast to other pieces of ice. Then they kept on until they met an obstruction, and this in turn gathered more ice until it formed a jam. But the mighty river tore it loose, whirling the big cakes farther on until they stuck on a sand bar.

I watched great piles of ice building up on the bar near my island. It kept on until it was almost as tall as the mill and looked like a Chinese temple.

I had been watching the river for days, and I realized it could not be long before it would be frozen over.

I hoped Davy would get back in time. What would the doctor tell him about his eyes? What could we do now that the mill was closed? These and many other anxious thoughts occupied my mind to the exclusion of everything else.

I went for a walk over to the mill, and I stood on the bridge, watching the swirling water and the ice cakes below me, wondering how the bridge could withstand the impact of the ice battering against it. I found relief from my worries and loneliness, as I continued on into the woods.

I did not realize I had walked so far. When I turned back, I did not know the way to go. I could not see the mill or find the bridge! I stood still, my heart racing. I told myself that I must not be frightened, that I must remain calm and look about. In front of me was a big log. I remembered climbing over it, so this was the way I had come. But as I started to climb back over the log, something moved in the bushes. Not stopping to look, I turned and ran in the opposite direction. It was growing dusk; in the deep shade under the trees it was almost dark. Suddenly a story popped into my head, one that the men used to laugh about, of the Indian who had said, "Me no lost; tepee lost!" I tried to see the funny side of my predicament—anything to keep up my courage; to stop thinking of what would happen if it grew dark and I had to stay out in the cold night! I wasn't lost, the mill was lost! But what if the noise I had heard was a bear? No! I must stop such nonsense! I must find the mill.

All at once, there it was before me! I ran over the little bridge toward my cabin; it did not seem lonely now. There I would be safe. But my relief was short-lived. I stood trembling, listening. Yes, there was the sound again. Snort! Snort! And then came the blowing noise I'd never forget. I had heard it on the trail at Lake Lindeman. It meant one thing only. A bear! I saw the creature now, dimly, in the shadows as he vanished into the bushes back of the cookshack.

I looked about, and at first I thought of running back over the bridge to the mill. But it would be better if I could get to the cabin. I would be safer there with the gun; I could shoot the bear if I had to. With another swift look around, I ran to my cabin, dashed through the door, and banged it hard behind me. Grabbing the gun from the wall, I climbed into bed, fully dressed, and waited—listening to every sound.

Something scratched on the roof, then ran along with tiny feet; the wind whipped the trees; the river roared and thundered. I must have gone to sleep. In the morning I found myself aching with cold, and regarding the horrid black gun with as much fear and distrust as if it were a bear!

By noon I was so hungry I had to do something, bear or no bear. I opened the door with caution and peered out; he wasn't in sight. I dashed to the cook-

shack and hastily ate a few bites while collecting
enough food to last a day or so. I waited, listening.
No bear. Clutching the little bundle of provisions,
I ran back to my cabin. Safe! Another long night
passed, and another day. Every one of my senses was
keenly alert.

At last I grew more at ease, less tense. I went outside for fresh water. Then I thought I saw the bear
on the other side of the mill and the same wild fear
returned.

I stood listening, ready to fly back to the cabin,
when down the river I heard a whistle — Davy's
whistle! Never had a sound been so welcome.

"Hello, hello!" called Davy.

"Hello!" I answered. "Oh, Davy, I'm so glad you
are back!" I no longer thought of the bear.

Davy and three men were poling a raft upstream
among the ice cakes. It had taken the four of them
three days to come from Dawson. Now there was
plenty of excitement. They brought news of Dawson; reports of a stampede; wild talk of staking
claims. There were warm clothes that Davy had
bought me, and a nine-hundred-pound outfit to examine. Plans and more plans to discuss. There was
a report of a strike up White River. The men were
talking of going to "stake."

Davy and the three men decided to build a stockade
house in the gulch opposite the mouth of White
River. By combining all our outfits, we could start
a roadhouse. Such a place would be needed in winter.

The gulch was overrun with prospectors, coming
and going along White River. A steady stream of
travelers arrived over the Yukon ice trail, bringing

merchandise to sell in Dawson, where there was a ready market for anything. They were looking for a place to eat, sleep, and rest away from the cold.

The roadhouse was to be built against the side of the gulch where it would be sheltered a bit from the wind. We planned on a big room, forty by forty, to be made of telegraph poles. These poles had been cut for a telegraph line in process of construction by the government, but plans had been changed. Since it would have cost more to move the poles than to cut new ones, Davy and his partners were given permission to use the poles. They were cut to the right length and then pulled on hand sleds over the ice to the sheltered place in the gulch.

The cook tent was put up, and the men used it for temporary sleeping quarters. Davy and I had our own tent.

Work was begun on the stockade roadhouse. By this time the ground was frozen hard, and it was slow, tedious work to dig the holes. Blocks of ice brought from the river were melted on the stove and the boiling water poured into the holes to thaw the ground. Once the poles were set upright, they soon froze solid in the zero weather.

It was my task to heat the water in coal-oil tins, and many a good burn I got in doing it. According to the old sourdoughs, the winning of the Yukon could never have been accomplished without these useful oil tins.

Davy used drums and oil tins to make the heating plant for his roadhouse. Pipes running about the sides of the drums carried the heat like a regular furnace. It was a fine heating stove, and was much admired. My cookstove was a homemade affair also, with a drum in the stovepipe for an oven. To an ingenious mind a substitute can always be found to take the place of the needed article, and Davy was a master hand at making anything he wanted.

The holes in the cabin were chinked with moss, and bunks were built along the walls and filled with spruce boughs—Yukon featherbeds. The floor was covered with sawdust which was brought from the mill, about three miles distant.

Before the roadhouse was even half finished, people stopped, begging for shelter. Each night the bunks were filled, and men were glad to spread their blankets on the sawdust—anything would do, just so they could be out of the bitter wind. Sometimes the floor was so covered with sleepers that I had to step over them in going about my work. Tired, weary, footsore, the men were grateful for a rest, and the chance to remove their moccasins and doctor tired, and often frozen, feet. They seldom complained, for if they did, they were sure to hear of a case much worse than theirs. They liked to tell stories and laugh to forget their misery.

We never had a dull moment; something exciting was always happening. Tales were told and retold. It was a wonderful country for adventure, but I thought it was prone to make liars of the men. I often heard the same story, but with a new hero. The one who could tell the most exciting tale naturally claimed all the attention.

I cooked for as many as twenty men at a time on my little thirty-six-inch stove. My experience in cooking for the men at the mill stood me in good stead and I was able to cook and manage very well.

We had room for only six at a time at the small table on which they ate, and each traveler must wait his turn.

All winter I cooked over the little stove. I had no time to sit down in any case, and when such a thing was mentioned I would laugh and say, "Anyway, there is nothing to sit on." It was almost spring when one of the men brought the stump of a tree for me to have a seat.

Our bunk was close to the door. Night or day the door was likely to fly open and a half-frozen traveler, hungry as a wolf, would dash in. On such occasions I always climbed out to cook a good meal, even though I might just have climbed in to get a little rest.

Our big, black, curly-haired dog slept with us all winter, and we were glad of his warmth.

The dog teams, coming over the trail, slept outside in the snow. Most of the men took good care of their teams and saw to it that they were fed; but others paid little attention. The tired creatures would curl up to sleep with their tails over their noses, glad of a little rest before they were kicked into action and readied for another grilling day.

The big stampede up White River continued to grow. This was the year of 1898, when thousands were coming into the country. It took only the slightest rumor to get abroad that a strike of gold had been made on a new creek and there was an immediate stampede. Each stampede developed into a race, the first arrivals having the best opportunity to stake valuable claims.

Practically every creek within a hundred miles of Dawson, on the Yukon and the Klondike River, was staked from end to end during this winter. The rule was that any person, having recorded one claim, could not stake another one in the valley or basin of the same creek within sixty days of locating the first. Men would stake a claim and then sell it, and rush madly to another stampede in some other district. These were known as "wild men," and the gulch was overrun with them.

As the travelers sat about resting and waiting for their turn to eat, they amused one another with stories and jokes. I could always laugh, no matter how old the joke.

The one about the "wild men" in Heaven was a favorite. It seemed an old prospector went to Heaven and asked St. Peter for admission.

"Well," said St. Peter, "I have so many old prospectors here now, I haven't room for any more. Wish I could get rid of some of them."

"I'll clear 'em all out for you if you'll let me stay," the old prospector said.

"All right," agreed St. Peter.

"Well, boys," the old man said when he got in, "I hear there's been a big strike in Hell—nuggets the size of goose eggs."

All the prospectors, after the custom of the "wild men," immediately stampeded for Hell.

As the old man watched them filing out of Heaven, he turned to St. Peter and said, "Well, guess I'll go along, too. Might be something in it, after all."

It was always known when a new traveler arrived. The men hallooed and yelled, the dogs barked, and the sled was pulled up the bank and brought to a stop in front of the door. I was ready with a warm welcome for each cold and hungry traveler. When the mummylike figure was unwrapped, often it would be a half-frozen dance-hall girl. I was always ready to offer a good strong cup of tea, then hot soup. Later I gave them a supper of beans, meat, and hot bread. Each traveler was fed, and then, if there were no empty bunks, I would show them how to spread their blankets close to the stove. Everyone received the same kind of treatment and a word of encouragement. I realized how strange and unreal was this land of snow and ice to one experiencing it for the first time—this soul-stirring stillness and loneliness. Many a frightened and homesick girl cried bitter tears on my shoulder, and told her sorrowful tale to my sympathetic ears. They were so young and lonely—it hurt my heart.

One night a lad came in who had "broke the bank" in Dawson. He was a common fellow, whom Davy referred to as a "pick and shovel man." He had won thirty-five thousand dollars and was on his way Outside. The men surrounded him like flies, while he was laughing and talking. Later we heard he had made it to Dyea and was smart enough to get out of the country and reach home with his fortune.

An old prospector who had gone up and down the different creeks, and who had often stayed at the roadhouse, was not so lucky. He struck it rich in the gulch and had sold his claim for fifty thousand dollars. He was bewildered by sudden riches,

and didn't know what to do. He went to Dawson
for a big time; he lost it all, over the gambling table,
the first night! Having nothing but his outfit left,
he grinned and said, "Well, boys, I'll go out and
bring in some more for you."

Then, for contrast, there was "Al."

"Al" struck it rich and cut a great dash at Dawson. He bought drinks for everyone, fur coats and
diamonds for the ladies, and paid a hundred dollars
for a bottle of champagne. His generosity made him
so famous his wife back in the States heard about
it. She at once brought her four children as far as
Skagway, then came in over the ice herself to see
about "Al."

She stopped a night at the roadhouse and told me
all about it. She declared that if she caught Al up
to mischief, she would shoot him. I advised her to
be careful and not do anything rash. However, Al
had been warned his wife was coming, and was prepared for her. He bought the finest new home he
could find, went no more to the dance halls, and
awaited her arrival with all the grace becoming a
faithful husband. Then, as long as his pay streak
lasted, there was not a better cared for family in
Dawson. Al fell back into matrimony as easily as
he had fallen out!

There was a tent back of the roadhouse fixed up
for Indians. Davy did not know much about Indians,
and I thought them a "dirty, filthy lot." A number
of them came one night with many bear skins, and
insisted on a trade. Davy never took advantage of
an Indian. He was not progressing very well when
a man rose up from the sawdust and said to him,

"Here, give me a pound of tea, and I'll show you how to trade with Indians."

He got all the skins they had. The Indians were up all night, making and drinking "white man's tea," laughing and having a tea party—the men drank the liquid and the squaws ate the leaves!

I was horrified to see one of the squaws give her papoose a drink of blood that she had saved from a caribou they had killed!

One unpleasant incident occurred that winter. The stage came in one day, loaded with passengers, hungry and cold. As I was preparing their dinner, a sled drove up. The single passenger was a rich and prominent man from Dawson. Two pretty dance-hall girls had come in on the stage before, and this man began at once to make himself known to them. When the food was placed on the table, he seated himself with the girls.

"You will have to wait," I said to him. "The people who came in on the stage got here first."

He paid no attention. I could not let this pass; it was the rule of the house, "first come, first served," and I was not allowing anyone to run my business for me.

I sent Davy to talk to him, but he was rude to Davy and still kept his place at the table. I could stand a slight to myself, but when an insult came to Davy, I was angry indeed. The man finished eating and went out to his sled. I left my cooking and followed him.

"I shall report you to the police for making a disturbance in my house," I told him.

He looked at me and realized I meant what I said.

He didn't know just how to get out of it and save his face. He knew it wouldn't do to let the police know about it, so he apologized and hoped I would overlook it. Having won my point, I let the matter drop.

The Gulch

SPRING WAS COMING along the trail; in a short time the breakup would do away with the necessity for the roadhouse. Travelers would no longer be going in over the ice. New plans must be made for the summer.

Davy settled with the men with whom he had combined outfits to build the roadhouse. They split the gold dust, supplies, and money four ways. Nothing was said about my part, although I had worked the hardest of all.

I felt hurt and angry, but did not say a word. To myself I thought: "Let this be a lesson to you; the next time—make your arrangements before you go into a thing—men never find it necessary to count a woman's work!"

Davy took the roadhouse as part of his share. In it we stored our heavy winter clothes, blankets, supplies, and Davy's buffalo coat that had been found and brought to us. The buffalo coat was in our first outfit, cached at Crater Lake and lost in the snowslide. In the spring thaw the things were found, but it cost us more to get them than they were worth.

We planned to go to Thistle Creek, about fifteen miles away, and work Davy's claim. He was sure we could take out a fortune.

With our outfit on the back of the horse, the dogs dragging the sled, and with what we could carry on our shoulders, we had enough for the summer. When

it grew cold, we planned to come back and get our
heavy winter clothes and blankets.

There were thousands going into the Klondike,
which was really a small district. When seen from
Midnight Dome, or King Solomon's Dome as it was
called, 4,220 feet above sea level, there is a panoramic view of the whole Klondike area. Davy used
to explain it to me, and he would tell me he would
show me just how it looked—drew it out on a piece
of paper. I grew almost as familiar with it as Davy,
for I felt we would soon get to the Klondike.

Creeks radiated from this dome like spokes from
the hub of a wheel. To the west is the Yukon River;
to the north is the Klondike and to the south, Indian
River; to the east, Flat Creek flowing into the Klondike and Dominion Creek flowing into Indian River.
It was in this small area that one of the greatest
mining dramas in history, the drama of the Klondike, took place. The ambition of everyone who
started North was to stake a claim in this Klondike
area. That was our dream—it almost came to pass.

We planned to go there as soon as we worked the
required amount on our claim at Thistle. The government specified that every year, work must be
done on each claim to the value of three hundred
dollars. An inspector made the rounds to see that
this requirement was met. If a claim did not pro-
duce, it could be abandoned and another started;
but the work must be done.

As soon as we got to the claim and began working, Davy decided he must buy a great deal of
machinery. He spent money lavishly, arguing that
we would soon take out pay dirt.

One day a man stopped and rented our horse to go a few miles up the creek to get some of his belongings. Later, when he returned the horse, it was raining. He was wet to the skin, and I asked him into our tent. He came in gratefully. I gave him dry clothes of Davy's and told him to step into the "lean-to" of the tent and put them on. He was a pleasant-spoken man whose good manners were such a part of him that he treated me with as much courtesy as if I had been a lady in a grand drawing room.

While we sat at the table to eat, he told of hunting trips he had taken in Africa and other parts of the world. The rain dripped through a hole in the tent into his teacup. He made no reference to it, but continued eating and talking.

Later I took it on myself to straighten out his dunnage bag. He seemed so helpless. In it was food, flour, butter, tea, cheese, rice, tobacco, hair brushes and papers, all in a hopeless jumble.

On one of his letters was his name, "Lord Talmash."

The pleasant summer was passing, but the claim was not coming up to expectations. Davy did not lose hope, though I began to have my doubts. I did not like the uncertainty; my practical mind must know where our winter "outfit" was coming from, now that Davy had spent the greater part of our money for machinery.

A friend came one day who had just returned from White River. He brought us bad news about our roadhouse in the gulch. Some people who had stopped to spend the night had carelessly caused a fire that had burned the house to the ground. The fine, heavy blankets, Davy's buffalo coat that he had never used, the winter clothes, and a carton of tea, rice, sugar, and other supplies were all lost.

"That is the third outfit we have lost." Davy heaved a long sigh. "One in a snowslide, one in transportation, and now this third one burned!"

It was well into July when Mr. Baxter came to us, making Davy a proposition. He had bought the mill and equipment on Sullivan Island from the Carey Mill Company and needed a good engineer. He asked me if I would cook for the men. I, remembering my experience in the gulch, made a hard and written bargain for my services.

We went with Mr. Baxter to the mill under this plan—Davy was to run the engine, I was to cook for the men.

But this was a different proposition from the one with the Carey Mill Company, where we had worked the summer before. At that time we had had plenty of everything; but Mr. Baxter was a poor provider, and I was often at my wit's end to know what to give the men to eat. It was hard when there was scarcely anything to cook except beans. One of the men was a good hunter and supplied fresh meat and fish, and this helped out.

The men grew dissatisfied. They knew there was money from the lumber shipped to Dawson. Lumber was used now in the mines and for building purposes, and the demand was greater than the supply. But Mr. Baxter was spending the money in gambling, and at dance halls. He did not come to attend to his mill, but depended upon the men to carry on the work.

The men at last selected a committee, composed

of Davy and others, to go to Dawson for a show-
down. They were just leaving when word came from
Mr. Baxter to bring everything from the camp—
machinery, equipment of all kinds, the horses and
supplies. Everything was to be sold to meet the demands of his creditors.

The men left with the equipment loaded on the
scow. They wanted me to go, too, but I said no—
that I would wait at our cabin until Davy returned.
I looked so shabby I was ashamed to go.

I was alone on the island just as I had been before,
but this time there was a very small supply of food.
It was lonely—seeing, hearing no one—my only company the river. I watched the boats pass, just to
see someone, to be sure I was not all alone in the
world. I used to dream I was the only person alive.
I found it a very lonely dream, but it was often repeated at this time. I would wish, even pray, for
someone to come, just anyone to talk to. My prayer
was answered.

One night a band of thirty Indians turned up.
They went into the mill and the storehouse and helped
themselves to my scanty supplies. I tried to stop
them, but it was no use. They took all of the tea
and coffee. When they had cooked and eaten, they
wanted to trade with me, showing me a few ragged
pelts. All this time they jabbered in their own language. Their beady black eyes that were never still
were watching me.

At last one of the bucks said: "When man come?"
I was surprised to hear him speak English. I was
afraid to tell them that Davy would not be back
for days, yet it was good to know they could under-

stand me. I began to feel less afraid. "Go string-talk to man—him come—talk furs." They meant by this that they wanted me to go to Stewart Island and telegraph Davy to come home and buy their furs. I was now satisfied that they were partly civilized.

As they sat or squatted in a circle about the walls of the cookshack, they began to make queer noises, drumming with their feet and hands. A young squaw, fine-looking, with sparkling black eyes, whirled out into the space in the center and began a weird dance. Wilder and faster, stomping and jumping, she came close to me.

She flashed a glittering knife in my face, then whirled away and came back again. The second time she grabbed my hair, pulling my head over and drawing the knife in front of my neck. I was frozen with fear—unable to move or cry out. The watching Indians laughed and grunted.

The young buck who had talked about telegraphing danced out. The two Indians stomped and yelled. Closer and closer they came to me. The buck thrust a gun in my face. Still I could not move or cry out. I was too scared. The wicked, leering faces, the gleaming, rolling eyes watched me, hoping to hear me scream, or see me struggle to get away. It was great fun to scare the white woman.

The dance grew wilder. The young squaw and the buck whooped and yelled, and the watching Indians drummed and laughed; the squaw drew close, ready to draw her knife again.

Suddenly I realized they were having fun at my expense, and it made me very angry. Waiting till the girl was in front of me, I pushed her in the stomach with all my angry strength, making her fall backward. The Indians howled and laughed. But this time at the young squaw. Before she could get to her feet I gave her another shove out of the way and took the center of the circle myself.

I would show these Indians a real dance! Tossing my head and humming the music, I danced the Highland fling for them, putting into it a gay spirit of abandonment, shouting in true Scottish style. The Indians were first surprised, then pleased. I had won my audience!

After the dance was over, the young squaw came to me and said: "You brave! You show me dance?" And for a long time I tried to teach the girl the Highland fling.

The Indians had now become friendly, and gave back part of the food they had taken; I made them a big kettle of hot tea. Along in the night they began trading with me again, but this time they brought out their best furs, pulling them from inside their shirts, while the squaws brought them out from under their skirts. I remembered how the man in the gulch had traded with the Indians. I had some money at my cabin and I went to get it. The Indian girl went along. I was afraid the girl might find the little valise with my old jewelry and pictures, so I hurried to get my money and a few pieces of clothing, an old hat, a cap, and a corset.

I began trading by putting the corset on the girl. This made the very best piece of merchandise. I had a hard time keeping the Indians from taking the other things from me. I would hold up something and ask: "How much you give?" and the

Indians would say "How much you?" And so the trading went on, the Indians enjoying the excitement. It was like gambling to them.

"How much you give?" "How much you?" One thing at a time I traded for furs. For the corset I got a beautiful silver fox, and the buck who got the corset had much fun trying it on; it made a fine belt in which to carry knives and hatchets! The young squaw got a red jersey; and an old squaw admired herself in the cap, for which she had parted with a fine red fox. By morning the Indians had the clothes and most of my money, but I had about three hundred dollars' worth of furs. They went on to Stewart Island.

The Indians stopped at the mill on their way back, having spent all their money at Stewart City. They had bought yards of red flannel, and shirts which they wore on the outside of their pants; white dress cuffs which they wore like bracelets; and hats and caps for the tribe.

"Man no come back?" asked the young squaw whom I had tried to teach the Highland fling. "You come," she waved her hand toward the Indians. "You come," the girl urged, nodding her head and smiling her good will. She apparently thought that my "man" had abandoned me, and offered me a place in the tribe.

But I refused the kind invitation to join the Indian tribe and stood watching them out of sight.

When the raft arrived in Dawson with all the equipment from the mill, the police were at the dock with papers to attach everything. Mr. Baxter owed more than he could pay. The men were hopeful of getting their money, but in the meantime they must eat, and no one had any money except Davy. So Davy fed them, believing he would get his money back when affairs were settled. However, Mr. Baxter was busy trying to dodge his creditors. He made flowery promises, and was always at the point of being able to put his hands on the money.

The men waited. At last he confessed he did not have the money. Davy remembered that Mr. Baxter owed me seventy dollars, so he went to the police about that.

The police asked Baxter, "Do you owe this debt?"

"Yes," answered Baxter.

"Well, pay it!"

And Baxter lost no time getting the seventy dollars and paying it to Davy, who promptly invested it in some supplies. Now he must get back to me.

Hearing that the *Willie Irving* was about to make her last trip of the year to Whitehorse before the freeze-up, he arranged to work his passage as far as the mill on Sullivan Island, where I was waiting.

Davy was having a hard time getting home. It was now along in October and the cold was increasing. The river was already running heavy with ice. On the boat much doubt was expressed about their making it through. Ice was forming on the paddle wheel; the engine would not work. Davy was sure he could make it run and spent hours trying, encouraged by passengers who would gladly have paid the price of the boat to get to their destination. Men and women waited anxiously for the engine to start and the boat to move along among the cakes of ice.

It meant going home — getting "Outside" once more — away from the long, dark days of winter. It meant many things of vital importance to all on board; besides, there was the danger of their being "froze in" and having to walk long weary miles over the ice back to Dawson.

"If any man can make the engine run, that's the man to do it," men who knew Davy told the others. Davy tried desperately not to fail them, but in spite of everything he could do, the engine would not run, and the paddle wheel froze solid. He was aweary and exhausted from working in the icy water that had flooded the engine room. His felt boots were soaked with the cold water that covered the floor.

They had actually traveled up the river to within a few miles of the place where Davy was to be put ashore. After a hard struggle, the boat was turned about in the hope that it would float downstream to Dawson. The idea was to keep it in the channel as well as possible, and let it go with the current. The fear was now that the boat might freeze solid in the ice.

Davy was helped ashore with his dunnage bag of supplies and roll of blankets. He was still three or four miles from the mill, but he was thankful to be even that close to me. His one desire was to get back to the cabin, to be warm once more, and to sleep. He was tired and weary, his head throbbed, and his feet dragged in his heavy boots. As he mushed along he felt he must rid his tired shoulders of their burden. He felt it impossible to keep going, and tried to lie down, to get his pack from his back; but something within him kept him moving.

I had been looking anxiously at the closing in of the ice on the river when I saw him coming. I fairly flew to him. He was muttering: "I can't make it —not another step. President McKinley put this pack on my back and I can't get it off. Peg! Peg! Come help me!"

I could see he had fever and was out of his head. "Davy, what is it? Tell me!"

"Take it off—this pack. He won't let me rest. He keeps prodding me, beating me, making me mush on. Take this pack from my back that McKinley has put there," he raved on.

I got him into bed and did all I could to doctor him. He never stopped talking—all night he complained about McKinley and the pack on his back. Trust a Democrat to blame McKinley. Davy always loved to talk politics. At first the pack was stones he carried. It grew until he carried a mountain; and at last, the whole world was on his frail shoulders.

Somewhere along the way he had lost the dunnage bag, and when I had found him he had only the blankets left. I had little food remaining; the Indians had almost cleaned me out. But I gave him the best I had and made shift with beans for myself. It was no consolation to realize that wood must be cut if we were not to freeze without a fire in the sub-zero weather.

"Oh, let me rest, my God, let me rest!" Davy moaned.

I wondered if I, too, would go mad, raving mad, like Davy. No, I must keep my senses; I must care for him. I prayed out loud: "Oh, God, send somebody, anyone, anyone—the Indians, that Indian girl —she would help me."

The ice in the river piled in great heaps not far from the cabin. It cracked and groaned and broke loose with a noise like a cannon, then moved on and more ice formed, roared and crashed. The horrid, deadly cold crept into the cabin and in the darkness came the sick man's continuous pleading, "Oh, Peg, help me, won't you please! Help me! You never failed me, gir-rul. Don't leave me. Help me get this heavy load off my back. I'm so tired, so tired."

Once he whispered, "Peg, I'm a very sick man. I think I have pneumonia." A short, dry, rasping cough racked his frail body.

I burned almost the last of my wood in the little airtight stove. A long night of darkness was before me, only one candle left, and I dare not let it burn too long. I crept into bed beside Davy. Darkness fell about us like a black velvet curtain—a breathtaking darkness in which we were helpless. No light came from the little window. Above the crash and groan of the ice in the river I heard the weird lonely cry of the timber wolves.

I could stand the darkness no longer. I crawled out of bed and put on my last stick of wood and left the lid of the stove part way off so a faint flickering light made mysterious shadows in the room. The wolves sounded closer and closer. The horror of the sound was almost too much. I crawled back into the bed, shaking with cold and fear, my arms around the sick man.

The cry of the wolves drove sleep from me. Davy's voice tore my heart asunder. The cold was an agony and the blackness a terror. The demons of fear were at me. I thought the night would never end. In the morning I knew I must cut wood to keep us from freezing.

I alone must care for Davy; I must not let him freeze. I put on my warmest clothes and opened the door cautiously; the wolves seemed very close in the night, and now they were gone. I took my ax and went out and hacked down a small spruce tree and gathered what wood I could. With this and a handful of sawdust, I kept the fire roaring. The next day and next again, I managed to cut down small trees, and at night I lay beside my sick husband. He wanted no food, but drank the cold water greedily. I made oatmeal gruel and he ate a little of that. I had only beans for myself.

I lost all track of time. Again and again I prayed for help as I toiled. I was becoming more apt at the woodcutting, and each day I tackled a larger tree. The cold bit at my face and my feet felt frozen. I was getting weak from lack of food and would stagger in, carrying my load of wood, shaking from head to foot with exhaustion. Davy's voice, ceaselessly pleading, drove sleep from my weary eyes as I lay beside him, staring into the darkness. I could hear the wolves about the cabin—jumping at the windows and scraping about the door.

"Help him! Help him! Oh, God! This darkness, the ice, the cold! Oh, God, show me what to do, and give me strength to do it," and Davy's voice, weaker and weaker, but still pleading, "Oh, Peg, don't fail me! Help me!"

He was growing weaker as the high fever took toll of his frail body and the cough tore him. How long could he hold on to the thin thread of life?

"Oh, God, don't, don't—please—I can't stand it! Let him live, let him live!"

Down the river came the weird, lonely cry; closer and closer the wolves came. I feared they would get at us alone in the dark. Only the one candle and then the horrible blackness. I crawled out of bed to put more wood on the fire, thankful for the boom and crashing of the ice in the river, for it drowned the wild, lonely cry of the wolves. At times I heard them outside the door of the cabin; again I was almost sure the door would give way. I was paralyzed with fear — I thought morning would never come.

In the morning Davy lay like a dead man, scarcely breathing. I felt the end was near. I went out and leaned weakly against the cabin. If Davy died—this was the last of life. I would stop struggling. It was all over. It no longer mattered that the food was gone; I would not bother to cut more wood. I did not care—it was all over. Life could not go on without Davy. I wanted it to be over. My dear life that I had loved was dear no longer; I was through.

After a bit I realized I had given up too soon. I opened the door and went in and watched the faint breathing, though no sign of life showed in the waxlike face. I took up my ax and saw and set myself to the task of cutting more wood. As long as that faint breath stayed in him, I would work—I would not fail him.

Late in the afternoon I was wearily carrying in my load of wood when I was surprised to hear a man's voice calling from the mill. It was Jack Mac-Donald!

"Jack! Oh, Jack MacDonald!" I cried. Before I could recover from my surprise and answer him, there came a noise like the bombarding of many cannons. A great jam of ice that had been forming for days broke asunder and the wall of water back of it came flooding over the slough, tearing away the bridge that connected the two islands, shutting Jack away from me and bringing the icy water about my feet. I ran to the cabin and Davy.

"God save Davy! Save him! Oh, don't let the cabin go!"

Davy lay like a dead man. In a panic I threw myself beside him. But soon the rush of water subsided. Then my heart froze with horror as I thought of Jack. Had he been carried away, crushed and broken by the mountain of ice? Struggling in the icy water, even drowning? Killed—trying to come to our rescue?

I rushed out the door into the cold water, calling frantically: "Jack, oh Jack! Oh, where are you?"

"Hi! That was some breakup! You all right over there?"

The bridge was gone between the mill and our cabin, but we could call back and forth to each other. Of all the people in the world that could have been sent, I could think of no one I would rather have seen than Jack MacDonald. Tears ran down my face. I laughed with relief and cried with joy.

Jack hurriedly lashed logs together with willow withes, and at last, just before dark, he was able to cross over to me. When he came to me and held out his hand, I dropped my head on his arm and sobbed out loud. Something within me snapped with relief. It was all right with Jack here.

Jack had never seen me lose my nerve before, and he had tears in his eyes as he held me in his arms.

When I had regained my composure I asked how it happened that he had arrived just at the time when I could stand no more. He told me that when he came in from his claim at Dawson he had heard about our trouble with Baxter, that we had not received our money. Also, he learned of Davy's going on the *Willie Irving*, of how it had had to drift back to Dawson, and that Davy had gone ashore some miles from the mill. It worried him so he could not rest, and he had set out to walk over the shore ice to see what was happening to his friends.

He carried a dunnage bag of things he thought we would like: tea, cheese, sugar, odds and ends, and a jar of plum preserves.

The time of terrible stress was over. Jack cut wood, brought in fresh meat, helped with Davy. Davy and I both slept. It was the turning point for Davy. Sleep was the best thing in the world for him.

Soon the river was silent—the big freeze-up was on. Jack gave me a hundred and fifty dollars' worth of gold dust, and the two of us took a sled and walked to Stewart City, about twelve miles, to get supplies. Davy slept on, resting after the weary days and nights of carrying the burden "President McKinley had put there." We spent the gold dust for the things we needed most, then hurried back over the ice. Davy was still sleeping.

Jack set about making bunks in the cookshack, in preparation for the time when people would be coming in over the ice trail. A boat was frozen in the ice on the river and the people on board came asking for food and a place to rest; they were on their way over the ice to Dawson. Not many miles away, another boat, loaded with fine groceries, was frozen in, and Jack went to it and bought things for our use. The superintendent of the White Pass, after hearing about Davy and me, had a really brilliant idea. He thought of having a few trees cut and putting up a sign, "Dangerous!" and this made a path that led right to our door. I never forgot his kindness. Everyone was very good to us.

In almost no time at all I was busy again, feeding hungry people who came over the ice trail of the river. Jack, who was young and strong, did all the hard jobs, cutting wood, hunting and helping in every way. Very slowly Davy crept back from the shadows of the "borderland" and began fighting to live. With a grateful heart I became my own self again. Jack and I could laugh as we used to do on the scow. I had never found anyone who enjoyed laughing like Jack. Davy was often annoyed at us, saying we acted like school children. Everything seemed funny to us.

I made biscuits, pies, and soup, and worked from morning till night, caring for Davy and doing all I could for the travelers who stopped and asked for shelter. I was so thankful for everything that I even tried to sing, until Davy objected. He said I was off key.

The little roadhouse prospered. By Christmas I was able to pay my debts and make Jack take back the money he had given me. I would never forget

how good he had been to us, for we owed our lives
to him. I could not have kept on cutting wood, and
Davy would have frozen to death.

It was almost spring and the breakup was not far
away when Mr. Smith, from Stewart Island, came
with the news that the Johnson Roadhouse was for
sale. He urged us to buy it, saying it was a fine
opportunity. We had no money, but Davy, who by
this time was able to get about a bit, went to a Scotch
friend and asked for a loan. It was granted and
Mr. Smith's advice was taken.

Jack was glad that we were safe and located in
a comfortable home. Now he must return to his
claim. He came into the kitchen to bid me good-by.

"Jack, I won't try to tell you what you have done
for us. My own brother could not have done more."
My hands trembled as I held them out to him. Jack
tried to smile, but he could not make it; tears were
too close to his eyes. We were such friends!

"When you are near, Peggy, life is gay and happy.
But now I must go back to my work and loneliness," he said.

He could not let go of my hands. All at once his
arms went about me and he held me close, kissing me.

"Well, if I'm like a brother to ye, lass, I'll claim
a brother's right," he mumbled, as he let me go and
hurried to the door.

I stood still—looking after him. It was so strange
to have Jack—like this; it was confusing.

Home on Stewart Island

THE TIME HAD COME for us to have a real home. "We had arrived in port and dropped anchor," as Davy put it. Stewart Island was just what we wanted. From the first, the little hotel was a success. Good fortune seemed to smile on us. The day we moved in, a friend shot a moose and gave us half of it. He was one of the men who had shared our tent the night of the terrible storm at Crater Lake in 1897. It pleased him to be the means of furnishing the first meal in our new home. A party of travelers left sixty dollars in my apron pocket. Everything had started off well.

Stewart Island is one mile long and three quarters of a mile wide. During the gold rush, in 1898-99, over a thousand persons lived on this island. It was called Stewart City.

The government put up substantial buildings along the water front—a recorder's office, where claims were registered; a telegraph office that connected with the outside world; the Mounted Police barracks; a general store and post office. Many cabins were built at this time. Streets and avenues were laid out. The hotel, or roadhouse, as it was called in the North, was on Waterfront Avenue.

At first the steamboats on the rivers were flagged for travelers who wished to go aboard. A gun was fired, or a flag (sometimes a miner's shirt) was frantically waved. In later years the boats stopped and put down a gangplank and the passengers followed a trail which led up two hundred feet to The Roadhouse. In winter a lantern hung from a tree to light the way, for the river was the highway in winter as well as in summer.

With the opening of the silver and lead mines at Keno Hill in the Mayo district, the transportation on Stewart Island increased. The smaller boats on the Stewart connected with the larger boats on the Yukon. Often there was a wait of two or three days, and during this time the travelers stayed at the hotel.

We took over The Roadhouse in 1900. At this time there were only about thirty people living on the island. A big stampede had called the others to richer fields.

The Roadhouse was made of logs and had seven rooms downstairs; there were five rooms and a big bunk room, which held thirteen beds, upstairs. At first it was furnished in "sourdough," or homemade, furniture, but as the years rolled by it was more comfortably equipped.

Davy took pride in making The Roadhouse comfortable. He could make anything he wished, and as he grew stronger he enjoyed this work. I was too busy cooking and caring for the guests to do more than the daily tasks, but I was proud of Davy's accomplishments. For instance, he made a stairway, turning out the round posts and spindles on his own lathe.

"It was a stairway fine enough for a gentleman's home," I always said.

Money flowed into The Roadhouse, but most of

it was put back, for both Davy and myself wanted
it to be a real home and not just a stopping place.

We now had a bedroom of our own. Davy said
it was never to be rented, no matter how crowded
the hotel. A cabin was drawn up and attached to
the house, and a door cut through. Here was a fine
big room, where we could be by our own two selves.
Some years later, when Davy was in Dawson, he
bought "outside," or factory-made, furniture. A
beautiful Brussels carpet with big red roses made the
room look cheerful and warm. We also had a brass
bed, a mahogany dresser, a desk, and, best of all,
my own low willow rocker, where I could rest when
there was time.

The years brought a sewing machine, and I sent
"Outside" to get a bolt of dotted swiss, and made
curtains for all the windows in the hotel. We were
happy and contented. We felt settled for life.

The garden was Davy's greatest joy. He loved
flowers, and gave them his most tender care. I
watched out for the uninteresting vegetables: carrots, onions, beans, beets, and cabbage.

"We must eat, you know, Davy," I'd say.

Many long winter nights were spent in shopping
in the seed catalogues for seeds, bulbs, grasses, and
anything that took Davy's fancy. He sent for things
that sounded interesting, even if we did not know
what they were. He liked trying new varieties and
never considered the cost. Saving seeds from his best
flowers and anxiously awaiting their return to blossom was a great joy. He was as proud as any pro-
fessional horticulturist when he propagated a new

flower, which he often did. He knew the botanical names for all of them.

Davy fenced off an acre for his garden. It was here that he spent his happiest hours. It was a perfect picture. The walks were outlined in border plants— lobelia, candytuft, pansies, and ten-weeks stocks. He raised beautiful delphinium, taller than himself, and having such heavenly blue and purple colors. I told Davy they had the shades of the distant mountains. There were snapdragons, scabiosa, zinnias, orange marigolds, and chrysanthemums, gorgeous gladioli, and dahlias as big as dinner plates. In later years the captains on the boats would tell the passengers about Davy's garden, and they liked to come ashore to see it and get some of the blossoms. Davy gave lovely bouquets to anyone who had an interest in flowers.

"The Yukon is a perfect heaven for flowers and vegetables," Davy said. "There are no bugs, worms, or pests of any kind to destroy them. The ground is a fine seed bed, just enough silt and sand to make them grow. There is a natural irrigating system 'that can't be beat.' The long, hot days of twenty-four hours of daylight, from the middle of May to the first of August, draw up moisture from the substratum of age-long frozen ground like water from a well. The heads of the flowers and vegetables are in the sunlight while their roots are cool and moist in the ground. They can't help growing, like the Hindoo Magic Tree."

The climate in this part of the Yukon District is dry and warm in summer, in winter, dry with light snowfall. The absence of high winds and the dryness, in spite of the extreme cold, make it a good place to live. Davy used to explain to me about the Japan Current and how it affected the climate. The moisture, rising from it, is carried inland by the upper southwestern air current, striking the Coastal Range. It is then precipitated on the sea face of the mountains in rain and snow. This air, freed of its burden of moisture, descends on the Yukon plains as dry air with a high temperature. The climate on Stewart Island was pleasant and healthful the year round.

I used to say no one need starve in our part of the country. With very little effort, the finest vegetables in the world can be raised. There is plenty of meat, fish, and fowl. Berries of all kinds are to be had for the picking. It is a homeland for anyone who is not afraid of work.

Davy built a greenhouse. He sent Outside for glass and cut it into small panes. These he fitted into frames. The outside and inside walls of the room were banked around with dirt to keep out the cold. In the center of the room was a table; this held the flats that were filled with rich river dirt and sand. The seeds were planted, watered, and watched tenderly. When they were coming through the ground, Davy could not stay away from them. I called them "Davy's babies." When it was warm enough they were taken out and put into the hotbed in the garden. This was a frame that could be lifted in the day and closed at night for there was danger of frost most of the time, except in midsummer. Here the little plants became acclimated to the outdoors. Later the small, young growths—flowers, cabbages, tomatoes, cauliflower, green peppers—were set out in the ground.

One spring Davy was ill and unable to place the flats in the hotbed. I thought to help, but I didn't understand the necessity of properly mixing the manure with the soil. The little plants could not stand the chemical change that took place. They withered and died. When I saw this tragedy I felt like a murderer. I could hardly bring myself to tell Davy that I had killed his "babies."

Early in February, Davy started a fire in the stove in the greenhouse and kept it going until the warm weather. A hole was dug and the stove was sunk partly in the ground. Pipes radiated about the room from the stove, keeping the temperature even. Davy worked out this system, which took him some seven years to perfect. He used to get up during the night when the weather was bad to keep the fire going so that the greenhouse would stay at the right temperature. Nothing was too much trouble for his flowers.

The first thing he planted in the greenhouse was cucumbers. The lacy green vines growing all about, hung down from the rafters, bearing beautiful cucumbers, ten and twelve inches long. The greenhouse was built onto the main part of the house next to our bedroom, and through a glass in the door we could see the beautiful cucumber vines.

I made pickles of the small cucumbers, putting in herbs and spices that grew in his garden. In winter these herbs hung in bunches from the rafters in the kitchen, giving off a good spicy smell.

In the very early days, when the caribou were traveling from one grazing ground to another, they would swim across the river almost in front of The Roadhouse. The hunters stood in the garden and shot our winter supply of meat. The carcasses were stacked up, one upon the other, like stovewood, in the dooryard. There would be thirty or forty, along with moose, which were not so easy to get, but each one taken represented from seven hundred to a thousand pounds of good red meat. The entrails were removed when the animal was killed, but they were not skinned until used. They were soon frozen hard, and made good food for us, and the dogs got their share, too.

Moose and caribou meat are considered good eating by most people, but bear meat is not so popular. Davy would have none of it, not even tasting it to see. One day I played a trick on him. A friend brought me some fine young bear meat. Davy had eaten heartily of it and had enjoyed his supper. I thought it time to break his prejudice.

"What kind of meat was that?" he asked. "It tasted like pork."

"Wasn't it good? I knew you would find it fine eating. It was bear meat," I teased. Davy gave a grunt much like the animal he had just finished and stomped angrily out of the room.

There were thousands of ducks, geese, and crane in season. At different times, hunters had brought me beautiful white swan, larger than turkey, and excellent food. I did not like to think of the lovely creatures being killed, but my practical Scotch nature would not allow them to be wasted, once they were killed.

Some of the hunters brought in ptarmigan, a grouse that in winter has beautiful white plumage and feathered feet. They burrow in the snow like rabbits. At times the trees are full of them, looking like tufts of snow among the branches. They are about the size of a pigeon, and are very easily killed. The men would bring thirty or forty at a time for me to cook. Some of the men cleaned their own game. I always appreciated it, for I did not like to handle dead birds.

Davy was no hunter, for he did not like to kill. But once when someone made sport of his hunting, he resented it. The next time he went to Dawson he came home with an expensive new gun. He told me that from now on he would keep the table supplied with meat. He went out hunting with a friend, and the story goes that he fired both barrels of the gun at one poor little duck, and all that was left of it were a few sad feathers that drifted to the ground. Davy came home, hung the gun on the wall, and never touched it again. It hung there for years. I used to tell with pride that Davy's kind heart would not let him kill any creature. But one of my friends who brought most of the meat to me said, "If everybody had the same kind of heart, where would the meat for the table come from?" I thought it better not to discuss the matter further.

In summer, meat was kept in a cache back of the hotel. A platform was built, supported by poles incased in tin to keep the squirrels and rats from climbing up. There was a roof, and the sides had tight screens. Here the meat was safe and kept well. The cache was always full.

At certain times of the year bushels of mushrooms could be gathered. They were splendid when served with caribou steak or moose roast. I dried some, stringing them in festoons over the stove along with the red peppers and herbs. I made soup of them, and sometimes baked or fried them like oysters. There was a kind of mushroom catsup that everyone enjoyed, but it was hard to make. I saved most of it for Davy.

Loads, almost wagonloads of berries grew on the island! Raspberries, blackberries as big as my thumb, squawberries, high and low bush cranberries, and red and black currants, fine for jam. The berries were so profuse one could pick almost a bucketful without moving from the spot. There were quantities of blueberries. I used to have some of the miners pick barrelsful for me, leaving them on their stems. They kept the berries in their shafts all summer, and in winter brought them to The Roadhouse on dog sleds. I put them on the shelf back of the stove to thaw out, for they were like little blue marbles. What pies they made!

I also learned to make vinegar. Once when we got a case of vinegar one of the bottles had some "mother" in it. A miner told me how to make vinegar by putting in berries of all kinds, molasses, water, and the "mother," which is a starter for the vinegar. After a bit I got the sweetest, best-tasting vinegar. Crosse & Blackwell couldn't outdo me. I had that vinegar barrel going for years.

I stumbled upon the making of wine by accident. A barrel of cranberries had begun to "work." Wondering what would happen, I put in some sugar and water, and a bottle of rum. Later, when I siphoned it off, I found I had a splendid wine. Captain Hogan, a connoisseur of fine wines who lived on the island, told me that it was the best he had ever tasted.

Davy and I liked to go out on the Stewart River in the early morning to fish. The light was opalescent.

"Look, Davy — the river — don't you love it?" I asked.

"Yes, the river sings," Davy replied. "This is the real music musicians try to reproduce in a symphony. No man-made instrument can make this sound. Listening to the night noises in the slough, I hear a regular orchestra. Never heard sweeter music in my life. It makes up to me for the music I miss. The orchestra in the slough follows its leader, stops and starts, fiddles away. Then the old frog, like a bass viol, booms in. I get a lot out of it! I think I hear a regular theme, parts of an opera. Sometime I'll write it all out so that it can be played by an orchestra. I'll call it 'Stewart River Symphony,' " Davy dreamed on.

Davy managed the nets while I poled the boat. Often the pole would catch under a rock and almost throw me into the water. It was great fun and we laughed like little children when by our own two selves.

The last of June, or the second week in July, we would go fishing for the lovely red king salmon, great beauties that Davy carried home over his shoulders, their tails dragging on the ground. The salmon weighed as much as thirty and forty pounds.

The first time we tried smoking salmon it was not a success. The pink beauties were hung by their tails in the smokehouse. Davy made a heavy smudge in the room. Later when we came to look at our smoked fish, there they hung like snakes that had shed their skins—the pink flesh on the floor. The hot smoke had been too strong. It was a loss of hours of labor, but since it gave us an excuse to go again on the river, it turned out all right.

In the fall of the year, before the freeze-up, we went fishing for grayling, making a dam in the little creeks in the slough. The fish were so plentiful that they could be shoveled out on the bank and left to freeze, and later put away in the cache.

I shall always mind the beautiful summer nights by the river! Davy and I used to sit out on the bench he made; below us was the river, flowing, flowing. Each year the river grew dearer to me. It seemed like a part of myself. "I don't know how I could live without this old river flowing along. It seems like a dear friend," I told Davy.

"It *is* nice," Davy answered.

I smiled. Davy felt it as keenly as I did. But, after all, you couldn't expect a Scotchman to show his emotions.

One summer morning, when we first went to live on Stewart Island, I started out to do the family washing. I took a couple buckets and hurried down to the river. Running lightly out on a tree trunk that had fallen into the water, I stooped down, dipped in the bucket and tried to pull it up. But its weight was too much and it pulled me in head first. The ice-cold water was deep. I was thoroughly frightened. Struggling and fighting to save myself, I went under. I came up for air. I knew I was not far from the tree trunk. I tried to grasp a limb but I didn't make it. I felt myself going down, down, and the water closing in about me, pulling me under deeper and deeper. I came up again, calling frantically for help. Davy was shingling the house and I knew if he could only hear me he would be able to see me in the water. But I felt myself going, going, down, down. Struggling and choking, I was going under the water again.

I felt this was the end; there was no help. Davy could not hear me or get to me in time. I did not want to die. "Oh, God, I can't die yet!" I pleaded. Just then there was a splash close by and a firm hand caught the knot of hair on my head. Strong arms pulled me out of the water. I was dragged to the bank and lay there exhausted.

I heard Jack MacDonald, who was staying with us a few days, calling loudly for Davy to come quick. I opened my eyes and saw Jack bending over me. He was white and shaking.

"Well, you were almost a goner that time," he said in a trembling voice. "I was on the other side of the slough watching you. I saw you fall in but I couldn't get here any sooner. Thought I'd never make it."

When Davy got to us, he, too, was frightened.

"Well, we'll have no more of that," he said firmly. "It's too dangerous. I'll fix it."

He went to Dawson on the next boat and got a pump and installed a good water system in the kitchen, cutting down my work by half.

All summer we enjoyed the fresh vegetables from the garden. I canned, dried, and put away, carrots, beets, turnips, onions, and cabbages in the root cellar. We bleached the celery and it came out white and crisp. Green tomatoes were wrapped in paper and put into milk crates.

Thanksgiving and Christmas we brought them up and put them on the big shelf back of the stove to ripen. It was a great treat to the men who lived alone on their claims and ate only dried beans and such things. I used to give them presents of cucumbers from Davy's hothouse.

Long before the freeze-up, loads of groceries came by boat, with the outfit for winter. Forty pounds of cheese in big boxes, crates of eggs, butter, sugar, oatmeal, corn meal, barrels of flour, big cartons of tea, bags of coffee, rice, and drums of coal oil. After the first year I made my own preserves and jellies. We had fine smoked fish and plenty of good fresh meat. The woodcutters brought us great barges of wood, which Davy had cut into stove lengths. Now we were ready for a long, comfortable winter. We lived like feudal lords. It did not matter that it grew so cold that the thermometer went out of commission, and that the men coming in from the trail declared "they dared not speak to a passing traveler for fear the words would freeze and not thaw out before spring!"

The light from the windows of The Roadhouse shone over the snow like a beacon. Weary men picked up courage and quickened lagging footsteps when they saw it. Inside was warmth, companionship, laughter. Whenever the door opened, in rushed a cloud of frost, almost hiding the traveler. Warm words of welcome met him, and with a sigh of relief in his heart, he felt he was home. The dogs, too, had a welcome. Davy saw to it that they were well cared for.

I always had a pot of hot soup and a cup of strong tea ready as soon as a man could get his frozen muffler from his face. Often their eyelashes were frozen until they could scarcely see. Sometimes they had to cut their mustaches to be rid of the long amber icicles that tobacco juice had made.

I loved an "open door." I enjoyed meeting people from all parts of the world, giving food and shelter to saint and sinner alike. Each person received the same kind consideration.

I took a personal interest in the men who lived on their claims. This interest was beyond price to the homesick men who longed to talk and tell their problems to an understanding friend. I sympathized with their hunger for companionship during the long, dark nights and short, dark days. This great overpowering country of vast spaces, strange, weird lights, and ghostly snow was too much to bear for most of the men who lived alone, and many a poor fellow lost his reason.

Our warm, friendly kitchen was a haven for these lonely men. They perched themselves on my big wood box beside the stove and watched me cook. We would talk and laugh together. It brought them back to normal, unwound taut nerves, scattered brooding thoughts, and made the world seem real again.

I had no favorites unless it might be the Mounties, that colorful body of men, the Royal Canadian Mounted Police. The North could never have obtained its high standing for law and order without these fine, tireless men. I found them true to the high standard set them by their superior officers. The barracks were about two hundred feet from The Roadhouse. Some of them were always in my kitchen. They were kind and helpful, ready to pump water, carry wood, wash and dry dishes. I used to tell Davy, "The better they are raised, the kinder they are."

I listened to men telling of their experiences in Africa, Australia, New Zealand, China, Russia, and India. Homesick boys away from their families for the first time, would bring letters from sweethearts and parents for me to read. A young Norwegian, who later froze to death, brought pictures of his fine home in Norway. I was very fond of this lad, and always glad to see him. I realized how he longed for home and mother.

Sick men came for Davy to doctor, and for me to nurse. It was a gratifying life, to be of service to others. It was almost like a big family coming home. Each one brought his own world with him. They would talk about their claims, their hunting and cooking, or their dogs. If you wish to find the way to a man's heart up North, talk about his dogs. Most of the men were kind to them and took excellent care. I never trusted a man who was careless and neglectful of his animals; I found him a bad lot.

In the early spring, when the sun shone brightly on the snow and ice, the men blackened their faces. They believed it kept them from snow-blindness. This gave them a fierce look, and a chechaco would get a real fright if he met one on the trail.

Summer was a busy time. There was no one to help me with the gathering and preparation of the vegetables, cooking and washing the dishes, and making the beds. My hands performed all the tasks, but never was my heart crushed with the labor.

Eight years passed, and I had not left the island. But in those years, I met more interesting people than if I had crossed the continent. The cry of "GOLD" had brought men from every land! Bishops and high church officials, governors and judges, military officers, professors, scientists, explorers, and miners, titled Englishmen, millionaires, writers, and poor men with their picks and shovels. I had the opportunity of meeting these world travelers in a way few had. They were guests in my home. Many letters came to us from faraway places, from people who had stayed with us, and remembered to write. It gladdened our hearts.

We had many laughs over funny situations. A well-dressed young man arrived to wait for the Mayo boat. He must stay at The Roadhouse in the meantime. Not seeing any porters to carry his luggage, which had been put ashore at his feet, he called out to some men in rough clothes who had come down to see the boat arrive. "Here, you fellows, do you want to earn some money? Carry my luggage up to the hotel."

"Carry it yourself. You look able," one of them answered. Then they all laughed. There wasn't a man there but would have given him a hand if he had needed it. But this was not a country of lackeys, and the chechaco had to learn this. Here, one man was as good as another. It was the *real* man who counted, not money and fine clothes.

An Englishman and his servant arrived. The servant told me his master did not wish to eat with "these people," and could he have a separate table? He would pay extra.

"No, not here," I told him. After a bit, the fine gentleman found himself hungry enough to sit down and eat. It happened that he was seated by Albert, a rough-looking old miner who, with the true spirit of the Yukon, wished to be kind and kept passing dishes of food and urging him to eat. His lordship looked at the old man haughtily.

Albert got the idea and said, "Well now, young feller, by the time ye're up here a spell, you'll get over that," and he paid no more attention to him. The valet floated about until I told him to sit down, that his master would get enough to eat, and if he didn't, it was quite his own fault.

The Englishman stayed with us a couple of days, waiting for the Mayo boat. He and Davy became quite chummy, exchanged tobacco, and discussed British politics. Some time later he returned and tried to get up a party to go hunting for "Big Heads," to be mounted as trophies. The boys did not want to go with him, although he offered more money than they were accustomed to get. I felt that we should help him. I explained to him, "You see, you do not understand the men. It is not the money, but the way you treat them that counts. They are not servants just because they work for you. In this country one man is another's equal. They resent your manner toward them."

The poor Englishman looked puzzled, but began to see the light. Davy helped him organize his party and get away on the hunt. By the time he returned, he understood the men much better. They, in turn, respected him, for he was sincere and a good sportsman. It had been a successful hunt. He sent out some fine specimens of Big Heads.

We had many calls in later years to organize parties for rich hunters. Though it was a lot of bother in the busy season, we made a good deal of money doing this.

People are queer. A man asked me to show him our garden. Upon leaving, he handed me a quarter.

"Here, this is for you," he said.

"What is it for?" I asked.

"Why, it is a tip for showing me your garden."

I handed it back. "If you were trying to pay me for my time, it would take a great deal more than that, for I am a busy woman, but as for showing you the garden, I was glad to do that."

A handsome woman arrived with her husband from Outside, waiting over to make connections with the Mayo boat. She learned her lesson, too. The next morning she came out into the kitchen to speak to me, dressed in a rose tea gown, with lace cascading down the front and in the sleeves. She looked very lovely, but out of place.

"Will you please give me another room? We're not comfortable. We don't mind paying more. I must be comfortable," she said.

"Well, you might look around and see if you can find anything you like better," I answered politely, but I had to turn my back to keep my guest from seeing me smile. I pitied the poor girl for I knew in what a hard school she would learn her lesson. Later we became very dear friends. We often laughed together about her tea gown with the lace, and her demand for comfort.

There was a big wood camp not far from The Roadhouse, and the men ate at the hotel. Wood was in great demand. It had many uses—for timbers in mines, for thawing out the ground to take out ore. The steamboats burned wood, taking thirty and forty cords at a time. Some of the rafts going to Dawson carried as many as sixty cords. Wood was cut in sixteen-foot lengths. The Roadhouse used as much as three hundred cords in a winter. It was brought in on a raft, then cut at the door into stove lengths. Woodcutting was a good job for men who needed work.

Each day I baked bread, cakes, pies, and puddings. I often worked till late at night. Sometimes eleven o'clock would find me baking bread for the next day, with a stack of dirty dishes still to be washed. By the time I had finished I often fell asleep with my head on my arm, resting on the table, too tired to get ready for bed.

But I was not always so driven. In the thirty-four years on the island, many things happened. When trade was not so heavy I liked to go to bed and read. Sometimes I would read the night through, and as I was strong and well, I would get up fresh and ready for another busy day.

The books I loved best were histories and poetry. The Bible, I had read through many times when a child in Scotland. There, no self-respecting person ever "walked out" on the Sabbath Day, except to church, and then home to read the Bible. The hours I had spent thus had taken up a good part of my young life. No passage of Scriputure was unfamiliar to me. I could repeat the Psalms at great length. I felt I had read the Bible enough. Now I chose to read the histories of Europe, America, South America, and other countries. I was fond of Emerson. I also loved to recite poetry—musical "Hiawatha," Sir Walter Scott's "Lady of the Lake," the poems of Bobby Burns, Lowell, and others. When I had an unpleasant task that took a long time to accomplish, such as cleaning fish or game, I would repeat poetry to myself. If I forgot a line, I must dry my hands and go into the bedroom and hunt up the poem. After a bit this taught me not to forget, whilse.

The Mounties kept me supplied with books and reading matter.

Hardly a mail arrived that did not bring me a package of letters from my beloved brother in Scotland. Each week, on a certain day, he wrote me a long letter, telling of the life at home. Great stacks of letters would come, and I hurried to sit down to read them in order, thus keeping in touch with my family and friends. Through the years, this was one of my greatest joys.

Our Years on Stewart Island

SPRING COMES in the Yukon at the same time that it arrives in other places in the Northern Hemisphere, March 21, with the vernal equinox. However, rivers and lakes do not open until much later—about the middle of May, when the sun becomes very hot and the surface of the ice begins to thaw. It is often as late as June 10 before the rivers are ready for navigation.

The breakup is the dramatic moment of the year. The miners and other folk from the inland hasten to the river to see the ice go out. Winter takes its leave, and beautiful spring comes in, with flowers and long golden days.

My heart was as gay as the birds, singing in the trees, as I stood watching the river. Each year it grew to mean more and more to me. I could hardly stay in the house long enough to attend to the daily tasks and cook the meals. Davy was busy in the garden, calling me to see the different flowers, comparing them to last year's, and showing surprise or disappointment at the yield. I would come running, glad of an excuse to get out in the warm, sweet air, all cares forgotten. When Davy was safely away, I would burst into song. I could never sing, really, but I had to let out my joy and happiness.

My strength seemed unlimited. I worked all day, and as night was almost as light as day, I did not know when to stop. Spring was too wonderful to

waste in sleep. Winter was made to sleep in. The
bears had the right idea. But even in winter I begrudged time spent in sleep. I often said: "Life
was not meant to be slept away, but to be lived."

Bets were made as to the exact time the ice
would go out. In Dawson, a flag was attached to
two steel stakes driven into the ice near the center
of the river, and these were joined by wires to a
time clock at the fire department. The clock stopped
when a stake moved three feet. This was judged sufficient distance to indicate that the ice was actually
on its way out and decided the time. The event had
all the excitement of the Irish Sweepstakes. Purses
were made up, and everyone who had a bit of sport-
ing blood placed a bet somewhere. One year I won
eleven dollars in a purse.

The "breakup" was watched with intense anxiety
by those whose homes were near the madly rushing
river waters. Davy and I were among those who
had good reason to watch the breath-taking sight.
With a noise like the firing of guns, the ice cracked
and crashed, jamming together, piling up with driftwood on the sand bars, sometimes damming the river
until it broke through and ran over the sloughs, at
times almost covering the island.

Again the river would slip out quietly, carrying
huge blocks of ice away. Then Davy would say,
"The river is just waking up from a long winter's
nap." We were grateful when this happened.

The ice cutting away the banks of the river had
changed the island, tearing it down. In the spring
the overflow built them up again. The river was
like something alive, fierce, merciless, as it tore along.

One spring I stood watching a small island, not far from Stewart, literally torn to pieces. The trees toppled into the water, and the great cakes of ice, like battering rams, tore away the helpless little island piece by piece. I shivered to think that this might be the fate of our own Stewart Island.

When we bought The Roadhouse, it had stood two hundred feet from the bank. But during the last few years I spent there, barely twenty feet separated the hotel and the mighty Yukon.

In the breakup, great cakes of ice came whirling along, turning and twisting in and out. Often some animal would be helplessly marooned on one, fearing to jump to another. The ice cakes tipped easily, and the poor creature would sometimes fall into the icy water and be crushed or frozen to death before it could reach safety. It was a common sight to see a moose, a timber wolf, or a caribou in this perilous position. The caribou seemed to be the only ones that ever escaped if they fell into the water. They could scramble up with their sharp little hoofs, get on top of another cake of ice, and sometimes reach the shore in safety.

One evening, about dusk, Davy and I heard a man crying for help. We ran down to the river. The man, on a whirling cake of ice, screamed for us to save him, waving his arms to keep his balance. He shrieked, "Help me, for God's sake. Save me! Help me!" We looked at one another. Between us and the frantic man the Yukon roared on. There was nothing we could do. We ran to the barracks, but even the Mounted Police were unable to help the poor fellow. He was soon out of sight around the bend in the river, never to be heard of again.

Davy and I were badly upset over this. It was hard to see the man going to his death and know we were helpless to save him.

Four times in the thirty-odd years we lived on Stewart Island the river went on a rampage. The ice dammed, causing the water to flood The Road-house.

The first time this happened, everything was at its best. The hotel was comfortably furnished in "Outside" furniture, the greenhouse complete. We felt we were settled for life. But we had not reck-oned on the Yukon, whilse.

A slowly moving mass of ice rapidly increased in speed until it jammed on a sand bar. Here it crinkled up and formed a dam against which the green, rushing water raised ten feet in a few min-utes. More ice piled onto the dam, and ice barriers that had formed in the fall came rolling and plung-ing down the river, forming a new dam which was only to be swept away again, with a thundering, crashing roar.

This went on along the whole course of the river, accompanied by a grinding, exploding sound that was terrific. The river, choked by a mountain of ice, tore itself free and ran angrily over the sloughs, causing the backed-up water to cover the entire island. We had climbed to the roof of the house with friends who had come to watch the ice go out. I ran downstairs to see if everything was safe, just in case there should be an overflow. I was in the

Public Room. Suddenly a little trickle of water came under the door, then quickly grew into a stream.

The three cellars under the house were soon filled with water. The trap door, which lifted by a ring, burst open with the force of the water back of it. The water came boiling up, filling all the downstairs part of the house. The old cat and her young ones ran along the fence, mewing pitifully for help. There was barely time to rescue them and call the dogs and get them all to safety on the housetop. The water tore in everywhere, even into the barn and chicken house, carrying the squawking chickens to their deaths. The horses, however, were rescued by a neighbor and taken with his own animals to higher ground where they were safe.

In an hour it was all over, we thought. Then the ice jammed worse than before and it was three or four hours this time before the water receded. Fortunately it was light all night. The river formed narrow lanes of rushing water that tore down between ice canyons, the walls of which were ground smooth by the descending ice. We watched fascinated, for we realized the danger.

After the flood had receded and we came down from the housetop, we found many things to be sad about. Poor Davy was grieving over his beloved greenhouse. The side facing the river had been jammed by a big cake of ice, tearing a hole large enough to drive in a team of horses. All the precious glass was shattered. The garden that was planted so lovingly was torn up, the seeds scattered.

Huge pieces of rotten ice, left to melt on the riverbank, looked like fairy prismatic castles. We took time in the midst of our work and worry to admire and watch one particular piece which was like an aquamarine jewel. We were even sad when the sun ate it up.

When we came to the reconstruction of the hotel, I felt optimistic. "Why, Davy, it could have been worse," I told him. "It might have carried our home away as it did some of the cabins on the island. Let's be grateful." I set about cleaning up the sand left by the water.

In my cozy bedroom I had many heartaches. The pretty room was badly damaged, the furniture watersoaked, and all the drawers warped. The fine Brussels carpet was filled with sand and silt, from which it was never after free. For years I thought of the flood every time I swept it. A friend had sent me a white silk waist. Still in its box, it was completely ruined by a piece of red ribbon which had faded on it. It grieved me very much, but I thought, "Well, I'd have no time to wear it anyway," and I set about cleaning and washing the soggy bedclothes that had to be carried outdoors to dry.

It was a big job to repair the damage, especially as people were coming to the hotel to be fed and cared for. The cellars must be dried out, and silt and mud were everywhere. Cold and dampness from the ice added to the unpleasantness.

Years later, after all this damage was repaired and forgotten, the Yukon again said, "Don't be sure of me." It flew into a rage, and when it was through, the poor Roadhouse was in a sad state.

I reminded Davy,

Ye'll ha' misfortune, great and small
But ha' a heart abinn them all.

Once more I set about to bring order out of chaos.

Years went by and this, too, was almost forgotten. The greenhouse was rebuilt, the furniture repainted, and a new garden fence put up. It was as if there had never been a flood. Then for the third time the river tore things up. It carried almost enough mud and silt to cover the hotel and garden. This time we had to dig it out with shovels and hoes before we could begin life anew.

As we were working, we heard someone grieving and moaning, "Oh, my friends, my dear friends! All gone, all drowned! Oh, my poor friends!" We found the good Dr. La Chapell of Dawson in our yard. When he saw us he came running, actually crying with joy that we were alive. He was at his hunting cabin on Stewart River, and hearing that the island had been flooded, he had come as soon as possible to find out what had happened to us. When he saw how badly things looked, he was sure we were drowned. This was a happy meeting with our dear friend. Our hearts were warmed by his loving friendship. We felt equal to the task that lay before us.

The fourth and last time the flood came to The Roadhouse it did not find us there. When I returned home, I found the marks of the Merciless One.

On November 11, 1909, after carefully packing three dog teams with supplies for fast traveling, Davy and I, with five men, set out for a three-hundred-

Photo by William Pierce, San Diego, California
AUNT PEGGY AND ORA M. SHAND
At home in San Diego, California, in the "Garden of the Singing Wind"

PLATE II

Photo by William Pierce, San Diego, California
PEGGY SHAND ON HER NINETIETH BIRTHDAY

PLATE III

Photo by William Pierce, San Diego, California
MRS. SHAND IN 1936
After she had lived in San Diego for seven years

PLATE IV

ROADHOUSE ON STEWART ISLAND
Mrs. Shand and the Mounties

PLATE V

HOTEL STEWART, AT THE JUNCTION OF STEWART RIVER
AND THE YUKON

PLATE VI

AUNTIE'S KIRK AT BUCKELIVY, SCOTLAND

PLATE VII

THE MILL AND OLD HOME AT ARNPRIOR, SCOTLAND

PLATE VIII

AUNTIE ON HER EIGHTY-FIFTH BIRTHDAY

PLATE IX

DAVID C. SHAND, PROPRIETOR OF THE STEWART CITY HOTEL IN THE
YUKON, AND HIS LEAD HUSKY

PLATE X

DOG TEAM READY TO START FOR DONNAHUE

PLATE XI

THE SHAND ROADHOUSE ON STEWART ISLAND IN THE YUKON RIVER

PLATE XII

A MEMBER OF THE ROYAL CANADIAN MOUNTED POLICE,
YUKON TERRITORY

PLATE XIII

AN INDIAN GIRL WHOM MRS. SHAND HELPED RAISE

PLATE XIV

PEGGY SHAND AND HER FRIEND, BELLE BRENNON

PLATE XV

FAITHFUL TO THE LAST

Prince by the side of Uncle Davy

PLATE XVI

ONE OF THE SHAND WORK DOGS

PLATE XVII

PEGGY WITH A GUEST'S SMALL BABY

PLATE XVIII

PACKERS ASCENDING CHILKOOT PASS, 1898

PLATE XIX

AUNT PEGGY AND HER NEPHEW, GRAHAM SHAND (1936)

PLATE XX

mile trip up the White River to stake copper claims. The range of mountains in which the copper was found was known as the Alaska Alps. It had not yet been decided if the valuable ore lay in Canada or Alaska, as the boundary line had not been established permanently.

It was a wild country; no white woman had set foot upon it. Many tales were told of the huge timber wolves. A lad came to The Roadhouse one night not long before we started on this trip, driven almost insane from fear and fatigue. He told us of timber wolves that had stalked him for days and nights along the White River trail. He had carried a little puppy with him through all his fright and it seemed to be his first consideration. As he put it down on the floor of the Public Room, he cried and laughed wildly about his frightful experience, and about a man he had passed on the trail. The police at the barracks listened to the hysterical lad, and later they set out to look for the man the boy described. The police sent back word that his story was true. They had found what remained of the man and his dog team, and had sighted a pack of five big timber wolves.

During the previous summer Davy and his friend, Walter Stewart, had gone up to this country to see what truth there was in the tales about a mountain of solid copper. They had returned enthusiastic and anxious to get back. They wanted to take me and some friends along to stake claims. It had been our intention to go at once, but many things had to be arranged before we could get away. I refused to leave my business of running The Roadhouse until I could find someone to take charge of it. At last we secured a young couple, and I was free to accompany them.

A friend who was a United States government surveyor sent word to me to go and stake and have the recording made. He told me he was sure he could sell the claim for me to a French syndicate interested in copper. He assured me I would be one of the world's copper queens. I smiled to myself as I made preparations for the journey. I was ready for the adventure. I did not need the promise of vast wealth for me to make any trip. The freedom from duties and responsibility, the joy of seeing new country were enough. I never saw a trail or river but that I longed to explore it. Hadn't I dreamed of following the mighty Yukon and watching it empty into Bering Sea? Often I made imaginary plans to see the source of the Stewart and White rivers. Now, one of these dreams was to be realized.

The trip over the ice worried me at first, as I had never liked this kind of travel. The open places, smoking as if a river of steam was running underneath, gave me a creepy feeling.

But it was foolish to worry about anything with Walter in charge. Davy and I knew how dependable he proved under any circumstances. He had been in our home for years, and was one of us. He became almost an invalid from an injury. As time went by he proved a valuable friend. Money was never mentioned. He took his part in the home. He was a fine hunter and kept the table supplied with meat and fowls. He cut the wood into stove lengths at the door. This he took as his work, and was faithful to his self-appointed task. When Davy sent to Dawson to buy our winter clothes, he bought Walter's. Whenever Walter wanted to take a trip, Davy had the money ready for him. It was a happy arrangement and we all three approved of it. Walter was our brother. We depended on him and he never failed us.

The White River rises in the Nutzotin Mountains. Davy and Walter told me of its wild beauty, the high-peaked mountains and chalk cliffs, the table-lands and fertile valleys. I was filled with the anticipation of seeing a new country.

The trip took careful planning. We must travel light, and yet take all the necessities. There were the three teams of five dogs each. The food for fifteen dogs was in itself a big item, and besides there were our own provisions, blankets, and cooking utensils. We set about cutting down, making the load as light as possible. It was decided to leave the tents and sleep in the open, to carry no stove, and to cook over campfires.

The temperature ranged from twenty to thirty degrees below zero, but there was little wind. Walter planned that I ride on one of the sleds, the men taking turns driving the teams. Everyone warned me to dress very warmly, that I would become cold without realizing it. One of the men gave me a fine parkee made of four different kinds of fur, with wolverine about my face. Over three pair of stockings I wore Indian moccasins. Everyone wore two pair of mittens. One pair was tied about the neck by a string, and the other, smaller pair was more glovelike and lined with rabbit skin, the fur turned inside.

When it was hard going and the ice very rough, I would get off and walk to make it easier on the dogs. I had a hard time keeping up, hampered by so many clothes. The men would not let me labor too long over the ice for fear my clothes would become damp with perspiration. They realized the danger of this. When the ice was smooth and the going good, I got back on the sled.

There were ice bridges out by the water. They were quite safe and strong. The river swirled and bubbled on each side of the bridge in such constant motion that it could not freeze even in the lowest temperature. The dogs picked their way carefully over these narrow bridges where there was hardly room for the sled. At least I was free if the bridge broke through. Though I was badly frightened, I did not allow the men to know how I felt, for I kept my face as blank as an Indian woman's. They never knew the fear that tore at my heart. I thought to myself, "Well, if I go in, it will be time enough to scream."

When the ice seemed dangerous along the trail, Walter removed his snowshoes, put them on his hands, and cautiously crawled out on the ice to test it before he allowed his party to cross over.

I was glad when we were traveling over a slough and I could see the dead tules sticking up through the ice. I did not consider that it would be just as easy to drown in five feet of water as in ten!

Walter was always very careful to keep the dogs' feet dry when there was open water, for if ice formed between their toes in hard marbles it must be cut out. If this happened, the party had to stop and go down to the beach to gather wood and make a fire. Then the feet must be dried out. All this took time, and it was not looked upon with favor by the leader. He insisted on the best of care for the teams. "Everything depends upon them," he said. "Frozen feet mean lame dogs, and we have too long a journey before us for this to happen."

In some places the ice on the trail would be like broken glass set on edge. This was bad for the dogs' paws. But Walter had provided for this emergency. We had made moccasins to be tied on. The dogs understood, and did not try to pull them off. Walter said, "Whenever they come to a bad place, they stop and ask for their boots."

We made twenty-two miles the first day and the men thought it not bad. Camp was set up in an open space close to the river. Two big trees were cut down and a fire built between them. A kettle at one end held our supper of beans and ham. One of the men made bread in a Dutch oven, pulling away the coals, putting the bread in the oven, and piling more coals on top. When it was opened, the best bread possible came out, baked a golden brown. At the other end of the fire, in a big copper kettle, the dogs' food was cooked. I was treated like a queen. The men would not allow me to help. I must sit by, wrapped in my blankets, free of all responsibility and "boss the job."

After all had eaten with ravenous appetites, more food was cooked and made ready for the lunch the following day so that it could be warmed by a small campfire along the trail.

This trip to the copper country was the high light of my years in the North. Along the sloughs there were beautiful snow flowers made by the hoarfrost. Davy was fascinated by them and called my attention to the brilliant flower patterns, sparkling like diamonds. "Tiffany's in New York couldn't put on a display like that," he said. I felt I was traveling over a lovely lace curtain. It was like a fairy dream I used to have when a wee lass.

The days were short. Walter tried to get in all the daylight hours possible. It was close to a full moon when we started, and each night grew more beautiful. The stars, twinkling and sparkling in the velvet of the sky, seemed very near and bright.

When we stopped at night, one man cut dead pine; the rosin in the wood made a quick, hot fire. Another, with snowshoes, and carrying an ax, cleared two feet of snow from the river and chopped ice to be melted for cooking. Close to the fire the men trampled down soft snow and covered the packed place with spruce boughs for our beds. On these they tossed the gear bags containing dry socks, underwear, and extra sleeping clothes. Blankets were spread upon the spruce boughs and each person put on all his clothes, wrapped his scarf about his middle, and curled up with feet to the fire. The dogs crept in near their masters and slept contentedly.

Only I lay awake, drinking in the beauty of the night. It was too lovely to leave and go away to sleep—sleep that could be had at home every night under a roof, with all this glory shut away! All about white, white ghostly snow and stillness, listening stillness. A silence that seemed to hold all the world in abeyance of anticipation. The tall pine trees, the spruce with their drooping branches heavy with diamond dust, sparkled in the starlight like a frosted Christmas card. I raised myself on my elbow, the better to paint the picture in my memory. Below, the frozen river, a shining crystal path. The dead white of the snow, the red glow of the big campfire, the sleeping forms of the men and faithful dogs. The Silence, the Silence like a living Presence, vibrated with ecstacy.

This night the northern lights were alive in the heavens. Across the sky flashed a stream of light, a band of gold in the eerie green, heralding the arrival of myriad rainbow colors, shaking down lavender, gold, rose, blue, orange—all the colors known to man and even more. A luminous curtain arched across the sky. Then the colors seemed to drop down all around like snow. The sparkling of the stars grew dim. Then I saw only the shimmering prismatic drapery, a quivering, living curtain that promised to draw aside and reveal all the mysteries of the universe. It was too much; no one could take in all this beauty and live.

From off in the distance came the weird cry of a wolf, the loneliest cry ever heard, then another and another. It was all out of keeping with the wonder of the night. It brought me back. I had seen the glory and experienced the greatest moment of my life, a moment of complete fulfillment.

Each person witnessing the wonder of the northern lights for the first time reacts according to his nature.

Some, full of fear, are driven almost insane by the weirdness. Others, who do not lift their eyes above the earth, are no more conscious of the lights than of the moon and stars. But there is a mystery about it that is terrifying to the average person.

Walter carried a thermometer and checked closely to see that all was well with his party, and that everyone watched his nose as the northern lights foretold a cold spell.

In the morning the men built up the fire and awakened the dogs. They were hard sleepers after a day on the trail. Curled up into little balls, their tails over their noses, they resembled balls of coconut, all covered with hoarfrost. They were pushed to their feet stretching and yawning like human beings awakened from a sound sleep. The men, too, covered with the hoarfrost, looked like animated snow men.

After a good hot breakfast we were ready to go. I enjoyed the excitement of the start. The dogs were in high spirits to be on the way, leaping and barking, their tails curled over their backs, for when animals are well fed and cared for they are happy to work. We were off in a cloud of soft snow, men shouting and dogs barking. It was all very gay. Walter never carried a whip, but controlled his teams by his own knowledge of the situation. The dogs had confidence in him, and, unafraid, they pulled with all their might.

The majestic mountains in the distance, peaked like cathedral spires, loomed before us. Between the near mountains were lovely fertile valleys in which there should have been comfortable farm houses full of

happy families. This was a homeland awaiting strong
men, helpful women, and laughing children. As I
rode along behind the fine team of willing dogs, I
dreamed of being young, of coming here and living
a long and happy life in this perfect setting, where
I could raise my eyes to the cathedral spires of the distant mountains and worship God in His own temple.

As we neared the end of our journey, we traveled
through a posted country—"Wolves—Watch your
dogs," read many signs. Passing the cabin of the
man who had put up the signs, we learned that this
part of the region was infested with immense timber
wolves. He had built his cabin wild-beast proof.
The windows were very small and the door heavy.
The night before our party arrived he had poisoned
thirty wolves. He would realize quite a sum of
money for their pelts. The wolves had eaten all his
dogs. The last one he had kept in the house but left
him out for a bit, and the wolves almost tore the
dog to pieces before he got it back in. The man said
that night he was almost driven insane by wolves
tearing about the cabin, howling and trying to get
in. Walter advised the man to get out of this part
of the country. He said he was going to do so as
soon as he had killed some more of the wolves.

That night when we camped, we could see here
and there the shadowy forms sneaking about among
the trees. The dogs were too wise to answer the
wolves' challenge for a fight. But in the night one
dog, with more curiosity than sense, ventured away
from the fire and was soon snatched up and devoured
by the waiting wolves. I called to the men that the
dog had left camp, but they went on sleeping. I

had borrowed this dog from a friend, so I felt responsible and blamed the men for not waking up when I called them.

I could see the wolves' emerald eyes flashing outside the light of the campfire. Shivers of fear ran over me, but Walter had said they were cowardly beasts and would not come close to the fire where there were people. I lay awake watching, nevertheless. Every night after this, the wolves annoyed us. I could see them on the ice, playing together like dogs, or sitting about, noses pointed up, now and again giving vent to the weirdest, most ghostly sound known to man. They were getting on my nerves. The beasts seemed like wicked Fate waiting to destroy. I did not enjoy the beauties of the night; neither could I sleep. Fear tore at me, but I did not mention it to the men. I was afraid they would think me a coward.

The party came upon a big moose that had been killed and eaten by the wolves. Walter told a story of seeing two wolves working to bring down a moose. They first hamstrung the poor creature. Then they sprang at his throat, and the whole pack was upon him and had him down.

After we passed Rabbit Creek, we came upon a fresh camp. At once Walter and Davy decided it must have been made by two men whom Walter had seen avoiding The Roadhouse at Stewart. One of the men he recognized as the man who had helped Davy during the summer when he was working on his copper claim.

"That fellow has gone to Dawson," Davy said. "He had told about this rich claim of mine and

persuaded someone to outfit him. They are on their
way up to stake as close as they can. We will have
to beat them up there and get stakes in first."

We camped at the mouth of Generac River. The
other party had gone on into Canyon City and stayed
all night in one of the two cabins which comprised
the town. A couple of our men had checked up on
this, and had come back to tell us. In the morning,
long before daylight, we packed up, quietly picking our way across the mouth of the canyon, ready
to make the steep climb up the mountainside.

At the foot of the ascent, Lem Lodge helped me
to scramble up, step by step, by giving me his double-
bitted ax to hold onto. If I had not held onto the
ax I'd have fallen backwards and rolled to the bottom. It was a straight climb up the mountain.

A band of raw copper ran through the mountain,
plainly visible to the eye. We came to the claim
that Davy had been working in the summer. He
pointed out to us the big rock where he had met
a grizzly bear. He had just put in a charge of dynamite and set it off and was going as fast as possible
around this rock to get away from the explosion.
Suddenly he met a huge grizzly, face to face. They
were both surprised. The bear raised up on his hind
legs, showing a red mouth full of big white fangs.
Davy said all he could see was the beast's mouth and
his great paws. He was scared so badly he could
not move. He had forgotten all about the charge of
dynamite and was as much startled as the bear at
the noise and shower of rocks. The old grizzly
turned about and scurried down the mountainside as
fast as he could go, the rocks bouncing off his back

and head. Davy threw himself upon his face, glad to have the rocks pelt him. Had the dynamite not exploded at the right time, it would have been the end of Davy.

It was a hard climb, and I was glad when we got to Canyon City, although our friend, Mr. McClain, was out when we arrived. Davy knew that it would be quite all right to go in and take possession of his cabin. What a little palace of comfort it was to us, after eleven days of sleeping beside a campfire, with everything so neat and clean! When our host arrived he was delighted to see us. Never do I remember being given a more royal welcome. He had a cache full to overflowing with fine meat: mountain sheep, caribou, moose, ducks, geese, crane—everything the land supplied. He had an outfit of the very finest canned fruits and vegetables. He opened can after can of his best provisions. He wanted even the dogs to be fed on the best in the cache. I baked bread and cooked great roasts of meat. We were all happy and our host could not stop smiling and urging everyone to eat more. After supper the men made me lie down on one of the bunks. I curled up, contented and comfortable. The men got out their pipes, smoking and talking long into the night. I lay there listening. Life seemed very good and satisfying.

The men in the other party who had come to stake near Davy's claim had gone on. We saw no more of them, but later we heard that they had staked twenty-five miles farther on.

The other cabin in Canyon City was now empty and Mr. McClain told the men in our party to occupy it. He insisted that Davy and I stay in his cabin.

We were here more than a week, the men going out each day prospecting and staking their claims.

I cooked a big supper, a regular banquet, every night. The surveyors who were establishing the boundary line between Canada and Alaska had sold Mr. McClain the goods they did not want to take back with them, so his outfit consisted of the best that Canada and America furnished. At the end of the week when we talked of going home, Mr. Mc-Clain pleaded with us to stay on, and each time we talked of going he looked so distressed that we stayed another day. At last, when we did get on our way, he loaded us with five fine mountain sheep.

A heavy storm overtook us the second day out. A deep snow covered the trail so that the going was miserable. We had cached our dogs' food on the way, but now everything was covered with deep snow and we could not locate it. We were compelled to feed our mountain sheep to the hungry dogs.

It took a much longer time on the way back; the second day it grew dark and stormy. The unbroken trail was difficult to make. Two of the men went on ahead of the dogs and packed it down with snow-shoes so that the dogs would not wallow in the deep snow. The snow was hard, fine, and dry, like little pellets of glass. The men ran and pushed on the handle bars of the sleds to help the dogs all they could. Poor Davy, not as strong as the other men, suffered most. I was glad when, on a smooth part of the trail, he rode on the back of my sled.

The wind blew, shrieking in our ears, and our lashes froze to our faces. Camping was now difficult. The dogs were tired from their hard pull through the deep snow. But our trip had given us valuable experience and we were more able to stand the strain. After fourteen days, we arrived home. How fine that home looked to us! We rested two days, and then set out for Dawson to record our claims.

The people we had left to run The Roadhouse had managed to care for the guests who had come during our absence. When we got back from Dawson they went to live in a little cabin on the island. Later, their baby was the first and only white child I ever heard of being born on Stewart Island.

The trip to the copper country was the finest one I ever had in my life. I often lie awake at night and think of the time I slept out under the stars beside a campfire, of the stillness, the northern lights across the sky, the weirdness, the howling of the wolves, and the danger of the ice trail.

It gave me a deep inner realization. I know why the Indians love their life in spite of the weariness and suffering. There is a fascination that only those who have slept under the stars can understand. A closeness to God, with nothing between. One must experience it to know what I mean.

A Tom Atkins came in from Thistle Creek. He had been suffering badly from rheumatism and his knees were so stiff that he was unable to walk and could only crawl along. Afraid he would freeze at home alone, he and his dogs had come to The Roadhouse.

We started "doctoring" him, and after a month he was able to get about and ready to go back to his home. His knees still pained him and I told him to wrap them in woolen kneecaps, but as he was ready to start, I did not have time to knit them. I looked down at the beautiful heavy white sweater I was wearing, the gift from a friend. I was very proud of it, so cozy and warm it was. But now I slipped it off, cut the sleeves out, and telling the man to roll up his pant legs, I put the warm woolen sleeves over his knees and told him to keep them there until it had warmed up in the spring. The old fellow went away thankful.

Men often came in from the trail, sick and discouraged. Sometimes I thought their own carelessness caused it. When I had them safely well and ready to start away, then I would give them a good talking to about their health. Davy, too, did this even better than I. He was a natural doctor, and knew intuitively the cause of the sickness and how to treat it. In an emergency he even performed minor operations. Still suffering himself from snow-blindness, he was especially good with these cases, and knew what to do for the one who needed help.

I was the nurse, and handled the unpleasant tasks as best I could. Frozen feet and hands were common. Men would come in with hands and feet festering, almost rotten from being frozen. Often they were wrapped in a dirty flour sack that had not been washed. There were many pitiful sights. We were happy to help save a man's feet for him. I kept a foot tub which served for these cases of doctoring of feet, and it was used many times as the years went by. When a sick man needed nursing and the hotel was crowded, I would fix a bed on three chairs near my bedroom door so that I could tend the patient in the dark hours of night. In and out of bed I would crawl, giving him attention. I was often up all night, putting hot compresses on a congested chest, working to keep away dreaded pneumonia, doing all I could to ease his pain.

In the morning I dashed my face with cold water, slicked back my hair, put on a clean apron, and started breakfast for some early traveler. All day I would divide my time between cooking and dishwashing and caring for my patient. I had good health and did not mind the extra work.

One thing I stressed with my patient when convalescing was for him never to start home before he was over the weak, discouraged stage. This was the dangerous time. If the man had little money and felt he could not pay his way, I would ask him to stay anyway and pay when he found the gold. A young English lad laughingly called The Roadhouse "Liberty Hall," and others took up the name. "Don't hesitate to go to The Roadhouse on Stewart if you are sick," he said. "You can stay if you have no money as well as if you are rolling in it." He knew by experience. I had nursed him back to health and saved his feet, which were severely frozen.

Well, we never lost anything by it. They always paid—well! At least they 'most always did.

During one quiet winter there were an unusual number of tragedies and deaths from sickness. I myself was ill, and it set me to thinking of what might happen if I died. I was not as busy as usual and never was a good sleeper. Long hours I lay awake, thinking, thinking. My mother had said when I was a young girl, "Dear me, lass, you never go to bed the day you rise."

The nights were long and I lived over my childhood days. The most vivid memories were of the funerals. Only the men were allowed to attend. We children would hide behind the hedges and watch with curiosity and horror as the great hearse came up, drawn by two big black horses. On top of the hearse, four black plumes nodded and beckoned in a frightening and mysterious manner. We shook with fear but did not dare miss the awesome sight, seeing the men walk behind the hearse in a solemn procession. They wore long black coats, and on their heads were tall black hats with streamers of black crape ribbon that hung down almost to their shoulders.

Every respectable member of the community had his mourning clothes, kept layed away to wear at funerals. I mind so well how my father looked in his. I was a bit afraid of him when he wore them. Mother always said he got his death by attending a friend's funeral. It was a cold, rainy day and they walked miles in the sleet and rain to sit in the cold kirk during a long sermon. He was never well after that.

I mind the time I was coming home from visiting a friend and hearing about a neighbor's funeral. I was told how the corpse had a long white shroud with a band of white cloth about the face, like a mummy, and the hands, in white gloves, were crossed on the breast. And there were ghostly tales, too. I was thinking of this as I ran through the thick woods in the dusk of a winter's evening. Suddenly I came upon this hearse returning from the burying.

My knees shook under me. I choked with terror. I never could tell how I got home.

It preyed on my mind that, in case I should die, there was no preparation for my decent burying. I must arrange it all so that it could be done properly. Next day I sent to Dawson for ten yards of white baby flannel, white gloves and stockings. I made the shroud to tie about my neck, so that in case there were no women to lay me out, the men could tie it about me without disturbing my clothes. I felt more secure after my grave clothes were carefully laid away.

About this time the river opened up and trade kept me too busy to indulge in any more of these gloomy thoughts. I kept my "grave clothes" for some time. The following winter I cut up my shroud and made it into a nice warm nightgown. After all, why should I worry about anything so far in the "dimmie dis?" Being sick can make one a bit queer.

A man was brought in that winter, not a violent case, but pitiful. He was a gentleman and unfit for the hard life alone on his claim. I realized that it was only the dark, cold, winter hours and the social starvation which had weakened him. We kept him with us for months. After the breakup in the spring, the rustling of the leaves in the trees almost drove him mad. He would run through the woods crying: "Oh, they're after me—after me!" Davy would go for him and kindly lead him back. Gently I soothed him like a little child. He then stopped trembling and listened to me while I told him interesting stories or quoted poetry. He changed, and came to himself, and began reciting verses, some of which he had written.

One day he came into the room where Davy was cutting out a sail for his boat. When he saw the white cloth he threw up his hands and shrieked: "My God! He is cutting out my grave clothes!" He had lost his reason entirely.

When the Mounties came to remove him to the hospital, I begged them not to take him away. "He has not long to live," I told them, "and he is better here with his friends than among strangers."

They would not listen to me, however, and he lived only a short time.

I had always had the peculiar gift of knowing when death was near. My family first noticed this when, as a wee lass about seven, I came into the house and said to my mother: "Why is God going to take Jessie away? I don't want Him to."

"What are you talking about?" Mother asked.

I began to cry and said I did not want my little playmate to die and be put in the ground in the kirk-yard. My mother hushed my "foolish talk," telling me there was nothing wrong with Jessie. In a few weeks little Jessie took sick and died. Then my mother remembered my prophecy. Time after time in my childhood, and in later life, when this warning of death came to me, it never failed. I myself did not understand it. I just seemed to know.

The Roadhouse

AN ENGLISHMAN by the name of John Lawrence came to the island. He was tall and very thin, with a long, solemn face. He was never known to smile or joke, and was often taken for a preacher. He started a general merchandise store in his cabin. At first he carried only goods for men, discouraging the women from coming. He made an exception of me. I would often go in to buy some supplies that I lacked. We wrangled over each purchase. I told him his prices were all out of reason. He defended himself. We learned to respect each other's integrity and grew to be friends.

There was a bull running loose on the island that summer, which gave me a good deal of fun. The store was about three hundred feet from the hotel. The bull, head down, chased me and I ran with all my might around the store. "He almost got me that time," I panted.

John Lawrence, looking up over his horn "specs" and drawing down his mouth at the corners, commented, "That animal must be shot. He'll hurt someone yet."

The bull, bellowing and pawing the ground, was waiting for me to come out.

"I'm not afraid. That bellow is only his laugh," I said.

John Lawrence took a stick of wood and drove him away while I ran home with my purchases. It was a sad day for me when the bull was shot by someone who did not appreciate his game. I missed the old fellow and refused to eat a bit of him.

John Lawrence had been living on the island about three years when he came over one morning and said, "I've something to tell you. My son, who has been living with his aunt in Vancouver, is coming to live with me."

We were surprised, as he had never talked of his life before he came to Stewart Island. We did not know he had been married, and had always thought of him as a bachelor.

In due time Johnny arrived, dressed like a young gentleman in a custom-made suit, and carrying a fine gold watch and chain. He took every occasion to tell the time to anyone who asked. His aunt had trained him to a fine way of living. He was never allowed to leave his room until properly dressed, his hair brushed, his face shining. It was hard for the little lad to understand his father's brusque ways.

Mr. Lawrence and Johnny lived in a small room back of the store. Here, economy was the greatest concern, for even food had value. The strict, religious father dictated all Johnny's movements. This was bewildering to the little lad. My heart went out to him, set down in this strange environment, and I went to his rescue. Every hour that he dared, Johnny spent at our roadhouse. His father did not understand what to do with the ten-year-old, so he felt he must be strict. Johnny slept in a bunk over his father's, up near the roof. It was hot from the stove when his father was baking the sourdough bread to sell in the store for fifty cents a loaf. Sweat poured off the boy, and when he could not stand it any longer, he used to run out into the snow to cool off.

If a customer came, the storekeeper took the small oil lamp with its tin reflector from the nail, and went into the store. John Lawrence never made idle talk, for he did not see any reason for a person staying longer than necessary. He did not wish to be bothered, or to burn up good oil. As soon as the customer was out the door he blew out the light and lighted a candle. He was a very careful man, John Lawrence.

In winter Johnny was allowed to stay at the hotel until nine o'clock, and then he must go home and to bed. Johnny and I became the best of friends. The boy needed a mother, and I had always wanted a son to laugh and have fun with.

Johnny told me, "I'll wash the dishes if you'll play jacks with me. First one game—the dishes—another game—the pots and pans." I stopped my work and we played.

He liked reading to me while I worked, or to have me tell him stories of my home in Scotland. We had happy, carefree hours together. I enjoyed his youth.

As the boy grew older, he became discontented and unhappy under his father's stern discipline. He often asked me, "How much longer must I be dependent? Why can't I be on my own?"

"Have a bit of patience, laddie," I would say to him, "the years go fast."

Johnny was a great favorite with the men. When he was fifteen, a man who owned a well-equipped cabin on the island went Outside. He gave his cabin to Johnny. Some of the woodcutters offered to help him cut wood and get a start for himself. Then he "histed" the flag of independence and went to the other general store on the island and got a three-hundred-dollar outfit. His father was surprised, and told Davy, "Well, Johnny got his outfit. To be sure, I'll have to pay for it, but it will be a good lesson for him."

The father never had to pay for it. From that time on, Johnny was one of the men and soon was getting a man's salary. He was busy making his living. I missed him. It was as if my own son had gone from home.

When Johnny left, a little girl came into our lives to compensate. A fur trader, bringing a tiny Indian girl about four years old, came to The Roadhouse. She was dressed in ragged dungarees and had a mat of uncombed hair hanging over her bright, unfriendly little face.

"What do you think of my daughter?" the man asked as he pushed the child into the room.

A baby girl was just what I wanted, and I opened my heart to the homesick child, so recently separated from her Indian mother. All the way to Stewart River, the father had fed her chewing tobacco. Now she cried and cried, and wanted to go back. The first meal she threw on the floor. She refused to have anything to do with her new friends.

I brought in a big washtub, filled it with warm water, and when I tried to bathe her she fought like a small tiger, but the bar of soap intrigued her. When at last she was clean, Davy cut her hair and she was made presentable. But there were no decent clothes for her to wear, I told her father, who was making a good deal of money at the time. He took her to Dawson and had her fitted out with the best there was to be had. Two dressmakers made her a wardrobe as fine as could be.

When the man and the child came back, he again pushed her through the door of The Roadhouse. But this time she looked like a little princess in her dark velvet coat and white fur, a muff for her little hands, a red silk dress and red shoes. The dress was her greatest joy. The men sometimes teased her and said, "We will have to send to Dawson and get another little girl."

She would run to the kitchen and pull on my skirt, crying, "Oh, don't let them get another little girl. Show them my red silk dress and white panties with the lace on them." She seemed to think these pretty clothes could work magic in any heart.

I was surprised to see how quickly she learned to take care of herself. Her father had brought her a comb and brush set, and it became her great pride to brush her shiny black hair. No child reared from babyhood in a well-ordered home could have attended to herself better. She washed her face and hands many times a day, saying, "Am I your little white girl now, Auntie?" Then looking at herself in the mirror, "No. Still no white girl," she grieved. Then she'd wash again.

Everything she learned she did in a careful, painstaking manner. Her clean, dainty ways were a constant marvel to Davy and me. She was very fond of Davy and would climb upon his lap and beg him to sing and play for her on the organ. One of the churches in Dawson had bought a new organ, and Davy had purchased the old one. For fun, he would play a wrong note, and she would stamp her little foot and say, "No, no, Uncle. Play right."

She had a beautiful voice, and Davy taught her many songs.

The little Indian girl never had anything to do with the Indians, but would stand silently watching them, her hands behind her. Once she said to me, "Auntie, why are they so dirty?" Then she went into the house and washed herself and brushed her hair carefully.

The child's father and Davy were engaged in building a big storeroom forty by forty feet in which they expected to put a stock of general merchandise in order to open a trading post to barter with the Indians and trappers for furs. However, they disagreed. The father determined to spite Davy by taking his little girl away. It was a great heartache to us. The last night, as she lay in my arms, her sweet little face nestling close, she sobbed, "Oh, Auntie, tell me this is not the last time I am to go to sleep with you! I don't want to go away. I can't leave you and Uncle. I want to stay here always!"

We held each other close, tears hot on our pillow. But nothing could be done. Her father was firm. In the morning, like a brave little soldier, she marched down the trail to the boat that was to carry her out of our lives. We did not see her again for years.

I shall always mind the first time I met my friend, Belle. It was a bright summer day that I wished could last forever. The steamboat from Outside was tied up. Our old friend, Captain McDowell and a party of travelers were coming up the steep trail to the hotel. I was standing in the doorway as usual, waiting to welcome them.

Captain McDowell said to me, "I want you to meet Mrs. Belle Brennon. I am sure you two will get alone fine together."

"She's an extravagant woman," I thought, as I looked at her black silk taffeta dress and big picture hat. "She doesn't know much about this country, to be dressed so fine." But in this I was mistaken.

The travelers were talking loudly and with great excitement about a new strike up Stewart. They were making preparations to go and stake.

There was another woman in the party, a well-known character, Stampede Lizzie, who always attended every stampede she could manage. She claimed to be a titled lady and was determined to strike it rich, go home to the Fatherland, and live in a style becoming her station. She liked to talk about herself and expected everyone to give her extra favors.

At the table I had a surprise about the good-looking Mrs. Brennon. She talked mining in the men's language. She knew all about placer-mining methods, about sinking and drifting, ground sluicing, hydraulicking, dredging, and thawing. The men accepted her as one of themselves, and talked to her about mining in the States. She had been reared in northern California. Her people were gold miners, the grandfather having come around the Horn from Virginia with his family in '49. Brought up on mining, she had now come to the Yukon to try her own luck.

Her husband, who had given up a position as violinist in the San Francisco Symphony Orchestra, had staked a claim on Thistle Creek and was there working it. Mrs. Brennon was returning from a trip Outside when she heard about this stampede, and she expected to stake a claim.

The excitement of the stampede ran high. Even the conservative John Lawrence, the storekeeper, got the fever. He rented his boat to the stampeders, and then, at the last minute, decided to go along. Now there were four men and two women. Although the boat was large, this made it quite crowded. Each was to do his share of the work, and the profits were to be divided equally. They were all ready to start when Mrs. Brennon discovered that the man at the head of the party had some liquor with him.

"I will not go along if there is any whisky to be taken," she said positively. "This boat is none too safe, and there is too much danger on the swift river to trust our lives to muddled brains."

Mr. Lawrence backed her up. After some argument, the liquor was disposed of and they went on their way.

Now, when Mrs. Brennon got into the boat dressed for the trip, I quite approved of her looks! She wore a neat corduroy suit, high-laced boots, and on her copper-colored pompadour there was a "Mountie" Stetson hat. She commanded respect from everyone. She knew what was to be done and stood ready to hold up her part of any bargain she made, and she expected no extra favors.

The stampede resulted in a few claims that were sold later, but the strike was not a success. Mrs. Brennon returned to our hotel to wait for the boat on the Yukon. Here began a friendship that Davy and I agreed was the greatest gold we ever found in the North.

Belle and her husband worked their claims on Thistle Creek, but after a time the musician went back to his profession in San Francisco. They both decided that mining was not the life for a man of his talents. Belle went Outside, but their mining interests often brought her back North.

When she was working her claim in Thistle Creek, she lived alone with her dog in her comfortable little cabin and managed her mine, which was worked by hydraulic power. Belle would often stop off and visit with us, always helping me in every way she could.

"Now, I will have to send to Dawson for a new broom, for you always sweep one out whenever you come," Davy teased.

On one visit I was begging Davy to open a stationary window at the head of the stairs so that I could shake out the blankets and the other bedclothes without carrying them downstairs. Davy was too busy. After he had gone, Belle took out the window and put on a pair of hinges, and when Davy returned, the window was in, and the summer breeze was blowing down the stairway.

Belle was clever with the needle as well as the hammer and saw. After supper dishes were done, we went to my room to sew. She was always making dresses for me. She liked to do things for Davy and

me. One time she made us a down coverlet, saving,
with patience and care, the down from the breasts
of about five hundred ducks and geese. She made
the big comforter of blue sateen and filled it with
the down. It covered us like a blessing for years and
kept us cozy and warm. There were few nights
that we did not send her a loving thought of gratitude.

Christmas was always a time of great festivities.
One year I planned a big dinner, inviting many
friends who lived on their claims, as well as everyone living on the island. Belle said I must have a
new dress, and she set about making me one. I never
had a chance to put it on, however. Long after the
dinner was cooked and the hungry people had enjoyed a bountiful repast, and after the stacks of
dishes were washed, I fell asleep in my chair, the
new lavender dress with its pretty lace collar and
cuffs lying across my knees.

One year the Mounted Police on Stewart Island
gave a big Christmas party at the barracks. They
spared no expense, sending to Dawson for everything to make it a success. It went down in sourdough history as something to be talked about each
time old friends met. Invitations were sent out even
as far as Dawson, a hundred miles or more. Friends
came from up and down the river and adjoining
creeks. Each dog team that arrived brought the
owner and his nearest neighbor. Jim McLaughlin,
at the mouth of Baker Creek, realized that some of
the ladies could not stand the ride in an open dog
sled so he fixed up a "hot air wagon" by putting a
wagon box on sled runners and adding a top like

a prairie schooner. Inside was a lantern to warm it a bit. He heated stones to put at the ladies' feet, and now they could ride the long cold miles in comfort. The men ran behind on snowshoes.

It was gay and exciting as each dog team drew up at the barracks. Dogs were barking and folks were laughing and shouting and clapping one another on the shoulders, shaking hands and greeting old friends, glad to be together again. Only people who live alone and grow lonely and homesick can know what it means to have a good visit and talk over problems, sympathize with each other, and laugh once more.

About sixty men arrived. There were only eight women, and two of these were young girls in pigtails. Inside was a joyous Christmas spirit, never to be forgotten. To add to the cheer, everyone had a drink of eggnog as soon as he arrived.

The Mounties had decorated the barracks with spruce and pine boughs. The hot room was filled with the spicy incense, which mingled with the appetizing smells from the kitchen. Everyone was hungry and ready for the feast.

The Christmas tree reached to the ceiling. For a week we had strung popcorn and red cranberries to decorate it. It was beautiful! Some of the old fellows had tears in their eyes as they thought of other Christmases in years gone by.

Everyone had brought presents of food, the best in his cache — mountain sheep, great moose roasts, caribou and bear, fine hams and smoked salmon, ducks, geese, crane, swan, ptarmigan, every kind of fowl to be had. Some of the men had roasted their fowl all ready to eat. The ladies presented their jellies, jams, preserves, pickles, and canned fruit. There were mince pies, pumpkin, apple, and blueberry, and cakes of all kinds. There was good old sourdough bread, too. Every man had learned to make his bread, and most of them were fine bakers.

Davy added tomatoes and celery, cabbage, and other vegetables from our root cellar. The tomatoes were put away green, wrapped in paper. A couple of weeks before Christmas he had brought them up from the cellar, putting them on the big shelf back of the stove to ripen. The celery was his pride; he wanted everyone to have a bit of it.

The Mounties had sent Outside for turkeys. One weighed thirty-five pounds.

Such a feast! The table was never empty for four days and nights. All one had to do was pull up a chair and eat his fill.

There was dancing to the latest phonograph records, and one of the boys played a fiddle, another the harmonica. There were square dances, too, and although there were not enough ladies to go around, the men tied handkerchiefs on their arms and stepped out into the part amid loud yelling and stomping.

A punch bowl was made of a big block of ice, and in it was a fine concoction. In the kitchen, the cook, treated a bit too generously by the guests, was feeling very happy. I went out to see how he was getting along. He was weaving gaily back and forth with a big "Outside" roast beef in his hand. This burden unbalanced his already unsteady legs, and the meat slid out of his hand, landing in the "swill bucket." I was horrified to see him pick it out, wipe it off, and put it back in the oven, in spite of anything I could do.

Most of the ladies at the dance had sent to Dawson for new dresses. One of the younger women had three sent out. She looked so pretty in each one that she could not decide which to wear so kept them all, wearing a different one each day. This same woman was flattered into running away from her husband while he was working in a wood camp to pay for the pretty dresses she had bought. She could not stand the hardships of the North, so went Outside with a miner who had struck it rich.

"Stampede Lizzie" was there in a fine black sequin gown, her hair, which had been braided for days in fine plaits, combed into a tall, fuzzy pompadour. Dances were her specialty. She shone in a dazzling manner. She was not a favorite of mine. I ha' me doubts about her being a fine lady at any time. Belle and I did not pay her any mind. But some of the men liked her.

The mother of a little lassie in pigtails thought her husband was too attentive to Lizzie. By and by she could stand watching them dance no longer, and cried into a ball of a handkerchief she held in her fist. Belle and I went to her rescue. "Don't feel badly," I said. "Come over to the hotel and I will make you a good cup of tea." This was my panacea for all the ills of life. The magic worked. Soon the jealous wife dried her tears and, forgetting her troubles, laughed and enjoyed herself again.

The Mounties had prepared some empty cabins for their guests to sleep in, but everyone wanted to spend the night at The Roadhouse. It was filled to overflowing. Those who did not have beds slept on the floor on bearskin rugs before the hot stove. They brought their own blankets. No one ever thought of traveling without his bedroll. That is one of the things the Mounted Police first taught the chechacos. Davy and I, as usual, gave up our bed to friends, and slept where we could.

Belle and I slept on a couch just wide enough for one. But what difference did it make where we slept? There really was not much time to sleep anyway. Besides, there were long weeks and months to sleep after returning home, when there would be little else to do during the long dark nights and short dark days.

Another year there was a birthday party at a German home on one of the creeks. Everyone around was invited. The hostess, a fine cook, enjoyed entertaining. The table was set in a "U" shape and there were so many dishes of food upon it that the damask tableclothes, which had been brought from the Fatherland, could not be seen. On the wall was a gold-framed picture of the Kaiser. The lady loved to tell of her happy life in Germany. She was the daughter of an army officer and had attended a beautiful court ball at which she had seen the Kaiser in all his glory.

The party was given in the fall of the year. The ice was not yet hard enough in places for safe travel. Davy, Johnny Lawrence, the little Indian girl, and I, were in a sleigh drawn by horses. The owner of the horses could not go, but sent a young lad who was experienced in handling the animals to do the driving. We were traveling on the river and were about halfway there when an accident occurred that came very near spoiling the party. There was an open place in the ice over a slough. The horses began to break through. In the struggle, one of them fell under the feet of the other. They got into a bad tangle. Davy and the boy tried to get them free. At last the boy jumped into the icy water to cut the harness so the horse that was down would not drown. Fortunately we were near the shore and the sleigh did not go in. From a near-by cabin a man came to help. The boy's clothes began to freeze in the stinging cold, and in a short time he was encased in a coating of ice. He could not move, and had to be carried to the cabin, where his clothes were cut off. A warm fire and a hot cup of tea soon brought him around. The horses, too, would have soon frozen if another driver had not taken charge and raced them at top speed to warm them up.

We arrived at the German home without any more trouble, stiff with cold and glad for a warm welcome and hot food. The party lasted two days and nights.

The start back was especially colorful. Hollering and laughing, fifteen or sixteen young men, with gaily colored knitted toques flying and axes in their hands to try the ice, ran ahead. Then we came next, in the sleigh, with dog teams following with the women and children. Belle and the rest of the party in a cutter brought up the rear. The whole group was in high spirits, laughing and calling to each other. All went back to The Roadhouse on Stewart Island to finish the party week.

At the end of one cold winter, when there was

very little travel, Davy and I were alone. Davy had been ill and was unable to rise from his bed. I was busy keeping the fires going and caring for the animals. I was glad there was no one but our own two selves, for I could give Davy more attention.

I was washing one morning when, stepping back, I tripped over a tub on the floor and fell. My left leg seemed not to be a part of me but stuck out at a right angle from my body. It looked so queer. I lay very still for a moment looking at the distorted member, then realized it was broken. Now, what could I do, with a doctor one hundred miles away? After a bit I called Davy. He knew something terrible must have happened to me to cause me to cry out. He was so weak he could only crawl on his hands and knees to me.

"Peg, gir-rul, what is the trouble?"

"Davy, I've broken my leg."

Davy crawled faster. There I lay, helpless, not daring to move. It was funny, too; I had to laugh to think of us both being such helpless old things, and no one to lend a hand.

"Well, I don't think I'd laugh if I were you; you may laugh out of the other side of your face when I have to set it," Davy said.

"Well, Davy, if I don't laugh, I'll cry."

"Then laugh, lass; I'll do my best."

He got to his feet and staggered about, holding onto things or crawling. He managed to get some thin boards from a crate. With these he made splints. He pulled and worked the bones into place and after he got it set, he padded rags about it to keep it

firm, and tied it tight. We got through the ordeal
at last and were both exhausted.

Weeks later, when the splints were removed, my
leg was as good as ever. But it was a long time
before I felt sure of it. For six weeks I lay on the
couch, while Davy brought me things to work with.
I mixed bread and prepared the meals, and Davy
tried to do the cooking. People who came to the
hotel were kind and helpful.

At this time, Belle was many miles away! It was
two months before she heard of my accident. She
got her dog teams ready for a man to drive for her.
When they reached the mouth of White River, the
ice was not safe. The driver warned her not to try
it as it was near the breakup, so Belle turned back
to Thistle, thinking she could go over the hills to
Stewart River. Here she could wait until some boat
came down the river to take her to her "dear little
friend," as she called me. The driver and the dogs
returned home.

For eleven days Belle sat on the bank of the river,
waiting for the river ice to break up so that a boat
might pass. There was a cabin near by that belonged
to a trapper who had gone to Dawson for the winter.
In this she slept, and ate what food she needed.

At last a little boat came down the river and she
signaled it. They made the dangerous trip among
the ice cakes to Stewart Island. When Belle got there
she found me sitting on the bank of the river, waiting for her.

"Why, how did you know I was coming?" Belle
asked.

"Oh, I just had an idea you'd be coming along

most any day now, and I've been waiting a week to see you," I told her. We were always such dear friends.

In the evenings the travelers at The Roadhouse would sit around the fire swapping yarns about their own experiences, or telling tales they had heard on their travels. Mineralogy and mining also came in for a share of discussion.

Belle and I would listen, often growing weary at some of the twice-told tales of the animals.

The dog and pet stories were prime favorites and were endless. Each man had his own particular tale which seemed to him most interesting. He was as anxious to tell it as a proud parent to tell of the smart tricks of the children. The dog teams made a topic they could continue all night.

Even Belle had her favorite dog stories. She had a very beautiful dog that she bought from the Indians. She was afraid people might think she beat him, because he always crawled into his harness as if scared to death. Indians were cruel to their dogs. In the winter they hardly fed them. When asked: "Don't you feed your dogs?" they would answer, "Huh, next summer get lots of caribou."

After a dog has a white master, he develops a great hatred for the Indians. He seems to remember his cruel treatment at their hands.

Belle liked to tell of her two dogs. When walking in the woods they always held the same position, Jip on one side and Captain on the other. Once a bear crossed the trail in front of them. Jip took out after it and did not come back for two days. When he went after the bear, he had a poke on his back, but when he finally returned, the poke was gone. Months afterward it was found in the fork of a tree where it had been caught and pulled from the dog's back. It contained four hundred and sixty dollars' worth of gold nuggets. The gold was returned to Belle by the man who found it and knew that she had lost it.

During the years we ran The Roadhouse on Stewart Island, we had a long string of pets. A friend brought a little moose calf. We fed it on warm milk from a bottle until it learned to drink alone. He was a cute little fellow and we enjoyed him, but he met a tragic death. I said never would I have another pet—never! But when someone came with a baby caribou, I forgot all about what I had said.

There were always squirrels, birds, even a tiny porcupine. He proved to be a terrible nuisance. He was always getting under the beds, and it took too much patience to get the prickly little fellow out. The dogs considered him an enemy, and always came out the worse for the battle. Davy would have to pull the quills out of their noses, a real operation. But the moment the dogs were free, they were ready to engage in another losing battle with the first porcupine that came their way.

Davy would say in disgust: "They are like some men, so blinded with their own hate they never use a grain of sense."

A man brought me a tiny mountain sheep. I was delighted and spent many happy hours feeding and tending the little lamb, and later many sad hours grieving when it was killed by a strange dog. Our own dogs never touched our pets—they soon learned that the pets *belonged*. Always, at the death of each successive pet, I would say, "Never will I have another." But friends who knew me realized how I loved young things. There was always a place in my heart, and time to care for each new one they gave me. Davy had the same interest in the pets as I, but somehow the care of them always fell to me.

Cats were rare in the Yukon in the early days. So I was delighted with a gift of a fluffy kitten that a friend brought from Dawson. The men liked to watch little Biddie playing about the stove during the long winter evenings. We gave her a character, and regular customers to The Roadhouse always inquired about her. For two or three years she was the only cat on the Island, so there was great surprise when Biddie presented The Roadhouse with a small kitten marked like herself! The mystery was never solved. Biddie was a devoted mother, and fed and washed the kitten tenderly.

Some half-breeds came one day with two dogs. The little kitten was out in the yard. She had not learned to fear the dogs belonging to The Roadhouse, and so saw no danger in these strange ones.

I heard Biddie crying pitifully. I went to the door to let her in, but she would not come; instead, she ran toward the garden and then back to the door. I followed her to the garden. There lay the two strange dogs with the kitten, dead, between them. When Biddie felt I was there to protect her, she dashed at the dogs and fought like a tiger. She jumped on the back of one, clawing, scratching and pulling his hair out in bunches. When she returned, she picked up her dead baby and carried it into the

house where she washed it, trying to bring it back
to life. When she found she could not, she came to
me, mewing and crying, then ran back to her kitten.
It was heartbreaking to see the poor creature.

Biddie lived for years. One time she ran away
and was gone a month. A friend brought word that
he was sure he had seen her in a cabin about eighteen
miles toward Thistle Creek. Davy paid a man fifteen dollars to take a dog team and go after her.
The trip took three days, but Biddie was brought
back home. She repaid her master by having the
largest family she ever raised.

Davy had many dogs, and Sandy was the outlaw
of the lot. He was a born thief, apparently stealing just for the sake of stealing. For a white man's
dog he was the worst ever known—I called him an
"Indian dog." He was full of mean tricks, but Davy
could never see it that way. I believed Davy was
just contrary about it. I can remember no time that
Davy ever treated me so badly as he did about Sandy.
I had raised about seventy-five baby chickens. They
were cute, fluffy little things. I loved every one of
them and they all knew me and came running about
me when I went to the henhouse. They were about
half grown when Sandy got in and killed fifty-seven
of them, one after another of those lovely young
chickens, and there they lay, that wicked dog not
even eating them! I was so angry I didn't know what
to do! Davy laughed—he just laughed! I could hardly stand it. I could have killed that dog, but Davy
would not even take a stick to him.

I said, "Look what he has done!"

"Well," said Davy, "I guess Sandy wanted a chicken dinner. It won't hurt him none."

Most of the time we had lots of fun with our dogs. Some of them liked me best, and some Davy. We raised a number of dogs, but it was always a heartache to give them away for fear they would not get good masters. Davy never sold a dog in his life. But we couldn't keep them all, though we always had a couple of teams of work dogs.

There was always plenty of meat, but one time Davy decided we must get some pigs to fatten. Previously we had bought our hams, bacon, and lard from Outside. The little pigs were purchased at great cost and brought from a long distance. They were cute little things, and afforded us a lot of fun, and proved fine pets, following Davy about the yard and trying to go into the garden with him. This was the only pleasure he withheld. He fed them on canned milk and oatmeal. By the time they were big enough to kill, Davy could not think of butchering them. Belle came to visit at this time, and he held out to her the prospect of a roast pig all during the time she was with us.

"Just stay another week and I'll kill a pig for Sunday dinner."

Belle at last went home discouraged; she came back months later to hear the same story.

The pigs were a problem, for they grew apace, and their appetites with them. They were like the dance-hall girl who was given her weight in gold, about whom Jack London has written. Those pigs were surely worth *their* weight! I figured out that it cost a dollar a pound to feed them. They weighed

eighty pounds when finally they were killed. Davy
had to go away, and I got a man to butcher them.
It was near Christmas and "they made fine eating"
for the Christmas table.

But of all the pets that passed through The Roadhouse, there never was one more dearly beloved or
more interesting than Jackie, the raven. Walter Stewart came to The Roadhouse one day, bringing in
his hands a raven, just out o' the nest, so young it
was still covered with down. We cared for it tenderly and kept it in a wire cage. Jackie grew fast and
soon became the pet of the house, strutting about,
sweeping his fast-growing wings on the floor. I
introduced him, "This is Jackie, my partner," and
Jackie would cock a bright eye at the stranger and
chitter-chatter in his own language as if he accepted the introduction. He was a regular clown;
everyone liked to tease him. One time Walter took
him outdoors and tossed him into the air to see if
he could take his freedom, but no, he flew about
in the trees and then lit on my shoulder and rode
into the house. He was somewhat of a nuisance for
he would wait his chance to steal things from the
table, and he always seemed to have designs on any
bit of bright ribbon or cloth. Hats interested him
especially.

In the summer, when he had outgrown his cage,
he had to be kept out of doors. When I went over
to Lawrence's store, Jackie delightedly flew in front
of me, or rode on my head or shoulder, chattering
at the dogs, often riding on their backs or catching
their tails, pulling with all his might. He would fly
down and share their food, and chatter and scold

them when they chased him. His gaiety suited me. When he reached the store, he apparently became possessed with a great desire to tease John Lawrence. His favorite trick was to clip off a bit of red geranium blossom from the plant that John Lawrence had so carefully placed on the pile of wood near the door to get the warm sunshine. Jackie would scream his loudest, and deliberately fly past the window or door, flaunting the bright flower in the storekeeper's sour face.

Once we were harvesting some tiny white onions, out of which I was to make pickles. Jackie's sparkling black eyes watched us. Soon he also began scratching with his claws, digging the onions out and pulling them into the rows. He kept busy as long as we stayed in the garden.

Another time when we were cleaning fish and laying them on the grass, Jackie watched his chance and, darting in, picked the eyes out of each fish. This worried me for fear he might start to do the same to the dogs, or Biddie, the cat, or even to a human being; but Jackie never did any real harm. He was full of mischief, and seemed always to be chuckling and thinking up new tricks to play. He would fly into the woods behind the house and have much fun with the wild ravens, but as soon as he was called he would come back in a hurry. When Davy and I sat out on the bench by the river, Jackie would ride on my shoulder. He had a trick of taking hold of my ear and biting it gently. When I would say, "No, no, Jackie, you hurt," he stopped. His chitter-chatter sounded like laughter. A favorite jaunt was to go down to the boat to meet the passengers. He always managed to get a ride home on the back of a certain dog, much to the amusement of the travelers.

He was very fond of flying down among the chickens and scaring them into fits of excitement. One of the old roosters was always ready to fight with him. They would jump over and over each other, making a tremendous din; but the old rooster seemed to be the better fighter and Jackie soon learned to fly away and leave the rooster to cool off as best he might.

One day I heard him making a great to-do in the woods. I knew by the sound that he was in distress, so I grabbed the broom and ran to his rescue. A flock of wild ravens had him down back of a log. They seemed to be motivated by the same jealous idea the work dogs had toward a pet dog that did not have to work. The ravens were trying to kill him. Jackie chitter-chattered to me, trying to tell me how his wild brothers had urged him to go with them, and how he would not go, and how they had almost killed him. He was in a state of great excitement as he rode home on my shoulder. But his curiosity was his undoing. He could not keep away from the other ravens, and at last they killed him. I often said he was the finest pet we ever owned.

One year, there was a plague of mice; thousands of them appeared on the island. They swarmed everywhere and got into everything. This was a great trial to my patience, but I could not help feeling a bit sorry for some of the poor little fellows that sat humped up, looking sick, lacking the strength to run away. They would topple over dead. But still they came in droves; they invaded the root cellar and ate the hearts out of all the cabbages—only the big outer leaves remained. Hundreds of them got into the bags of carrots. They ran all over the food and spoiled it. They even got into the beds and ate holes in the bedclothes. Davy said the plagues of Pharaoh were as nothing compared to the plagues we were having. Then all at once the plague was over—and dead mice everywhere. We swept them into baskets and dumped them into the river.

CHAPTER TWELVE

The Middle Years

ON THE FLOOR of the Public Room there was a bearskin rug fourteen feet long. It was a Kodiak bearskin that a man traded Davy for a shaggy black puppy. Davy was very fond of this particular puppy and had been talked into the trade much against his will. He heard a year later that the man, coming home in the early dusk of a cold fall day, had shot the dog, thinking it was a bear.

"Just like that old fool bear hunter," said Davy. "Wish I'd never traded."

I, too, wished the same, when I had to drag the big bearskin out to clean it. It was a harbor for dust. Just the same, it was a good warm bed for many a man when all the other beds were filled.

In those early days bears were frequently seen. One day I noticed a mother bear with her two cubs in the slough back of the island. The mother took the younger cub and threw it on her back where it clung to her like a monkey; the other one, last year's cub, swam along beside its mother. They crossed over safely, and I had an idea that they were going to a berry patch for a feast of raspberries. I saw this same bear put her cubs up in the tree while she went away to hunt food. However, the baby wanted to go along and, sliding down the tree, started after his mother; she waited till he got up to her, and then spanked him, much after the manner of a human mother. The little cub cried like a real baby and, scampering back, climbed up the tree, whimpering to himself. I think I never saw a cuter sight. The mother bear went on about her business with the air of a stern parent who had done her duty.

Once Davy was given a cub. He would take out a little box with food in it and the little fellow would come walking on his hind legs, take the box in his paws, and walk away, making a funny shooing noise. He grew so fast and became such a nuisance that we had to give him away.

One evening, as I was coming in from the chicken house, right in my own dooryard I saw a shaggy old bear shambling away, grunting and complaining. At least he was going; for that I was grateful. Bears are mischievous animals. They have been known to come down the chimney, tearing it to pieces, when the windows and doors were too securely fastened. They are fond of sweets and would tear a cabin apart to get something they want. One of their tricks was to tear open a sack of flour and scatter it all about the cabin.

One bear got into a cabin on Thistle Creek and tore the owner's suitcase to pieces. The man killed him and brought his hide to The Roadhouse. His story was that he had found the old fellow trying to dress himself up to go to Dawson. He said the bear already had a necktie about his neck and a cap on his head, and when caught in the act, he was getting into a can of tooth paste! Even the man who had lost his suitcase thought it a good joke.

Once Belle Brennon and I went out with some of the men on a bear hunt on Thistle. We got a big bear all right, but one of the men had a terrible fright. Thinking the bear was dead, he bent over it and the animal gave him a swipe with his paw which almost knocked the breath out of him. The other members of the party had a good laugh at his expense.

Bear stories were great favorites with the men as they sat around the fire those long winter evenings. If they had no new one of their own to tell they retold the old ones, turning over each incident, so that not a single point escaped.

A favorite was the story of Carl Swanson and the big grizzly. Carl had killed a moose and was getting ready to put it into his cache. He went into his cabin for something and when he returned, found a big grizzly bear at his meat. He never understood how the bear got hold of him, but with one swipe of his huge paw, it tore a great hole in his scalp, so that the blood ran into his eyes, almost blinding him. The creature hugged him and crushed him until he felt as though he were being broken to pieces. Its horrible mouth chewed at his face; he felt his jaw bones break. Thrusting his knees into the bear, he was able to loosen himself sufficiently from the animal's grasp to reach the hunting knife at his belt, and with one desperate effort, he lunged it deep into the bear's stomach, ripping it open. It was a question which would die first, the man or the bear. The stench of the hot blood from the wounded bear nauseated him. He tried ever more desperately to loosen the great, cruel paws. Gradually he felt the creature beginning to weaken; it let loose and fell away, groaning in its death agony.

Carl lost consciousness. Hours later, weak from

the loss of his own blood, he crawled away from the dead bear and made his way into the cabin. Fortunately, his partner, who had been in Dawson, returned a day sooner than had been planned. He found Carl in a very bad condition. After months in the Dawson hospital he was sent Outside to have a silver plate put in his skull, and a partial jaw bone made. When he got back to the Yukon he stopped at The Roadhouse at Stewart for a few days' visit to tell his friends that he was glad to see the North again. He confessed to me:

"I'm afraid I've lost my nerve, for I never want to tackle another bear."

When the first World War broke out he went over as a sharpshooter. He must have borne a charmed life, for he returned to his beloved Yukon at the close of the war.

There was one bear story that had a rather comical side. The little Frenchman who told it to me would laugh and clap his hands on his knees and say, "My leetle dogs—garr—if it was not for ze leetle dogs, Frenchee would not be sitting here telling you about dees."

He expected everyone to laugh with him, glad of his rescue, and amused at the funny sight. He had been in his cabin getting his evening meal when he heard the dogs baying wildly in the slough. He thought it might be a moose so he went out to see. In a clump of willows there was an old bear, the dogs excitedly circling about. At once he joined in the fight, urging his dogs to greater effort; but he dared not shoot lest he kill the dogs. The old bear turned, and as quick as lightning, chased him. Frenchee looked about for a tree to climb. The only one close by was a small one, but there was not time to make further selection. Frenchee scrambled up the tree and it bent dangerously. The dogs kept circling about, taking nips here and there at the bear, but keeping close watch for its sharp fangs and claws. Around they went, the bear ever alert. It is remarkable how quick a clumsy bear can be. While the bear and the dogs were fighting, Frenchee was trying to climb the tree, keeping a watch out for the bear. All at once the bear had him! Standing on its hind legs, it tore a good bite from the back of his neck and another out of his wrist. He felt its hot breath.

He said, "Holy Mother, save me, save me!" And she did.

"Zose leetle dogs, they nip ze bear and he stop biting me and chase my leetle dogs, but back he come to ze tree, bite my heels and try pull me from tree. 'Go 'way, go 'way, bear, please go 'way,' I say to ze bear. I pull up my boots ver' high, the bear he jump and catch seat ze pants. My leetle dogs they tear off skin from back of bear. He get mad and go 'way. Night come, I climb down, go cabin, tie up neck from which bear take big bite."

In the early days bears caused many tragedies. Two young men who were strangers in the North had a sad experience. They started out one morning for an old prospector's mine about twelve miles from Mayo. They had not been warned about bears, and when they saw one on the trail they took a shot at it, though they had only a .22 rifle and a hunting knife. The wounded bear came at them so quickly they were taken by surprise. The furious creature caught Tom, slashing and tearing at him with its great claws. Sam was afraid to shoot, for the bear had Tom in its paws and they were rolling over and over. Tom was a big, strong Irish lad, and put up a good fight with the hunting knife.

Sam clubbed the bear with the butt of the gun, using all his strength. The bear was a match for the two boys. In the terrible struggle, both boys were badly mauled. Sam beat the bear until it gave up and staggered away in the bushes down by the river.

Now the question was, what to do about Tom, torn and bleeding, almost unconscious, and so badly hurt he could not move. Sam knew he must get help at once or the boy would bleed to death. It was impossible to carry his friend the twelve miles to Mayo, and there was no help to be had. He dragged Tom out of the thick woods and leaned him against a tree, but he could see this would not do as it made the blood flow faster from his open wounds. He was injured himself.

Poor Tom sobbed, "Don't leave me! My God, don't let the bear get me again! Shoot me, please, Sam, shoot me! Don't leave me. Finish me off. Let me die, let me die! Shoot me! Shoot me!"

Sam staggered to his feet, turning away from the dying lad. He could not shoot his friend. Using all his strength, he ran, falling, getting to his feet, falling, crawling, making the long bitter miles, crying, praying, leaving his own blood on the trail, spurred on by the thought of Tom, the horrible thought the bear might have him again. Not a person to help him in all that distance until he reached the Mounted Police and sobbed out his story. He wouldn't listen to the Mounties, but insisted on going with them to help find his friend, Tom.

All this time poor Tom was in terror, thinking every moment that the bear was coming back. He thought he heard him crushing the underbrush; he heard him groan—he was coming back! Tom's cries came fainter and fainter as his blood, flowing, flowing, made him weaker. Asking God for protection, he prayed to be out of reach of the bear.

"Don't let him get me, oh, God, don't let him come back," he cried over and over.

When the Mounties got him to the hospital he still feared the bear, calling and calling for Sam to help him. At last death released him from his agony.

In the early days of the great gold rush there were forty-nine men named John McDonald in and about Dawson, and it was difficult to get the right mail to the right man; we knew several by this name.

A John McDonald lived not far from us. One spring he came on a friendly visit. The previous winter, after striking it rich, he had gone Outside and had purchased a fine black horse which he named Danny. Danny had a good stable and a fine warm blanket and the best of food. When John and Danny made the visit, part of the trip was by barge. A raw wind had swept up the river, chilling Danny and giving him a bad cold. By the time they reached The Roadhouse, Danny was a very sick horse. Davy was ill in bed at the time, but he crawled out and went to the barn to help doctor Danny. Nothing was too expensive for the beloved horse. His master sent a hundred miles to Dawson for a doctor and medicine. Danny was shaking with cold, so his master bought all the liquor on the island to pour down him. He never left his pet, but spread his bedroll close by the horse's side.

He could not keep back the tears. Each morning when he came to the house for his breakfast I could tell how Danny was keeping by looking at John's face. In the winter when he had been down on a visit he had asked me to knit him a sweater. Now that he was so worried about Danny, I hurried to finish it, thinking it might cheer him a bit. It was of a nice, bright navy blue. When I gave it to him, he put it on and smiled and said, "I'll go show Danny."

It was not long before Davy came in saying Danny was dead. I ran out to the barn. John stood beside his dead horse, tears streaming down his face. When I entered, he brushed his arm across his face like a small boy, wiping his tears with the sleeve of his new sweater.

This picture returned clearly to my mind when I heard about John's tragic end. He had gone Outside a couple of winters, but he was always "back with the ducks." His home was on the hillside by Indian River, and while he liked people, he didn't want neighbors too close. He was no longer young, and this last winter he had been sick much of the time.

Two of the Mounties went over to find out if he was all right. About a hundred feet from his cabin they found a sleeve of a torn blue sweater on the trail. One of the boys stooped down to examine it, saying, "This looks like a bear's work. My God!

Look!" Inside the sleeve was a badly mangled fore-
arm of a man. They ran on up the trail and halted
in horror as they almost stumbled over the half-
eaten head of John McDonald. The inside of the
cabin was a wreck; flour was strewn about, supplies
and clothing were in a tangled mass on the floor.
The supposition was that the bear had surprised the
sick man and he had been unable to use his gun
in self-defense.

Davy and I were grieved over this. John Mc-
Donald was buried in the little graveyard on Stewart
Island.

Sometimes the men around the fireside turned to
stories of the Mounted Police, and how they always
got their man and brought him to justice.

It was near the Christmas holidays when two men
stopped at The Roadhouse. They had just come from
Dawson on their bicycles, and were finding traveling over the ice very satisfactory. It was the first
time bicycles had been used in this way. They were
to be joined by another man along the trail, and
the three of them were to go to Skagway to spend
Christmas with their families. They brought their
bicycles into the Public Room, putting them back
of the stove, spent the evening discussing whether
or not it would be advisable to put on glass wind-
shields to protect them from the wind. Then someone suggested that they blacken their faces to keep
off the glare. They did this before leaving.

Everyone who knew about their traveling was interested in their safe arrival, and when nothing was
heard from them, relatives and friends of the miss-

ing men reported their disappearance to the ever-vigilant Mounted Police.

Nothing could be found out about them after leaving Minto until Major Walsh, of the Mounties, found evidence of a murder having been committed. Further search revealed that the victims had been put into the river through a hole in the ice. The murderer had thought to destroy evidence by putting even the bicycles under the ice.

The evidence pointed to the guilt of a man named O'Brien. He was captured at Tagish Post. The trial proved holes had been bored in the wooden runners under the steel shoes of his sled, and that in these he had placed about six thousand dollars, mostly in gold dust, which he had taken from his victims. He was tried at Dawson and speedily executed.

One bitterly cold night we heard cries of distress down the river. Some of the men went to the rescue and came back carrying a man who was screaming with pain. The man who was with him was also exhausted. The dog team was starved, and they had all they could do to crawl up from the river trail to The Roadhouse. In the sled was the suffering man, his feet frozen to the knees, and his hands almost beyond saving. We set about to doctor the poor fellow until they could get him to the hospital at Dawson. But a bad cold spell had set in, and it was impossible to leave the house for a few days. His cries of agony were hard to bear, for he had no self-control.

As I stood watching him, I had a feeling that I had seen him before. His face was familiar.

All at once it came to me that he was the man I

had cursed on Chilkoot Pass for abusing the beautiful horse until it leaped from the cliff. I was frightened as I stood looking at him, suffering so horribly. I had wished to see him suffer. I had cursed him. It might be that God had listened to my prayer. His feet and hands were tormenting him. He shrieked in agony. Appalled, I stared at him. I prayed under my breath, "Oh, God, forgive me, forgive me! Don't let him suffer so. Forgive my wicked curse. I'm sorry. I don't want him to suffer. God, forgive me!"

I was tireless in nursing him. When they started with him to Dawson, I gave him a beautiful new sweater I had just finished knitting. I thought about the bitter curse I had put on him. Fearing I had had something to do with his agony, I was badly upset. Never again would I be guilty of such a sin as wishing evil on anyone, no matter what the cause.

The first time Fred Wilson was frozen was on the way to Nome. He lost both heels and his hands were frozen badly. The thawing was so terrible that he said if he was ever frozen again he did not want to be thawed out, but left to finish freezing. He got his wish. He was found frozen, on his way to The Roadhouse. He was frozen in the form of a cross, both arms outstretched, his face and body covered with hoarfrost. It was impossible to get him into a coffin until he had been thawed out. An old man took him to an empty cabin to do this. It took two nights, his old friend talking to the corpse all the time. After he got the frozen man into the coffin, he put a pipe and tobacco into one pocket, and into the other a plug of chewing tobacco, saying, "Well now, old fellow, ye can have yer tobaccy along the trail."

Friends built a big fire where his grave was to be dug, and in this way the ground was thawed out. They had to wait to get permission to bury him as he had died on the trail, and the permit did not come until after dark. The funeral took place on a cold winter night.

Before the coffin was nailed, I went over to see him, all ready for his last resting place. I was all alone at the time. As I stood beside him, his head fell forward and rested on his breast. Although I knew this was caused by the body's thawing, it startled me. After the nails had been put in the coffin lid, I took my lantern and followed the men who were carrying the coffin to the lonely grave in the island's burying ground. There John Lawrence read the burial service, and one of the men sang "My Wild Irish Rose." I had seen to this, because I had often heard this man say when he was alive, "When I die, I don't want a lot of things sung I don't know—just 'My Wild Irish Rose.'"

The following is the original story given to the author by J. R. Slaggard, written at the time by one of the Mounted Police.

J. R. Slaggard, the man to whom Solomon Albert owes his life, in a rescue from almost certain death, arrived from Stewart City. It is some days since Albert was brought in, and Slaggard had been spending the interval recuperating from the heavy mushing that he did in order to get the frozen man out. Slaggard says he must have covered nearly six hundred miles in thirteen days, and that he is about exhausted.

The pathetic part of the story was the way in which Slaggard had to leave Solomon Albert, after having carried him almost one hundred miles. Both of Solomon Albert's feet were frozen, but he stumped along for many weary miles before he had come to Slaggard's Camp. He had killed and fed two of his sled dogs to the remaining two. The will power of the man was tremendous to keep going on those dead feet. He had gone after dynamite to Copper River, and got his feet wet and frozen, but had come along for almost twenty miles on his frozen feet.

He had been with the Bratnober party and had gone by the way of Tanana. He tottered into the camp at the head of White River. They "toted" him to a creek called Kolotsun, about ninety-eight miles farther on. Here they had to stop. They had no more grub, but to go on with the helpless man was impossible, as they themselves were weak from hunger and the dogs about spent. They made camp and rested and talked things over. Solomon Albert was a brave man. In spite of his suffering, he persuaded the men to go on.

"Boys, you go on; I'm done for—I can't go on. You hitch up and go as fast as possible to save yourselves; I'm dying and I don't want to think I'm guilty of your deaths."

He turned over, groaning in his agony: "Go along; I'd just as soon die alone. It makes no difference to me. Got to go sometime—mush along—you can't help me die."

They hitched up and set out, telling the dying man they'd be back after him. They had little idea where they would get grub for themselves, and had no hope of ever seeing Albert alive. It was a question if they could get out alive themselves. Their dogs were weak from hunger. Albert had one dog left and he urged the men to take it; but when they tried, the dog turned on them fiercely, and crawled closer to his suffering master. So the men left him, thinking the faithful animal might be a comfort to the dying man.

Down the White River the men went, breaking a trail in two and three-fourths feet of snow. It was a wonder, under the circumstances, how they made thirty miles. They came to a cache of Billy Roup, the fur trader. Here they found some rolled oats. They cooked the food and fed themselves and the dogs. They made about thirty-eight miles when they met Billy Roup with his horses. He was going on to the Tanana. They made camp with him and had a good supper for themselves and their dogs. They told of the frozen man alone by his camp-fire.

"We'll go get him," said Roup.

The men told him they had no grub.

"Rats—I have enough for that trip," Roup told them.

Slaggard was to go back with Roup to find Solomon Albert. The other men to go on and inform the Police. They were about thirty miles from the mouth of White River. In one place, Slaggard and Roup had to break trail through the water for the horses, so they would not cut their feet with the ice. To do this, they had to wade to their hips, and then stop and make a fire and dry their clothes. They traveled as fast as possible, but could not get to Albert that night, and it was after midnight before they made camp. Next morning they were on the trail and at last came to Solomon Albert.

The men had left a bountiful supply of wood for a fire to keep away prowling wolves, as this is the country of immense timber wolves. When they found him he was a sorrowful sight. He was alive, white and sick—a brave smile lit up his face when he said, "I'd no idea you'd get back, boys."

He had had to kill his faithful dog, and that was not easy to do. He had the last hind quarter in the snow back of him. Roup was in a bad way, and his horses had eaten nothing but a hand-ful of rolled oats for two days. The men started back to Roup's cache where there was hay for the horses.

The next day they met a Mounted Policeman with a dog team, at the mouth of White River. Solomon Albert was trans-ferred from Roup's to the Policeman's sled, then on to the Shand Roadhouse on Stewart, where Solomon Albert had a little rest before they made the eighteen hour trip to Dawson.

Albert had an operation and had all his toes taken from both feet, the next day. Friends gave a benefit for him. (End of Slaggard's story.)

Later, after Solomon Albert grew better, he set about doing something for his feet. He got a set of bear claws, and in some way was able to strap them onto the stumps of his own feet. In this way he could find a balance that helped him walk. He would go stomping about in Dawson, the toe nails of the bear claws scraping on the boardwalks. For many years he had been known as the "Bear Man."

June 6, 1912, was a day never to be forgotten. I was alone; Davy was in Dawson. Suddenly there was an explosion, as if a thousand cannons were bombarding the country. I could see steam coming out of the rocks on the other side of the river. The night before we had heard a boom, boom, in the distance, but had thought little about it. One of the men suggested that it might be the old extinct volcano up White River becoming active again. Someone else thought the Japanese and Russians might be fighting. The noise was terrific, though far in the distance. It kept increasing in volume.

After the men had gone away in the morning and I was left alone, the noise got on my nerves. I had a helpless feeling, not knowing how to get away from it, nor where to go, nor what was the cause of it. I decided I must do something, at least get to the mainland. Hurriedly I collected my clothes and valuables into a big basket and carried it down the riverbank. The noise was now terrific, as if the whole island might be torn to pieces at any moment. I waited anxiously for someone to come along in a boat that would take me to the mainland. The thundering noise, like distant cannon roaring, might at any moment be followed by an explosion.

But after hours of waiting, while the noise continued and still nothing happened, my fears subsided and I carried my basket back to the hotel and began to prepare the evening meal, calm as usual. When the men returned, they discussed the increasing noises with anxious voices.

Next morning everything was covered with a deep, gray, volcanic ash. It was so heavy on the windows of the greenhouse that it shut out the light. All about lay a thick coating of gray dust; even the river was filmed with it. Everyone was excited, but it was a long time before we knew what had really happened.

It was caused by the eruption of Mount Katmai, in Alaska, one of the most tremendous volcanic explosions ever recorded; a mass of ash and pumice, whose volume has been estimated at nearly five cubic miles, was thrown into the air. In its fall this material buried an area as large as the state of Connecticut to a depth varying from ten inches to over ten feet, while small amounts of ash fell as far away as nine hundred miles, according to the report.

Kodiak Island, Alaska, one hundred miles from the volcano, was buried nearly a foot in ash. It seemed to everyone a hopelessly ruined waste, from a "Green Kodiak" to a gray desert. But after two years the barren country was covered with rich grass as high as a man's head. The growth was almost like a luxurious tropical jungle in its lushness. Kodiak still enjoys the distinction of having benefited from the explosion.

During the eruption, dust fell as far away as Juneau, Ketchikan, and the Yukon Valley, distances of 750, 900, and 600 miles, respectively, from the volcano. When the expedition of the National Geographic Society in 1915-16 first looked through Katmai Pass and beheld below them the Valley of Ten Thousand Smokes, it was at once evident that one of the wonders of the world had been discovered. We heard all this much later. The men who had the privilege of seeing this great sight reported it was beyond all power to exaggerate its magnificence. The year after the Valley of Ten Thousand Smokes came into being, we had the finest garden we ever had. Like the Kodiak Islands, Stewart also benefited by the eruption of Mount Katmai. We never had such a garden.

One day a letter came telling me that my dear brother Jack was very ill. From then on, every moment was a prayer for his recovery. It was winter and the next mail was long in coming. The suspense almost killed me. I could not eat or sleep. If Jack died, how could I stand it? How could I live without this beloved brother? I had always depended upon him. When I was a wee lass he had carried me in his arms about the old home in Scotland, guided my faltering baby footsteps over the stone flags, stood between me and the strict mother who never understood my love of adventure. I had always poured out my heart to Jack. In all my perplexities he had given wise counsel. How could I get along without him and his letters? Never had a week passed since I left my home that he had not written a long letter, full of good advice on subjects I had written to him about. There was always word of the dear ones at home, too. Each mail had brought a great sheaf of letters from him. Reading them, I would be back again in the peace and quiet of my home in Scotland. His letters had bridged the gulf that separated us; they were "like prayers answered." Now I was driven almost frantic with the suspense of not hearing from him or about him. Waiting was agony; I went about my work in a daze, praying every minute, "Oh, God, don't let Jack die—oh, don't let him die!"

Then, one day, I knew there was no more use in praying. That old, uncanny ability to feel the coming of death told me Jack was gone. He had always been a wall of strength between me and any danger. He was security. Never again could I turn to his protection when things got too hard. The time when Davy was blind and sick and we had no money, when first we came to the North, I had not felt afraid, for I knew that Jack would send help if I asked for it, would even come himself if the need was great. I knew he was back of me, always ready to give his last cent, just as he did when I started to America. Then, putting his bankbook into my hands, he had said, "All I have in the world is yours."

I was never without help while Jack lived. I tried to pray, but my prayers fluttered about aimlessly. I felt as if God had deserted me.

I went out and sat upon the bench by the sleeping river. All was cold and still, with a stillness that was unearthly. It was as if I existed in a strange world of Silence. No sound, only Silence. All about lay the blue-white snow, wrapping the world in ghostly sheets. I raised tired eyes to the mountains, shadowy and awesome. My soul filled with fear— fear I had never known clutched me. Unbearable loneliness crushed my heart. All was gone from me. The stillness was driving me mad. "Oh, God, don't leave me. Don't desert me," I cried in terror. Silence —Stillness—Silence!

Then a voice seemed to speak to me, hushing my grief. I grew quiet like the sleeping river. The Great White Silence came close about me, like a Presence out of the vast Stillness, "Peace, be still. He is not dead. Life is eternal." Peace enfolded me, assuaged my anguish, strengthened my heart. I took hold of life once more with a new grip.

It was many weeks before the letter came telling me Jack was dead.

Winter crept away. Spring opened her heart in song. Sometimes, when I could not sleep, I would work all night in the garden. I whispered to myself, "God is in the Silence, and Jack is close to God." I felt that I should not worry nor want Jack back. It seemed selfish. Friends felt the change in me. Friends said I was a different person, quieter and more gentle. People would look at me quickly sometimes, as if there were something about me they did not understand. They said they felt a new contentment in my presence. While they missed my carefree laugh, they felt that I had a greater wisdom, strength, and courage.

I told the discouraged and heartsick men who came hating the country and its loneliness: "You must learn to understand this great land of high mountains and rushing rivers, of vast snow-white Stillness, if you would find peace and contentment. You must feel toward them like friends to get companionship out of them. Look at the river; it is an ever-constant source of contentment. It is a power. Watch it flowing past. It's just like life—changing, changing, never two days alike. There is enough pleasure to be had in watching that river to keep a person interested for the rest of his life."

I would stand on the bank of my river — not moving. Many of the captains of the boats said that I was there when the last boat went out in the fall, and when they returned, I was still standing beside my river, as if I had been there all the time, like a figurehead on a ship.

Election time at The Roadhouse was one of high tension. Men came from Dawson to take charge of the election. Both Conservatives and Liberals made long treks up and down the river and the creeks in the district. At one election, sixty or more were staying at the little hotel. It was a fair rival for the Christmas festivities. I was as busy as it was possible to be, cooking and caring for my guests. Since there were just so many beds, after they were occupied the others must sleep where they could spread their bedrolls, on chairs, on tables, on bear rugs, on the floor—anyplace that was available. There was so much excitement, no one cared to sleep anyway—plenty of time for that when they got home. I did not mind the work, for as I worked I listened to many interesting discussions as the men sat upon the wood box or leaned against the pump. I enjoyed hearing both sides of the question. I did not always agree with Davy on politics. The men were very kind in helping me with the work, ready to carry food to the table and bring back dirty dishes, to wash and dry them, to pump the water and peel potatoes, helping while they talked.

Tact did not permit me to take sides with either the Conservatives or the Liberals. I had friends on both sides, and would laughingly tell each one that I was supporting his side; no one knew for certain who was my favorite candidate. It was my business to feed the men, and I got as much fun out of it as possible. I would rather listen than argue, and I kept my own counsel. Davy was not that way. The men all knew that he would rather argue than listen. After the election was over and the men on their way home, we would have a good laugh over it all. It was altogether "pleasant as well as profitable." On one occasion we took in seven hundred dollars, which was gratifying.

I made it a rule never to go down to the boats, that is, to meet them. It did not seem the thing to do. However, when a boat tied up, waiting for the Mayo boat to arrive, the captain would often send up an invitation to come down and eat supper on board. If I could manage it, I enjoyed accepting these invitations. I had many good friends on the river boats.

One of the boats had just left; on board was a couple who had been staying at The Roadhouse for a few days. I watched the boat going up the river, around the curve of the bank, and out of sight. Then I walked past Mr. Lawrence's store, on by the barracks and the little telegraph office to the post office farther down the island. Along the path the grass was about knee high. Suddenly I noticed something beside the trail. I stopped and picked up a leather wallet stuffed with a big sheaf of bills of large denomination, as well as gold pieces. I was stunned at finding so much money.

"Oh, I know who that belongs to. They had sold out their holdings and were going Outside, whilse. I must hurry and get it to them when they get to Selkirk," I told myself. I ran to the telegraph office to tell the operator to wire on to Selkirk and let the owners know that the wallet had been found. The operator counted the money, which I, in my haste, had failed to do. There were $11,800 in currency, besides other securities of even greater value.

After the owners received the money, they sent the telegraph operator a meerschaum pipe, and me a small handbag. A few days later the sergeant of the Mounted Police came up from one of the boats and said to me: "Well, if you don't need a guardian! I always thought you a smart woman, but I've changed my mind. Why didn't you turn that purse over to the Mounted Police and get the 10 per cent that you were legally entitled to? You would have had over a thousand dollars—it was coming to you by law."

But my idea had been just to get the money to the owners as fast as possible. I had never forgotten my early training, and the thought of keeping the wallet for a reward had never entered my mind. The only regret I had was that, when the couple went Outside, they disagreed over that money and separated. It seemed too bad that the money caused the trouble.

The wicked war bird cast its shadow over the Yukon Territory, just as it did over the far corners of the earth. Men wore serious faces now when they came to The Roadhouse to get the news. Twice a day, the telegraph operator typed an official report of what was going on across the sea. He left it on the table in the Public Room. Though eight thousand miles of land and sea separated London from Canada, England was still the Motherland, and England's king the head of the great Empire. Canada was British and her loyal Yukon sons traveled to Dawson to enlist and join troops going overseas. One lad walked five hundred miles to Stewart, and then on to Dawson, to enlist in the World War that was to "end all war." George Black, Commissioner of the Yukon, had resigned his office and proceeded to organize a Yukon Infantry Company, of which he was appointed captain.

The war worried me so that I could not sleep, and to ease the strain, I knitted every moment I could steal from my duties. I was never without a sock on my knitting needles, and many a pair of good, warm socks, as well as sweaters, I turned out. The Roadhouse was filled with men talking of war. Men in small boats from up and down the river came to hear the war news. In winter they would come in over the trail on their snowshoes. Each battle was reported as quickly as the news could come across the wires from Dawson.

There was bitterness, too. One old German who had been a favorite among his friends became an enemy because of his boasts that the war would soon be over and Germany would rule the world. As the war feeling grew more intense, this loyal

German was warned to hold his tongue or go home to his Fatherland.

My heart ached for one poor German lad, Caleb, whom we had known on Thistle Creek. He was alone now, since his friend had gone Outside. Many cruel and undeserved things were said to this gentle boy. They preyed on his mind, and when he came to see us, we begged him to stay with us, as we saw that he was not well. But no, he would go back to his claim alone.

Later, word came that he was ill. As Davy was sick in bed and could not leave, I got a man to drive me in our dog sled to bring Caleb back to the hotel, where I nursed him until spring. He was out of his head much of the time, crying pitifully, "I can't help it that I was born a German. Why do they hate me? I have no part in the war. I'd fight for Canada, too. I will when I get so I can."

I would allow no hatred of the Germans expressed before Caleb, and many a man was surprised at me, who had usually been too meek. When Caleb grew better, he returned to his home on Thistle. In the years that followed he was never found or heard from. It was thought that in his condition he might have shot himself. He was known to have borrowed a gun from one of the men, and he could have hidden his body by falling into some old mining shaft. The Mounties finally gave up the search. Poor Caleb had joined the Army of Missing Men.

The war worried Walter a great deal. When Captain George Black organized his infantry to go overseas, Walter enlisted and was impatient to be off under his friend's command. However, he was taken

ill. Since it was something that we did not understand, Davy went with him on the boat to Dawson,
where he was in the hospital for some time. Captain
and Mrs. Black were very kind to him. Davy had
been home only a few days when Captain Black sent
word for him to meet Walter at the boat, as they
were taking him Outside to Vancouver in order that
he might have special treatments, as his condition
was serious. Davy went down to see him when the
boat stopped, but I would not go.

I have loving memories of the man who lived in
our home so many years. His death was the saddest
thing that had happened to us since brother Jack's
death. Walter was like a brother to us—always so
good and kind and dependable. He was the best
known man thereabouts. Travelers always remembered him and on their return would ask, "Where's
Walter?"

He had a personality people liked and trusted, and
was a leader in his own quiet, gentle way. In all the
seventeen years he lived with us, Davy and Walter
never had a cross word. Nothing was ever said about
money; it was just understood. The clothes Davy
bought pleased him. He would say, "Dave knows
what I need better than I do. He gets the best; they
always fit."

In all those years I never received anything but
kindness and consideration from Walter. He was a
gentleman in every sense of the word, looking out
for our interests as if they were his own.

He took it upon himself to keep the table supplied
with meat, which meant a great deal in a hotel like
ours. He always cleaned his own game, too. He liked

to cut wood into stove lengths and carry it into the house. He did more for us than we did for him. Word came to us that our friend had died at White-horse and that he was buried in the cemetery there. Davy and I both grieved that he could not be with us at the last, among his friends, and be buried here at home in the little graveyard on the island.

CHAPTER THIRTEEN

The Fire on Stewart Island

ON DECEMBER 29, 1918, The Roadhouse burned to the ground. The old-fashioned Christmas party that had lasted from the twenty-fourth to the twenty-eighth had been a big success.

Belle was ready to go Outside to spend the holidays with her husband in San Francisco. She had stopped for a little visit with us before she left the North. I had begged her to stay and eat Christmas dinner and visit with her old friends, and she was persuaded to do so.

The hotel was filled with fun and laughter; good friends were enjoying a fine old-time visit. There were twenty-seven at the dinner table. They stayed four days and four nights. We had never had a better time. Davy and I had given the party. The Roadhouse was decorated with incense pines and spruce. Everything on the table had come from the Yukon. The hunters brought the meat. I had raised the chickens. There was good smoked salmon. Davy was very proud of the vegetables he provided. There were even cucumbers and cantaloupes which he had raised in his hothouse. Everybody brought gifts, the best in the cache. It was a fine dinner, with plenty of good homemade wine. We laughed and visited those happy days we were together.

The time passed all too soon. Friends dreaded to say good-by to this jolly cheer, to go home to dreary cabins and lonely lives.

The next morning after they were on their way, Belle was helping me as usual.

"Now, see here, Peggy, you are all tired out with so much cooking. You go up the stairs and get a little extra rest." She pulled me to the stairway and gave me a push. "Run along, now," she said. "I don't want to see you for two or three hours. I'll finish up these dishes and then I'll have a few winks myself."

Davy was in his bed. After all the excitement, and not being well, he needed to rest.

I was just drifting off to sleep when a terrible explosion shook the hotel. Before I knew what was happening, the flames were roaring and crackling through the house. Belle came dashing halfway up the stairs screaming, "Hurry! Come at once! Don't stop to dress."

It happened so quickly I did not realize what I should do.

"Come, Peggy, come, for God's sake, come!" Belle called frantically.

Flames were racing up the stairs. I ran back. I couldn't go through that fire. I stumbled to the little window at the top of the stairs, the window Belle had opened and put hinges on. I looked down; it was too far to jump. I dashed back. Fortunately I had not undressed, and had on a heavy sweater and woolen clothes. I pulled the sweater over my head and ran into the flames, the fire licking at my stout woolen clothes. I struggled down the stairs. Belle caught and dragged me out the door.

There was a horrible sound of crackling wood and a roaring of flames. Everything was ablaze. Belle had helped carry Davy and lay him in the snow out of reach of the fire.

She had on only a house dress, not outdoor clothing. Nevertheless she ran a quarter of a mile to the telegraph office for help in the bitter cold. She was speechless when she got there. The operator, seeing her scorched hair and face cried, "My God, it's a fire!" Belle could only nod her head. He shouted, "Fire! Fire!" as he ran.

It was early in the morning and very cold. Most everyone on the island was indoors and did not hear the explosion or see the fire.

Soon everyone was there. It was impossible to save the hotel. But next to it was another building that had been put up by Davy and the little Indian girl's father, Rook, for a trading post and general store. It had not been finished and stood empty. If this could only be saved! Belle was the first to think of it. She worked like mad and encouraged the others to help, using poles to push the burning timbers away from the building, and shovels to put snow into the fire.

The greatest horror in this cold country is fire. It takes away shelter and protection.

The big store building was only a very short distance from The Roadhouse, and it was nothing short of a miracle that it was saved. Fortunately, there was no wind. This was in our favor.

"What happened?" everyone asked. "How did the fire start?"

"Old Irish Bill put on too much damp wood in the airtight stove and it exploded," Belle explained, as she kept on working. She seemed to think of everything, and kept everyone working with all his might.

"Why are you patting my head that way?" I asked Belle.

"Well, my dear, your hair is on fire," she answered.

I put my hands to my head, and the knot of hair came off in them. Even then I did not realize my face was scorched.

"Where is Mr. Dennis?" I gasped.

"Oh, I'm afraid he's burned to death! Has anyone seen Mr. Dennis?" Belle cried above the noise.

"Oh, try to get him out! The last time I heard him was when I started down the stairs," I called. "I heard him screaming, 'Now they will believe me —now they will believe it is the wrath of God that is burning up the world!'"

Mr. Dennis was a religious fanatic, a self-styled prophet. He was always telling everyone who would listen about the wickedness of this world, and how it was doomed to be burned up by fire. Belle and I were grieving over him when we saw him come staggering toward us, his face like wax.

"Oh, we were afraid you were burned!" we both cried at once. "What kept you so long? The house is almost ready to fall in."

He staggered toward us, eyes staring, hair falling over his wild face.

"Not me — I'll not burn — God wouldn't let me burn. But I had a hell of a time getting out of that damned little window and I almost broke my neck falling to the ground. First I couldn't get my clothes on, and then I couldn't get my shoes off, and then I couldn't get them back on. I thought the house would fall in before I got out. I could hardly make it through that little window. Any feller ought to be hanged that would make a window like that!"

Belle and I exchanged glances.

"Well, if it hadn't been that I got my pants on wrong, I'd got here before. The damn things don't seem right even now." He gave them a much-needed hitch.

"You've got them on backwards, Mr. Dennis," I told him.

How he had ever been able to get his two-hundred-pound body through that window we never could understand.

Poor Davy was lying in the snow. Fortunately, someone had grabbed blankets for him, but he was almost frozen. Forty degrees below zero is cold, even at the height of excitement. At last some of the men carried him to a friend's cabin. After the danger to the store building was passed, Belle came to my rescue and took me there, too, and gave me emergency treatment. I had worked frantically to throw snow on the blaze, and my face and hands were scorched. I did not realize it until Belle began treating them.

The first night was the worst. While the burns tormented us, we had little time to think of our losses. I wouldn't cry, but my stoical manner couldn't fool Belle, who knew me. I would never let anyone see me cry. All night this faithful friend sat by me and kept warm olive oil on my face, forgetting her own face that was both scorched and frozen. Her ears had been frozen so badly that it was years before they recovered.

Davy had suffered so much from the shock. He was unable to walk for months.

A big scab formed on one side of my face; when it came off, that side was as smooth as a baby's—not a scar. "Too bad both sides didn't get burned," I used to say, "then I'd be all new."

After the terrible pain had eased and we were getting well, I looked at Belle. "My, but you're a sorry-looking sight! With your hair gone and your eyelashes and eyebrows singed away—your face scorched and your nose and ears frozen!" I teased her.

Belle looked at me and commented: "Well, my dear, you don't look so fine yourself!"

Then we both laughed.

The news of the fire flashed to Dawson. Friends came to the rescue as soon as it was possible, but it took days to get clothing and merchandise one hundred miles by dog team over the ice.

The hotel and winter supplies were a total loss. The warm winter clothes and blankets, furniture that had taken years to accumulate, dishes, and the cooking utensils—all gone.

But the greatest loss to me was the contents of the little valise which I had cherished all through the years. Each trip I had made over Chilkoot Pass; the weary hours of climbing, struggling through the bitter, biting blizzard at Crater Lake—every step of the way—this little valise had stayed close by me. And now it was gone, gone. Nothing left but ashes! All the dear, intimate things from home, the family portraits, the little treasures, the old-fashioned jewelry; the precious letters from brother Jack that meant all the world to me! Nothing could replace these things; they were the last tie that bound me to the old life at home.

Kind friends lent blankets and clothing. An old miner gave us his cabin, and went to stay with a friend who was also glad to give shelter to Davy and me.

Mr. Lawrence, the storekeeper, came to us and said, "Come over to my store and get anything you want. Your credit is good." Later, when we paid the bill, he took off fifty dollars.

Our friends, the Lees, in Dawson, sent one hundred dollars and a big duffle bag of warm garments on the first dog team that left town. Other friends sent money and gifts. Even people we did not know, who lived miles from us, sent blankets and many useful things. A man who owned a team came to fill up the three big cellars and smooth the ground. Everyone was more than kind to us.

Then began the construction of the new hotel. Belle took charge. The men worked willingly under her direction.

Belle had not a word to say of her own losses.

"She lost more in real money than we did," I said to Davy.

"She took it like a man," Davy replied.

I thought, "No man I ever knew could have done the things Belle did, though she never said one word about it. All my life I shall always mind how good she was to us. We could never have come through without her loving help. She was more than a sister.

No one ever had a better friend. Davy used to tell me, "Belle is the best feather in our wing."

Belle had stored two trunks and several boxes at The Roadhouse. She did not want to leave them at her own cabin while she was Outside. She had intended taking them sometime in summer, when she went out on the boat. In the meantime there was plenty of room to store them at our hotel. The contents represented twenty years of collecting— valuable ores, beautiful native crystals, gold nuggets of unusual size that she had washed out of her own claim, and other things she could never replace. There was a thousand dollars' worth of furs. Just the night before she had bought a beautiful silver fox fur for one hundred dollars.

"Don't you wish you had not given the money for that fox fur?" I asked her.

"No," answered Belle. "If I had not bought it, the money would be with the six hundred dollars that burned. As it is, someone will get some good out of it. I felt worse about the loss of my husband's black opal ring. I should not have left it in my bag, but kept it on my finger where he put it."

The new mink coat that she had worn only a short time was burned. It had taken her several years to collect the perfectly matched skins. Belle lost many valuable things, but she was too busy now to think about it. She ran back and forth from the home of the postmistress, where she was staying, to the cabin where Davy and I stayed, a distance of nearly a quarter mile. She cooked our meals and cared for us, keeping hot oil on my badly burned face and hands.

Clothing for Belle was a problem. The postmistress, being a small woman, found her clothes fit me, but Belle, being much larger, had difficulty finding enough warm clothing. Someone gave her a coat and cap, and later she made a very good-looking Mackinaw from a Hudson Bay blanket that was given her.

Belle saw the possibilities in the big trading-post building. Partitions must go in to make the rooms; a stairway must be built, and so on. She immediately sent to a sawmill eight miles up Thistle Creek for the lumber. She knew she could count on the men to help her, and now was the time to do it.

It was slow, tedious work, for the winter of 1918 was very cold. She gave up all ideas of going Outside, and stood by Davy and me. No sister could have been kinder. She took all the hard places and saved me in every way. What a friend! No one ever had a better, whilse.

The trading post had not been finished. Fortunately, before the building was put up, two big cellars had been dug, which was a great help, for now the work inside could start at once. There was a door on the building, but the openings for the windows were only boarded up. It was necessary to let in the light to do the carpenter work. Davy thought of a roll of drafting paper he had put away in the barn. This was fastened over the kitchen window to let in the light and keep out the biting cold.

The men worked faithfully under Belle's direction. They found her a good manager. The ashes were hardly cold when she started the reconstruction of the hotel. The first thing she did was to have the old steel kitchen range dragged out of the ashes and put up so she could cook good hot meals for the men working on the building. She even managed to give food and lodging to travelers coming in over the ice trail. This made a little money for Davy and me.

Everyone was kind and considerate and put up with the inconveniences, feeling sympathetic when he looked at the deep burns on our faces. My hands were so badly burned it was months before they were free of bandages. It was a long, drawn-out time as there were so many things we needed, and it would be months before the breakup and supplies could come in. But Belle never stopped; she was always working with all her might and encouraging the men and keeping up their enthusiasm.

The winter dragged along. The fire was the last of December—spring was long in coming, but Belle never lost a day; she planned everything. Men came from the near-by creeks, offering to help. She always had a job for each and every one. Two of the men she sent to her cabin on Thistle Creek to get most of her furniture and bring it to the new Roadhouse. A couple who lived miles away, and who were going Outside, sent a nice extension table and side dishes and cooking utensils. We did not know we had so many friends.

There was one thing that happened that humiliated us very much. An old rascal went about on the creeks begging for money in our name. He collected quite a good-sized sum from the kindhearted miners—enough to get himself out of the country before the disgraceful robbery was found out. We felt very bad at being put in such an embarrassing position.

The Roadhouse was quite comfortable by the time Belle went back to her almost-bare cabin. She gave up going Outside for another year. I could now take care of my duties. Davy had been very ill all winter, but he was feeling better and was now able to help finish the inside rooms and build the stairway. His lathe had been put away in the barn and had thus escaped the fire, so he set about making another stairway quite as fine as the one in the old hotel. There were five rooms downstairs besides the kitchen, and sixteen beds in the upstairs bunk room. Things were taking on an atmosphere of comfort.

One of the things Belle and I laughed about was my fine gray suit. "Well, it's better to laugh about it than cry. Neither can help, but laughing makes you feel better," I told her.

The summer before the fire, a government official and his wife stopped off at Stewart three or four days to wait for the boat to Mayo, and the lady enjoyed our company so much that she decided to stay while her husband attended to his business in Mayo. When she was leaving, she said to me, "Now, if I can do any shopping for you in Ottawa, I'll be glad to do it."

Davy, listening, said, "You can buy her a new suit and outfit. She hasn't had new clothes for ten years."

"Well, I haven't needed any," I answered proudly.

Davy gave the woman a hundred dollars for my new outfit. When the lady went home she sent me a lovely silver-gray suit that cost seventy dollars, and a hat to match that cost fifteen, and a fine white silk waist—the best outfit I had ever owned in the North.

I was delighted when they arrived and I tried them on. Looking at myself in the mirror, I decided I was not such a bad-looking little Scotch-woman after all. Twice I had tried them on and dreamed of someday going to Dawson to visit my friends.

After the excitement of the fire was over and we were thinking of the various things that had gone up in smoke, I said to Belle, "If I had only gone to Dawson and worn my new suit, I would not care so much. Oh, well, it may be years before I get there again, and that suit would be all out of style."

Life ran along at The Roadhouse about the same. I was always busy. There were little things to laugh about among the worries. A tourist came up to The Roadhouse from the boat and said to me, "Do you know where the old Scotch couple live? They are about a hundred years old, and I am told they lived here on this island."

There was a twinkle in my eye as I answered, "No, I dinna know if any such old Scotch couple aboot here."

Jim McLaughlin gave us all a good laugh. He rescued a worthless old fellow from drowning. Someone said to him, "Jim, you old fool, why didn't you leave the scalawag drown? All he does is cost us money and food!"

"Yes," said Jim, "but I had sent him to the river

to get some water to make us a cup of tea and he had my teapot with him."

This same old fellow had a dog, Morley. The dog had a reputation of being a thief and a rascal. He was known to steal food in such a way that it could easily have been laid to a man. It was unheard of for a dog to open doors, climb through windows, and drag home to his master pieces of meat quite as large and larger than himself. Of all this, Morley was accused. His master gloried in his wicked ways. Davy would sometimes smile at me and say, "Old Fagin is proud of his pupil."

His master boasted, "Why, I've seen that dog when the meat was hung too high for him to reach, drag up a box and stand on it. Then he'd get up on his hind legs and pull down a hunk of meat as easily as a man could ha' done. That dog can always get his grub, and don't you forget it."

Old Tompson, Morley's master, also had ways of helping himself that might be a bit questionable as to real honesty. But he was such an interesting old teller of tales that he was always welcome. He was like Scheherazade of the Arabian Nights. He could always keep a room of people entertained with his wild tales, which would wind on and on from Australia to the South Seas, where he had been a pearl diver; or to the Inlet, where he smuggled liquor into Alaska. He had traveled all over the world and, if anyone doubted this, all he had to do was to speak of some foreign port and at once Old Tompson could give a good description of the water front. Davy liked him for this reason; he, too, had traveled over the world, and the stories of the sea always intrigued him.

Old Tompson and Morley would come to the hotel and stay for four or five weeks at a time, and on leaving, never mention money in any way. But we never cared. After all, it was worth his feed to have him there to entertain us through the long winter evenings. "What are a few meals?" asked Davy.

But sometimes I wondered about so many guests who did not pay, and I would think, "Well, they have to eat someplace, the poor old ne'er-do-wells. It is not for me to begrudge them a meal or two."

Old Tompson shared everything with Morley, and the dog got the best. At night it was a rule that all dogs must go out of the house to the barn. Old Tompson would call Morley: "Here, you old rascal, get up. Time for you to go out and find new lodgings."

He would get a big piece of meat, or anything he could find that Morley would like, and with loud talk about being put out, the dog would have an extra supper. Later, when the house was quiet, Old Tompson would sneak cautiously to the door and let the waiting Morley in. Then the happy old dog would curl up in bed beside his master and the two contented rascals would go to sleep. This little act was put on every night. We paid no attention to it for it was not in our hearts to hurt the old fellow or his dog.

At last his claim did begin to pay, and with the first money he sent to Dawson for a case of the finest whisky. Then he hired some men to do the work. He sat and watched them, holding onto his

bottle, weaving back and forth and yelling orders
down to them like an old sultan. He was an old
man when he came to Stewart, "not a hair on his
head," thin and frail-looking, but he and Morley
had always managed to eat. He always had hopes
of gaining wealth and going back to North Africa
and starting a coffee shop, where he could sit out
in the sun all day on the sidewalk and listen to tales
of Morocco and Algiers.

A friend thought if Davy got away from home
for a while the change might be good for him, so
he arranged a comfortable trip in a motorboat up
Thistle Creek. My idea was that it might not be
so good for him, but Davy and his friend overruled
my judgment and Davy went. There were a few
quiet days between boats and I was all alone in the
house. I never liked going to bed early, and as the
violet light of night came, I grew a bit lonely. The
house was unusually quiet and filled with shadowy
dusk.

I started to go down to the river. It always comforted me. It was like a dear, understanding friend.
Going from the kitchen through the dining room,
suddenly I ran into a tall, black figure. Backing
away, I looked up to see the white-turbaned head
of a Hindu. I was badly frightened. His dark face,
piercing black eyes, and flashing white teeth were
entirely strange to me. He was like no one I had
ever seen before. I was shaking. It flashed through
my mind that I had never had such a scare since I
was a tiny lass in Scotland and an old beggar woman
had come to the door and had tried to catch hold
of me with her withered, claw-like hand, the other

hand pointing to her horrible mouth where her tongue had been cut out. I had screamed and screamed; my mother could not stop me. I felt like screaming now. I could not move. This strange man was like a genie, stepping out of a bad dream. He bowed, and in broken English tried politely to explain his presence and what he wanted.

At last I got the idea that he was asking for food. This made it more real. He told me he and his companions, about twenty of them, had come from Whitehorse. They had given a man ten dollars a day to pilot them and their provisions down the river to Dawson. They came ashore to cook their own food. They believed no one must handle it but themselves. No human shadow must fall upon it. They were East Indians, British subjects, who, after the war, were sent to Canada as an experiment to mine gold and establish homes to which they could bring their families. All were fine, aristocratic-looking men, clean and neat, wearing black coats and white trousers and white turbans.

The government gave them work on the road at Henderson Creek. They were unfit for manual labor and it was not long before the government shipped them all back to India. The night they were on the island they went to an empty cabin to cook and to sleep.

I still felt a little uncomfortable to have all these strange foreigners so close and no one but myself in the house. I wondered what I could do about it. I did not want to let Mr. Lawrence, who was my closest neighbor, know I was afraid; still I did not like being alone. A happy thought struck me. Why not take a bedroll and climb up on the roof of the house? From there I could watch everything, and not be seen.

I did this. It was midsummer and the birds were singing sweetly. All night there was a lavender and golden light about. From the roof of the house I watched my lovely river glide by, rippling and ever moving. I could see the white-turbaned figures going and coming from their strange, boxlike boats that they themselves had built to pattern after the boats of India—boats with two tiers or decks.

I grew sleepy when the Hindus showed no more activity. After a refreshing sleep under the sky, I awoke with the sun brightly shining in my face. I could hardly get the sleep out of my eyes. My eyelids seemed too heavy to open. A wet dew sprinkled my brown hair with diamonds. I washed my face like a kitten, wiping away the dew. "Ho, hum," thought I, "this is the real life. Everyone should sleep out under the sky." I turned over on my stomach and looked to see if my new neighbors were about. They were not, so I sat up, yawning and stretching and looking down at my beloved river.

In the morning the Hindus left for Dawson and there was no reason for me to climb to the roof the next night, but I did, and every night until Davy returned—just for the pure love of sleeping out in the open.

Many strange people came into the country. A family of gypsies tied their craft and climbed up to The Roadhouse. They were truly Rumanian gypsies. Seeing them made me a bit homesick. It took me back to Scotland and to my childhood when my family used to visit the gypsy camp near our old home.

These gypsies were a certain tribe that came each year. They cooked their food in great iron pots and all sat about eating and laughing, dancing and making music. There were many children and dogs. I liked the colorful scene, and remembered the time a gypsy told my fortune. The woman had told my mother's fortune and I held out my little hand. The gypsy said, "Ah, the child will travel far and live amid snow and ice." Little though I was, I never forgot this.

Remembering these things, I welcomed the colorful family. The father was a fine-looking fellow with flashing smile and a yellow scarf tied gracefully about his head under his hat. He had big gold earrings and a red sash about his waist. The mother, pretty and young, was wearing many gay petticoats, a bright red silk scarf about her head, and big round earrings in her ears. The two little girls were dressed like their mother; and the baby boy was fat and healthy, with an enchanting grin. I was excited, and my welcome was so warm I had a hard time getting rid of them.

They wanted food—they wanted everything. The children were all over the place in a moment. The parents had no idea of paying, but generously insisted on telling fortunes. There were several people at The Roadhouse at the time, and the gypsies picked up a few dollars. One of the bachelors, who was **very shy of women**, blushed and paid out a dollar to the pretty gypsy who held his hand. She looked into his eyes and told him, "You will marry a beautiful lady and have many nice babies." He had a hard time living down his blush—and fortune. It was much fun. The tale went up and down the creeks, and he was teased about his wedding.

The gypsies had to put up a bond of five hundred dollars to get into the country and they proved they were not paupers by showing two thousand dollars in money. It took work to get them off the island and on their way to Dawson.

During this period there was an old Laplander who lived in a cabin on the island. My heart went out to him in his loneliness. He had come from Norway, bringing fifteen reindeer with him. The project was financed by a rich Dawson merchant who thought of starting a herd of reindeer in the Yukon, as was done later in Alaska. On the way over, the voyage was so rough that most of the creatures died. They landed in Montreal and it was not long until more died.

The old man arrived in the Yukon with only one of his reindeer and this one did not live long. Old Andrew was sick at heart. His herd had been his pride and joy. He knew all about reindeer; it had been his life work and that of his family for generations. To see them die, one by one, was almost more than he could bear. It was like losing his own children. The agreement had been that he was to stay five years and care for the herd of reindeer, then return home to his wife and children in Norway.

He would come to my kitchen when his heart could stand no more, and cry and cry for his loved ones, and his beloved homeland away across two oceans. He never had enough money to go back.

The man who had brought him to the Yukon lost interest because his herd had died.

The poor old man, a stranger in a strange land, knowing only a few words of English, led a lonely life. I taught him to read. I used to tell him that if he learned he would not be so lonely, and he accomplished the difficult task of learning to read and write. He would lie long hours in his bunk, studying, and at last he could read. He was very proud and happy over it. Before he learned to write, I used to write long letters to his wife for him, and when the answers came (someone had been kind enough to write her letters to him), I read the letters while old Andrew sat by, crying lonely tears. He loved his wife and family, and when his wife and two of the children died, he was sorely grieved.

He liked to sing his old Lapland songs. Whenever there was a party he would get dressed in his Lapland clothes and sing until someone stopped him, or he would have kept on through the night. A kindly old fellow, and deeply religious.

CHAPTER FOURTEEN

Davy

DAVY WAS TAKEN ILL and I decided to get him to Dawson to see if Dr. La Chapell could help him. I had no clothes fit for such a trip and I did not know what to do about it. It was a long time since I had been there and I did not want to go looking so very shabby. Trying to get someone to run the hotel while we were away was another source of worry. However, I made up my mind I must wear the only dress I had. Davy had to go to the hospital. What did my clothes matter?

That night on the boat from Mayo, a pretty dance-hall girl whom I had known for years stopped off at the hotel on Stewart Island to see me. I had tried to help her the first winter when she was so lonely and strange. She had never forgotten me. The man she had married bought her a lot of pretty clothes. She came into the kitchen and stood near the stove talking to me.

"I heard about your fire in the winter. Did it burn up all your clothes?" she asked.

I told her about the fine gray suit and laughed. "Oh, well, I had very little use for it here, as I seldom leave home."

"But what will you wear in the morning when you go to Dawson?" the girl asked.

"Oh, I'll get along," I answered more cheerfully than I felt.

That night, when the girl was going to her room,

she said, "I have been repacking my clothes and I have so many I don't need. I'm going to leave this brown coat and hat here." She looked into my face, hoping not to offend me.

I smiled. "I'll be glad to accept them, and thank you," I said to the kindhearted girl.

When she knew I would not be hurt, she got a fine suit from her husband for Davy. She also insisted I take twenty dollars extra. "Why not?" she laughed. "It will be our wedding present."

The man looked pleased about it and gave me the money.

The coat was a beauty, with a lovely mink collar. There were gloves to match a nice warm dress, and a hat. I had sent away for shoes some time before, and they had, fortunately, just come, so I was fitted out "like a lady."

The coat had not served its usefulness, however, with this trip. One cold fall day another dance-hall girl, on her way to Mayo with a party in a small motorboat, stopped at the hotel. I told her she would be sick going all that way in an open boat. The girl had no other clothes but the thin suit she was wearing. I brought out my fine brown coat with the mink collar and put it on the girl, who promised to send it back as soon as she got to Mayo. But she never reached there as the boat wrecked and the girl drowned. A lawyer who settled the girl's estate, and who was a friend of mine, sent me seventy-five dollars for the coat.

When Davy was able to go home from the hospital, I went to the Mother Superior to pay the bill and was told I did not owe one. The Sisters would not accept a cent. They had often stopped at The Roadhouse on their way to Mayo and Davy and I had never allowed them to pay, and this was their time, they said. Everyone was good to us. I can never repay all the kindness Davy and I received.

Back home again after this trip to the hospital, Davy was better for a short time, but it was plain he was losing strength instead of gaining. I did not know what to do for him, and this worried me a great deal.

Davy was taken very ill. Dr. Chapell came over the ice with his dog team and did all that skill and devotion could do. But the rest of the winter Davy remained in a dangerous condition. There were not many travelers at the time, for which I was thankful, as it gave me more time to devote to Davy.

"If he is only spared to me, that is all I ask; nothing else matters if Davy can only live," I thought.

One night, when Davy was first taken ill, and Dr. La Chapell was there, we both thought he would not live until morning. I looked into the doctor's anxious face and for a moment I, too, lost hope. I ran out of the door and down to my river for comfort. It was silent and peaceful there. I remembered how peace had come to me when brother Jack had died. I asked for the same peace now. I prayed in agony: "Oh, spare him, spare him! Davy must not die." Something within me willed it so. "No, no, Davy must not die." I hurried back to his bedside.

The faithful doctor looked up. "Do you know, I believe he is better. Look, he is sleeping quietly. Why don't you go and rest? You will need your strength."

I only shook my head. "No, I am not tired."

Placing my hands on Davy's brow I gently stroked him. I mind the anxious hours I had stood beside him, soothing his aching head when we had been at Lake Lindeman and Davy had been almost wild with the pain in his eyes. My hands were the only medicine that helped him then. And it was this way now.

I was busy all day and long into the night. But no matter how busy I was with my work, Davy always came first. I gave him sweat baths, heating a big tub of water and wringing out hot sheets, twisting them tight on a broomstick. Placing a piece of oilcloth over the mattress, I put him into the hot sheets, covering him with blankets so that he would sweat. Then I bathed him in soda water, keeping him carefully wrapped all the time. He wanted these baths at least once or twice a week. It was a hard task, but I managed it. Davy had taken Turkish baths in San Francisco and he claimed they were the best medicine he could have. This was the nearest we could come to them.

"Oh, Peg," Davy would look up at me and beg, "if I could have a breath of salt air I think I could get well. I think of it all the time. I want to feel the salt spray on my face. I want to smell that tangy salt air. Peg, I know it would make me well."

I longed to grant this wish, but I didn't know how I could manage it. It took more money than I had to go Outside. Beside this, there were other considerations. So I put him off.

"We'll see. It's winter, Davy. Wait, whilse. We'll see when the spring comes."

But he kept longing for the ocean. He would lie on the couch, his cat in his lap, looking out of the window. Prince, his faithful dog, lay beside him.

"Peg, I dreamed of the ocean last night," he said. "I was back home in Scotland, sailing my boat. The white sails overhead. I could feel the roll of the boat under me. Not long ago I dreamed I was sailing out over a sea of gold as I did in the Bay of India. I went so far that time I almost lost my way and had a hard struggle getting back to you. But I wouldn't leave you, Peg. You've been a good wife, my gir-rul. When I get better you won't have to work so hard. I don't want you working for all these people; it's not right."

"Davy, I'm glad I can make our living," I answered. "I love my life as it is. I wouldn't change it. I've had a fine life. I wish I could live it all over again, every day of it. I love my life.

"Mind how our friends who never left Scotland lived such monotonous lives? Each day like the one before. The men coming home after a day's work, eating, sleeping, going to work, no change, just the same old thing over and over; the women keeping house, cooking, gossiping, going to church, maybe a holiday once a year, and then the rest of the time just drab sameness.

"Mind how Maggie Cameron never had anyone come to her house for a meal? All those years she kept her wedding silver wrapped up in flannel bags, never using it for fear it would wear out; and when I asked her when she was going to use it, she said, 'Well, John and I thought we might have a party on our silver wedding anniversary and use it then!

Look, it's just as good as new!' And she showed me.

"She did not like it when I laughed. If I had it, I would want it to show wear. Think of it, Davy. In all those years they never left Stirling. John never took a holiday; and there they still live, saving money, saving their silver, saving, saving, never any change or experience. Oh, that kind of life would have been the death of me. She can have her 'bonny hoose,' and money in the bank. Oh, Davy, I've never regretted our life. I always say, I wish we could live it all over again."

After Davy's "bad spell," he grew somewhat better. But his right hand remained useless and he dragged his right foot. It was months before he could go about the house with my help. The extra care of Davy and my other work kept me busy. But I did not mind; all I wanted was for him to get well.

I was happy to hear him ask for his pipe, though he could no longer manage it himself. I put the tobacco in, and between the two of us we got it lit; Davy enjoyed a good smoke. The next time I filled it I put it into my own mouth and gave a big draw to get it going, then gave it to Davy. It made me ill at first. The pipe was very strong, so I cleaned it. I wondered at a boy learning to smoke, keeping on trying when it made him sick. I kept on, as Davy had to have his pipe, and it took much less time if I started it. Davy would watch me with satisfaction.

"Take a good puff, gir-rul; it won't hurt ye," he would say.

I rather liked it.

"Get ye a pipe, lass, and take a few puffs," Davy

encouraged. All at once it had happened! I was smoking a pipe! Davy laughed and enjoyed it. It was our secret. I would light Davy's pipe and then, if there were no people in The Roadhouse, Davy and I would smoke together, but if strangers were there I went into my pantry off the kitchen and smoked my pipe in comfort.

Davy would manage his pipe with his left hand after he got it going. He was always anxious that I have my smoke, and would say, "Let them wait. Go have your smoke, gir-rul."

This same winter I started going out to the chicken house to skip rope. I had to keep up a fire in the chicken house in very cold weather anyway. Going back and forth to the barn to feed the horse, there were times when I was not dressed warmly enough, and rheumatism began to bother me. In the morning I would be so stiff I could hardly get out of bed.

"This won't do, to get old and stiff. I've got to exercise," I decided. So I went to the barn, got a piece of rope, and began skipping in the chicken house while the chickens looked on and made all kinds of excited noises. "Just laugh if you like. I'm not going to be a stiff old lady," I told them.

The first week I could skip twenty-five times. At the end of the winter I could skip one hundred without stopping.

"Pretty good for an old lady?" I asked the chickens.

In my school days I had been the champion rope skipper. It pleased me to see I was not bad after all the years.

Following the breakup, Davy thought of nothing else but getting down to tidewater. I planned and planned how I could manage it. In the morning, as I went about my work of caring for Davy and cooking for people who came to The Roadhouse, I kept praying my own special prayer that had bolstered me so often, "Oh, God, show me what to do, and give me the strength to do it."

I set about getting him ready to go Outside. We could take the boat at our own door and go to Whitehorse. That would be easy. We knew all the captains on the river boats. I did not know how I could get him the rest of the way to Skagway by railroad but I felt sure I could manage it somehow. I even made arrangements for a cook to run The Roadhouse. We must start soon. Davy and I planned it together. It gave him new life. His dog, Prince, would come close and look up into his face, putting a pleading paw on his knee.

"Peg, I believe this old fellow knows we are going to leave him. Doesn't he look sad? Never fret, old man; you and Pussy stay here and keep house. We won't be gone long and then I'll come back all well, and I'll take you hunting."

Now that the day was near for Davy to have his breath of salt air, time went faster.

We were planning to go by the next boat to Whitehorse when Davy was again taken sick. I was in a panic. I didn't know what to do for him. There was a boat tied up waiting for the Mayo boat. We could leave sometime in the night for Dawson. It seemed best to take Davy to the hospital to Dr. La Chapell and the good Sisters. They had helped him before; they would again. We got him aboard the boat and managed to get him to the hospital.

But after a few days the gentle Mother Superior said to me, "Don't you want to take your husband home? He might be happier there."

I knew she had no hope for him. Yet I did not allow myself to believe it. I could not face his dying; no matter what anyone said, I did not believe it. Yes, he would be better and happier at home. They had failed me. I would take him back and care for him myself. Just so he lived—that was all I asked.

Davy wanted no one near him but me; no one else must help him or do anything for him. My hands were shaking so I could hardly take care of him. He held onto me, not allowing me out of his sight. Men carried him to the boat, but I must walk close beside him. When we reached home, he did not want to be alone for a minute. I made a bed for him on the couch in the Public Room and tried to be gay and natural, but it was no use. I saw how tired he looked.

"Davy, you look so weary, let me take you to your bed."

"Yes, Peg, I am awearying," he answered.

I helped him to rise. The others in the room were on their feet, wanting to help. But no, he would not allow it.

"My wife will help me," he said.

We made our way slowly, slowly, to the bedroom, I holding him with loving arms. All at once he collapsed and would have fallen, had not anxious hands stayed him. He was carried to his bed. Slowly his breath ebbed away.

I went out alone and sat on our bench by the

river. I was thankful no one came near me. It was the quiet hour in the night; the birds had ceased their singing. The Great White Stillness was close about me.

All at once I saw a beautiful white sailboat come sailing toward me, the sails spread like great white wings. On and on it came. I watched breathlessly. The sails dipped. It turned about, then sailed away over a golden sea. I covered my face with my hands. Davy was to have his breath of the sea, and I was left alone.

Two of Davy's friends had made his coffin from rough pine boards, smoothing them and giving them a fine finish, as they knew Davy would want done. Another friend neatly pleated two sheets as lining for the inside of the coffin. Davy had a good suit that he had worn when he went to Dawson, and he looked very much like his old self.

I had taken one of the pillows from our bed and covered it with some white material I had in the house. I worked through the night, making a big ruffle all around it. I regretted stitching it on the machine. I should have liked to do it all by hand but there was no time.

Prince knew that something terrible had happened to his master. He would not eat, but lay under the coffin all the time, Pussy beside him.

In the morning when I had finished the pillow, I waited until I was all alone to place it under Davy's head, that I might stoop down and kiss his dear face.

I could stand no more. I went out to the river. As I walked along the bank, my heart breaking, I saw some beautiful white lilylike blossoms. I had never seen flowers like these before. They must have grown for Davy, because he loved flowers more than anything. I picked a great armful and, carrying them into the house, I placed them in the coffin, some close to his waxlike face. The rest I made into a wreath.

Friends closed the coffin. I stood by. The little procession started to the lonely cemetery, among the tall pines. The day we buried Davy in the little graveyard on our beloved island the August sun shone brightly upon the little group. Old Albert, who had dug the grave, started first, carrying a shovel over his shoulder; then Mr. Lawrence, who was to read the funeral service; and Davy's friends carried his coffin on their shoulders. I followed closely. No one offered to walk with me, I did not want it. I was alone. From now on I must walk alone. Prince was close by my side, and Pussy, too, was not far away. The sad procession wound its way to the burying ground, about a quarter of a mile from The Roadhouse.

That night I went back alone to the grave, only Prince with me. I sat quietly near Davy as long as I could. I knew the time would come when I could not be near him. The saddest moment is when you have to close the door on your loved ones who are dead, and shut them out, leaving them all alone.

Davy was buried before the news reached Belle, who was busy working her claim up Thistle Creek. Later she told me how, when she went down to Veal's Trading Post at the North of Thistle for the mail and groceries, she overheard some men talking of Davy's death. She did not wait to go back to

her cabin four or five miles away, but said to the
man who worked for her, "Get ready, Sam, we are
going down to Stewart Island at once."

They were in an unsafe, tipping old boat, not
strong enough for the twelve-mile trip in the whirling, dangerous Yukon. Sam was a poor boatman.
A friend of Belle's had often warned her never to
get into a boat with him if she did not want to be
drowned, as he had little idea of how to handle the
oars. However, Belle's only thought was to get to
me. When they started, one of the men at the trading post called out, "You'd better not go down the
river in that old wreck of a boat. You'll be drowned,
sure and certain."

"Go ahead, Sam," Belle commanded, "we'll make
it. I must!"

They spun around and around helplessly in the
swift, dangerous current. Time and again they almost upset, the boat whirling, spinning around as
if it could never get out of the whirlpool of the
current and on into the flow of the river. Sam was
helpless with the oars. Belle directed him, as she
held on tightly to the side of the boat. She could
stand it no longer.

"Give me those oars. You change places with me.
I'll crawl over there." As he hesitated, she cried,
"Do as I say!"

"You sit still, you'll wreck us," Sam yelled back.

They were in one near-accident after another.
First they landed on the bank and then on a sand
bar among driftwood. Then they were whirling,
rocking, tipping, all but upsetting in the fierce current. Belle had never experienced such a trip. After

hours of terror and excitement, expecting every moment to be thrown into the river, they arrived at Stewart Island. She hurried up to The Roadhouse.

When I felt the comfort of Belle's kind arms about me, I slept for the first time in many nights.

Belle arranged everything so she could take me home with her. We went back on the river boat to the mouth of Thistle, stayed all night at the trading post. In the morning the men who ran the post took us up to Belle's cabin.

During all the years of our friendship I had wanted to see Belle's little place, but this was my first visit. I was always busy, and Belle did the visiting for both of us.

I was pleased when we reached my friend's comfortable little home on the hillside. Bright flowers were blooming in front of it. Surrounding the place was a strange-looking fence, made of ancient mastodon tusks. Belle explained she had washed them out by hydraulic pressure from the overburden found close to bedrock. There were twelve or fifteen of the big tusks, huge, dark-brown in color, and shaped like a scimitar. The others averaged from seventy-five to eighty pounds apiece. They had been lying about until one of the men who worked for her thought of making a fence out of them. Many teeth and jawbones of other prehistoric animals were gathered into piles beside the cabin.

The fence was always a curiosity to strangers. Not until later did Belle realize the value of these mastodon tusks.

Inside the cabin, I sat down in a comfortable chair and gave a sigh of relief. There were clean

white curtains at the windows. Vines were growing in an old copper teapot which hung in one of
the windows. She had built cupboards about the
room and painted them a pretty light green. On the
steel range the shining teakettle would soon be boiling and we would have a good cup of tea. A nice
airtight stove came into the same flue with the range
so there would be plenty of heat in very cold weather.
The windows in the room faced to the south, and
the sun shone in all day, making it cheerful and bright.

The view of the river and valley from the hillside
was unobstructed. It lay before us like a beautiful
picture.

Belle had often told me about her view. I could
now understand, for I knew it meant the same to
her as my beloved river did to me. There was a
sweet peace about it. I stood looking far away at
the winding river and the green valley. What a truly
beautiful country!

Belle had sent most of her furniture to us after
the fire. Later she had only bought what she needed
in Dawson. But I thought I had never seen a more
comfortable and tidy little home. It looked as if
she were expecting company.

The men who worked for Belle lived in the bunk-
house down by the creek.

When the word got about that I was visiting Belle
on Thistle, friends came on foot and by boat, up
and down the "Creeks," to visit with us. Sometimes
there would be two or three at a time. They brought
meat, fish, and the best in their caches as gifts to
the "Little Mother of the North," as they called me.
Everyone was good to me, and wanted to show sym-

pathy; at times I had a hard time to fight back the tears.

We were invited out to dinner at different miners' cabins. We walked miles through the woods. We always took the dogs. Belle said we need not be afraid. The dogs were fine bear dogs.

Lew Bower gave us a good dinner of grayling and vegetables from his garden. He opened two cans of tongue for Captain and Jip, who were with us.

Next day we went to another old friend's cabin and enjoyed a good supper of a different kind of food. He could bake pies and cakes. His specialty was big white sugar cookies; he had a batch for us to take home. Before coming to the Yukon he had been a superintendent of schools in eastern Canada. It pleased him to have company and to talk books. History was my special interest, and since this was his favorite subject, we had a fine evening. He insisted on walking the four miles to Belle's cabin with us.

I felt more like myself, listening and laughing at the stories the men brought to amuse me.

One of the men liked to tease Belle. "You know," he said, "Mrs. Brennon won't stand for cruelty to man or beast. I've known her to spring many a trap when she'd heard some little critter howling. She'd take the traps and throw 'em down old prospectors' holes—at least, so they say. One mean old rascal told how he was going to kill her if she didn't leave his traps alone. He didn't say a word to her face, though."

"Well," Belle said, "I told him, after Captain got his foot caught in one of his traps, that he had better

not set any more of them on my place, and I meant
it, too."

"Yes," laughed the old miner, "and by golly, he
believed you! Guess he didn't come about your claim
after that. The men around here know Mrs. Belle
Brennon. They know it's best not to get her mad;
a red-haired woman has a temper, you know."

He roared at his own joke. "Well, she got her
Irish up last winter, all right. There was an old feller
up the creek about twenty miles, mean old cuss.
Treated his old woman like a squaw. Some of the
boys were a-layin' for him, and just waitin' for her
to say the word. If she'd asked for help they was
a-goin' to give him a good lesson, but she never did
say a word. No one would have anything to do with
him but a few old rough ones like himself. One of
the boys told Mrs. Brennon how he treated his wife
and she got mad." He looked at Belle now, and
laughed as the angry light flashed in Belle's eyes at
the memory.

"The poor old woman took sick and when Mrs.
Brennon heard about it she got a couple of her men
and her dog team loaded with food and warm blankets and set out to bring that old woman back to
her cabin to take care of her. When they got there,
three or four of those old fellows were holdin' a
wake and drinkin'; the poor old woman was out in
the shed, a corpse.

"Well, did Mrs. Brennon fix those men! She didn't
say a hell of a lot—all she did was look at 'em. Jim
told us how she looked, and how those old boys got
out of there in a hurry. She told them what to do,
and did they do it? Let me tell you, they did! She

made them build a fire where the grave was to be dug, to thaw the ground. When she told that old man what to do he was so scared he kept sayin' 'Yes, ma'am,' 'Sure, ma'am,' keeping his eye on her all the time. Jim said he never saw a feller get over a drunk so fast. Jim said he was sure afraid of her —didn't know what she would do to him." Here the old miner laughed and clapped his hands on his knees, enjoying Belle's embarrassment.

"Mrs. Brennon made the old man go out and get the corpse and bring her into the shack. She washed the poor old thing and dressed her in some of the things she had brought. She made the old feller get busy and help make the coffin. No one got a wink of sleep, I can tell you, until Mrs. Brennon got her way.

"She done most of the coffin makin' herself. There wasn't any back talk from any of the men; they were all too scared. Most women, when they get all het up over a thing like she was, would have given that old scalawag a good tongue lashin', but not her; she never wasted a word on him. When everything was done for the old woman, she told Jim to hitch up the dogs, and without another word to that old feller, she left. We've often said if she had talked a week she couldn't have given him a better tongue lashin'.

"That's a sample of Mrs. Belle Brennon," the man continued. "She'd never set eyes on that old woman —only heard about her; yet she'd go forty miles in the dead of winter—" He shook his head. Belle Brennon was too much for him to understand.

The men told us about a tragedy that happened

up Pelly in the winter, which caused a good deal
of talk. Everyone knew of the blind Indian woman
whose white husband used to lead her around by a
string on her wrist. He took her everywhere with
him, leading her like a dog. She carried burdens
like any other squaw. When he jerked the string,
she knew the signals and would jump over logs.
When some of his people, who were very important
folk in the States, came to the Yukon, they hunted
up the black sheep of their family and dressed him
in new clothes, even to a new hat, which he promptly
traded to one of the Indians. He knew what he
wanted, and it was not new clothes and white man's
ways. The life of the Indians for him. He was said
to be good to his blind wife and baby.

It was the beginning of the freeze-up. The ice
was running in the rivers, freezing over along the
creeks, but not hard. The Indian woman took her
baby in a sled, drawing it herself, and went out on
the river to meet her husband, who was hunting. She
had a good sense of direction and would soon meet
him, for she knew he had gone down the creek.
Once out on the ice, she realized it was not frozen
hard enough. It began to crack about her. She
grabbed her baby from the sled, holding it tightly
in her arms as the ice gave way and they slid into
the water and under the ice. A long time later,
their bodies were found in the frozen river, among
the piled ice cakes. The wolves had almost destroyed
them.

A good story for a laugh any time was what happened in the early days at the very beginning of
the gold rush. An Irishman had brought in his pretty

young bride with him. He was very jealous of her, and as he was away at his work days at a time, he feared she might not be safe from all harm. He knew an old Indian and his squaw, so he took her to their cabin and left her for them to care for. When he returned she was very angry with him. She had never lived in such a dirty place, she said. There was no floor, only the hard-packed dirt, and the food and bed were beyond endurance.

"I'll not stay in such a place—I'll run away," she sobbed.

"Now, you just wait. When I get the money, I'll get you a better place to live. Be a good girl and I'll buy you a fine present."

He did. A pale-blue, silk-quilted Japanese kimono, for which he paid most of what he had earned!

The poor girl had to stay on with the Indians until he had earned more. It was a good joke in after years when they were far away from it. Even the wife laughed when her husband told how pretty she looked in the sky-blue kimono in the dirty Indian shack. "As pretty as a peach," her husband always said.

One spring, when Belle was with us while Davy was still alive, he was setting out some plants. Before she went home he gave her some—tomatoes, green peppers, cabbage, and eggplant. Belle had never tried this type of fancy gardening before, and she was anxious that the plants should have every care. One day she carried twenty buckets of water. Then she had the men carry more water, only to see it sink down into the sandy soil. Still the sickly plants did not grow. Belle was the type that would not

give up without a struggle, so she kept at it. At
last she sent to Dawson for a pump. After all these
trials, she learned from Davy that when she watered
the plants, she stopped the natural irrigation system
and froze the plants. Davy explained to her how
the sun draws up the moisture from the substrata
of age-old frozen ground which never quite thaws
out, even in summer, bringing about a natural irrigation system. Belle had interfered with Mother
Nature's own plan for a Yukon garden.

The miners laughed at her and told her she was
a better miner than gardener. They would bring
things from their gardens as presents, to tease her.
No one told her why her garden would not grow,
because they thought it so much fun to see her fail.
She could run the hydraulic plant and knew as much
about mining as any of them; that she couldn't
grow a garden was a laugh.

Belle and I enjoyed going to the mine to watch
the men at work on the hydraulic plant, washing
out the gold. Belle took a picture of me using the
monitor. She gave me several large gold nuggets,
and these I tied in my handkerchief.

After two weeks, I said I must go home to see
how The Roadhouse was getting along. Belle went
with me, intending to go to Dawson on business.
The morning after we arrived at Stewart Island, I
had an idea. "I wonder if you can do something for
me?" I asked Belle.

"Why, certainly I can. What is it?" she asked.

"Well," I said, "will you cut off the legs of the
cook table and these other small tables by the window, about two inches? They are all too high. Davy

used to say, 'They the all regulation size,' but he forgot that I wasn't.''

Belle soon had them my size. This made my work easier.

When Belle had gone to Dawson, I began straightening out all my accounts and looking over the bills incurred during Davy's sickness. I had spared no expense to give him everything he asked for. The only thing I had not succeeded in doing was taking him to tidewater so he could smell the "tang o' the sea." It grieved me not to have been able to grant this last wish. A big box of medicine that had come from Dawson the week before he died was still unopened. The bill was twenty-seven dollars. I poured out the medicines, planning to pay the bill very soon.

There were many bills I did not know we owed: seven hundred dollars, I counted, for materials of various kinds, for Davy's "ice machine." He had worked for years on this invention; a sled with two engines for power, to carry freight on the river in the winter. It had always given him great hope, and promised to be a big success. He had worked faithfully until the last few years, when he was too weak to make further venture. Many of the bills had stood for years. He had kept it from me, expecting when he had made a big success of his ice machine he could easily pay them and buy everything else we needed and wanted.

While Belle was in Dawson she met a man who asked about the "Scotch couple who ran The Roadhouse on Stewart."

"I'll never forget that little woman," he told Belle. "Years ago I was there in a spell of bitter

cold weather. The house was full to overflowing.
I was new to the country, sick, and in bad shape,
without enough blankets in my bedroll. She doctored me and put mustard plasters on my chest, and
soaked my feet in hot water and did all she could.
She had fixed a bed for me on some chairs near the
stove, but I was chilling and couldn't get warm.
She didn't have any more bedclothes to give, but
she got her coat and took off her petticoat and spread
them over me. That was the best little woman in
the North. I'll never forget her. She wouldn't remember anything about me, there were too many like
me that she doctored. I've heard other men call her
'Little Mother of the North.' I found out why.
Will you give her my best regards and tell her I
never forgot her kindness. I was sure down and out
at the time. Take her a box of apples for me. I saw
some fine 'Delicious' apples at the store."

Belle promised to do this on her way back to
Stewart.

People were always sending me presents. A minister, his wife, and two children stopped over on
their way to Mayo. They had met a friend of mine
in Vancouver who asked if the minister would take
a little present to his friend at The Roadhouse on
Stewart. The package was a long roll. I thought my
friend's wife had sent me some jelly, as she had done
once before, in just such a roll-shaped package.

"Wait," I said. "I'll open it and give the children
some jelly with their breakfast."

The children and their parents were watching me
as I worked at the dining-room table, trying to get
the package open. When the wrapping came off,

to my horror I saw that it contained two bottles of rum! The minister, having a kind heart, helped me to take the bottles away from the children's inquisitive eyes, and to get their minds off the nice slice of jelly bread they had been promised.

On this same boat, waiting to change to the Mayo boat, was a woman the worse for too many drinks. She came out into the kitchen and asked me if I knew where she could get a "drink."

"I have both tea and coffee on the table," I said.

"You know what I mean. I've been sick and must have something; I can't stand this pain. Don't you know where I could get a drink of whisky?"

I thought she had already had too much for her own good. I did not know what to do for fear the woman would make a scene, with the minister and his family there. Besides, I was quite sure she would not get any of the rum which I had safely hidden away in my own bedroom.

"Have you got any Jamaica ginger?" the woman asked.

I gave her the bottle and she emptied it. On a shelf over the work table was a row of flavoring extracts. The woman looked them over, and while I was busy with my cooking, she drank a whole bottle of lemon extract. I began growing uneasy as to the woman's condition, so I said, "You might find what you want over at Mr. Lawrence's store." She left at once.

Later that night I heard the rest of the tale. One of the men came in, laughing, to tell me.

The woman insisted the dignified teetotaler, Mr. Lawrence, give her something to drink or she would scream and cause a scene. The storekeeper ordered her out of the store, but she said she was sleepy and went into the room back of the store and crawled into the storekeeper's bed and went to sleep. The disgusted man sat out in his garden and waited until the purser of the boat came to get his passenger and put her safely aboard for Mayo.

On her way home from Dawson, Belle had a little visit with me while the boat stopped to unload some freight going to Mayo. I tried to get her to stay a few days, but she said, "No, I must get back to my work."

My days were very busy now that summer was on the wane. The vegetables from the garden must be put away in the cellar, and all preparations made for the coming winter.

Each year, less and less mining was being done along the creeks and rivers. More men were going Outside. The prospectors were hunting new fields. This had its effect on The Roadhouse. Fewer people stopped over on the trail in winter. Sometimes it worried me, but I would throw off the thought, saying to myself, "There's just as much gold here as there ever was. All they have to do is get it out."

I was lonely without Davy. At times I felt that I could never be as happy and contented again. One evening, sitting on the bench by the river to watch a boat tie up, I was surprised to see my dear Belle coming up the trail. I saw immediately that something had happened, for Belle's face was white, and there was not the usual smile. She had come to bid me "good-by," and she was taking the first boat Outside. She had a message saying that her husband was critically ill at the hospital in Oakland. She had attended to her affairs on Thistle Creek as best she could in so short a time, and now she was leaving.

"It may be some time before I can get back," she said. "I paid off the men and closed things up. I am afraid I shall be a year or longer.

"Sam did a foolish thing while I was in Dawson. He sold all those old mastodon tusks to a purser on one of the river boats. He got only twenty dollars for all that old ivory. When I was in Dawson I heard of a man who would have given me two dollars a pound for all I had. They are making beads and little trinkets out of it. The older it is the darker the color and the more valuable. Sam had no business doing it, of course, without permission. He did not know they were so valuable, and he thought he had made a good sale; the poor fellow was pleased to give me the twenty dollars! I didn't have the heart to tell him. If I had the time I'd make that purser give them up, but I can't bother with it now. I must get to Oakland as soon as possible."

Belle was worried about her husband, and grieved to leave me. We did not talk as we waited for the boat coming from Dawson and bound for Outside. We sat on the bench in silence. I knew how it hurt her to leave me alone.

"You must not get sick when I'm away," she chided me tenderly.

"I won't," I assured her. "I hope your husband will soon be himself. You let me know all about it."

She promised. Then we sat silently. The boat was coming upstream, around the curve of the riverbank. Looking into each other's eyes, we knew it was "good-by." There were no tears, no clinging. Side by side, we walked down the trail to the boat just as if the separation would not be long. But in the heart of each of us was a sense of fear that this was not like other times. It might be years before we should meet again, perhaps never. Captain walked beside his mistress. I laid a hand on his head.

"He will have a good home with Hughie. I never knew a man better to his dogs than Hughie is," I told Belle.

"Yes, both dogs have good homes," she answered. "It's too bad to separate them, but Hughie did not want them both, and Lewis always liked Jip. He will feed him and treat him well."

The boat was pulling out soon. Belle stepped up the gangplank. She stooped down and kissed me lightly on the cheek. I could not speak, but patted her shoulder with a trembling hand. How dear and dependable was this kind friend! No sister could have been a greater wall of strength to lean upon.

Belle went up the gangplank.

I walked back alone to my favorite spot on the riverbank and stood watching the boat pull from the shore. Belle waved from the upper deck, trying to smile and shouting words I could not hear. I watched the boat until it was well under way upstream. Then it was lost from my sight by a bend in the river. She was gone.

A feeling of loneliness came over me so that I felt I could not live. I was all alone in the house. It was so still and forsaken—empty—I could not bear it! I went back to sit by the river, all that was left to comfort me. There I sat the night through. It was the saddest night I ever spent in the Yukon.

In the morning a Mayo boat arrived with a load of people who needed my care. I was thankful to be busy.

A Scotch friend of ours, captain of one of the river boats, brought material for a fence to put around Davy's grave. Another captain on one of the Mayo boats, also a Scotchman, came with him to help put it up. They made a fine marker with Davy's name, his birthplace, age, and death clearly carved into the wood. I had not known they were doing it till I found it, all finished, when I went there one evening after the day's work was done.

It was cold now, not long before the freeze-up. I sat beside Davy's grave until I was chilled and shaking with cold, his dog beside me. We walked back with heavy hearts—poor old Prince. He, too, seemed to have lost his nerve. The next day I was taken with a bad cold which developed into influenza.

Hughie, who lived at the hotel and carried the mail, was anxious about me. Mr. Lawrence, too, realized I was seriously ill. When the operator came for his supper he at once telegraphed to Dawson to Dr. La Chapell. The message came back, "Put Mother on the boat at once and send her down to me."

Hughie promised he would look after Davy's dog and cat. I was bundled up and taken on board the last boat to Dawson before the freeze-up. The doctor met the boat and helped me into his car. I was burning with a high fever, but I managed to keep my senses long enough to ask, "Aren't you taking me to the hospital?"

"No, Mother, you are going to my own home, so I can watch you day and night. I'll have a nurse to help me," the doctor assured me. Comforted by his loving care, I knew now that I would have the heart to get well.

It proved to be a pleasant winter for me. I was soon well again, and able to do the work of keeping the doctor's home running smoothly. He would often tell me I was a "godsend" to him, that he would have been very lonely without me. His wife and baby had gone Outside for the winter.

Everywhere the doctor went among his friends, in the evenings, he took "Mother." The Lee family were especially good companions, but even with all this kindness, my heart was back in my home on the island. I kept wondering how things were going. I knew Hughie and Mr. Lawrence would do the best they could to carry on. I worried about Davy's dog and cat, and Davy's lonely grave.

The night before Christmas I was alone. How happy I had been just a year before! Davy had been so pleased with the new sweater I had knit him, and the new pipe I had put into his pocket. He had laughed at my fixing extra meat for Prince and Pussy (enough to make them sick, I said, so that they would know they had had a Christmas dinner). Belle had come down to spend Christmas. Friends were in for dinner, only ten of them, but we had had a big feast. Everyone was happy. Davy had seemed strong. He fed Prince a bite and then Pussy a bite. When Belle brought a towel and wiped the grease from his fingers, he had looked up and smiled. She came next to me in his affections. It had been a happy day, though we missed many of the old friends who had gone Outside, and some who had gone over to the "Other Side."

I thought wistfully of it now. It was all over— Davy was gone. Belle was worried about her husband's serious illness, and I was not there to comfort her. In spite of all the dear doctor's kindness to me, I had a feeling of being all alone.

Just then the doorbell rang and the Lees rushed in, laughing and calling "Merry Christmas." They had no more than gone, their voices ringing out on the Christmas air and the dry snow crunching under their feet, when the doorbell rang again.

I had not even time to open the gaily tied packages they had left before other friends arrived, fine Scotch folk whom the doctor had brought to meet me just the week before. In they came, laden with gifts and carrying their curly-haired little daughter, Frances. "Merry Christmas" they called, and so it was all the evening. By the time the doctor arrived home, twenty-seven friends, old and new, had come to wish me happiness. I must not be sad when so many kind hearts wished me to be happy!

I thought about the doctor's offer of a home with him a long time. At last the doctor overruled all my objections. It was settled—I was to go back to the island on the first boat in the spring, sell my hotel, and make all arrangements to live in the doctor's home.

It was the Oakland letter from Belle that decided it. She told of her husband's serious illness, saying that he could never be well. She was taking him to Southern California, intending to buy a home and stay. She had given up all hope of ever seeing her beloved Yukon again, and wished that someday I would come and live with her in California.

That settled it. I had no more reason to stay alone on the island if Belle was not coming back to the Yukon.

Peggy Alone

ON THE FIRST BOAT after the breakup, I went home to the island. I thought I would sell my hotel and go back to Dawson. The doctor had insisted, and he made me promise to do this.

There was no one to meet me, for Hughie and Jim McFann, who had been keeping the hotel open, did not expect me so soon. I walked up the trail to the building. A sorry sight met my eyes.

At the breakup, the river had gone on a rampage and flooded the island. The door of my home stood open; silt and mud filled the doorway. I was shocked to see my cooking utensils and clothing, along with furniture and other household things, scattered about in the yard. The fence was gone from the garden, the whole place a pitiful wreck.

I stood still. I could not believe my eyes. From a bush where it had caught, I picked up my tea-kettle, a lovely white enamel one that Belle had brought me after the fire, and of which I had been very proud.

However, gratitude began welling up in my heart that at least my hotel was still there and had not been carried away. I could clear up the wreckage and set it right. But now Davy was not here to tell me what should be done. How it would have grieved him. His poor garden!

I turned to look for our bench where we had sat together the many long hours throughout the years,

gazing down at the rushing Yukon. It was gone.
Pain stabbed my heart. Davy had made that bench
with careful, painstaking hands.

I wondered if his grave had been harmed. I found
myself hurrying, running to the little graveyard,
but I knew even as I ran that it was unharmed,
because it was far from the river and on higher
ground. I sat down beside Davy's grave.

It was hard to clear away the marks of the tem-
pestuous river. The cellars, all the downstairs rooms,
were covered deep with silt and mud. The upstairs
had not been harmed, nor the mattresses watersoaked. The men helped, but summer had almost
passed before the damage was repaired.

The garden must wait until the next year for
another fence, but I managed to get the vegetables
planted, beets, carrots, potatoes, and turnips, and
by fall they were ready to go into the cellar which
had taken weeks to dry out and be made ready for
use. It was heavy work. I wondered why it seemed
so hard to do; it had never been this way before.

When I was sick and taken to Dawson, I had
asked Hughie to take Prince to John Larson, a man
I thought could be trusted. I had insisted they put
the poor cat in a box and send her, too, because she
would have better care. Hughie had eight dogs of
his own, and John only four. Prince had never been
among other dogs, but had slept in the house near
his master, with little Pussy snuggled close to Prince's
fur.

The work dogs hated Prince, and he was never
able to eat with them. They would have killed him.
It was more than a month before John Larson's

partner came with his team to get provisions at
Mr. Lawrence's store. John was sick and had gone
Outside. I went over to ask his partner about Prince
and Pussy.

"There's Prince," he said.

I looked to see a poor, starved dog sneaking around
the house. If I had been struck in the face, I could
not have been more shocked and horrified. That pitiful old dog couldn't be Prince, Davy's pet, Prince,
who had a lovely cream ruff, a sunburst of beauty
around his neck, a shining coat, and a beautiful plume
of a tail!

I called to this poor, miserable creature. He
crawled on his stomach and sneaked up to me, his
string of a tail between his legs. Suddenly I felt
sick. I staggered. Feebly I pulled the screen door
open and tried to coax him into the house, but the
poor animal had been taught in a bitter school not
to go into the house. He stood there trembling and
whining, trying to tell me what he had suffered,
how hard he had found life since I had gone away.
It was all too plain in his pitiful body and fear-filled
eyes. He was a ghost of the Prince that had lived
there with his kind master, Davy.

Tears, hot blinding tears, ran down my face. I
could not see as I stumbled about trying to find
food that he used to like. He ate ravenously, gulp-
ing in terror lest the other dogs come and drive him
away. I went into the house for more food, and
when I returned I saw the poor, bewildered dog
running after the man and his team as he drove
away. Poor Prince! Poor, brokenhearted thing! He
did not know where to turn. Everyone had failed

him since he had lost his master. He had come with the horses and he must follow them.

I waited most of the night, thinking Prince would return. When Hughie came, I sent him many miles to try to find him. I was sick with grief. I could not rest. When Hughie returned, he had not found the dog. No one ever knew his sad fate. I learned that little Pussy had frozen to death in the winter.

I felt that I had failed Davy in not standing by his beloved pets. The work had not been as trying as the grief that tore at my heart about the dog and cat he had loved so well and had treated like children. At night I would go to Davy's grave and cry and grieve as I had never cried over anything before. Never before had I been unfaithful to a trust. I had always done what I thought was my best. Now I had failed poor Prince and Pussy, Davy's friends. Nothing that happened in the North hurt me like this tragedy which came to Davy's pets.

"I should never have gone away," I mourned. "I was not so sick but that I could have stayed at home and taken care of Davy's dog and cat. I never failed Davy while he lived, but I certainly did after he died."

I was thankful for work. It helped. It made me grateful for the quiet hours when they came. I would steal away through the pine trees to Davy's grave.

In my sleep, half waking, I listened for him to call, missing the care of him. It seemed strange to put out my hand, as I often did, to see if he were covered, and now, not to find him there. It was queer, even when he was so sick, that it had never occurred to me that life could go on and Davy not be there.

One day I found his old pipe in the dresser drawer. I held the pipe in my hand. I pressed it to my cheek. I could see his delicate, sensitive fingers on it. Poor Davy, his pipe was always a comfort to him. I smiled sadly as I minded how he had enjoyed having me smoke with him. Yes, he would want me to have this comfort now. I took out his leather tobacco pouch and filled it, closed my door, and smoked Davy's pipe. It was the first time I had smoked since Davy died. I was comforted. This was the closest I had come to Davy since he left me.

I set about improving the hotel. I must be active, make things move. The place looked forlorn and shabby since the flood. Things needed paint and fixing up. I worked hard, scrubbing, painting, cleaning, making everything look as it used to look. I welcomed the work. It kept me from thinking.

"Nothing else can happen," I thought.

Then came the message that the Lee family were moving from Dawson to live in Vancouver. I always felt I had these dear friends close. Now I must give them up. Even Mr. Lawrence, my close neighbor, talked of going Outside.

A year after Davy was gone a letter came. I opened it anxiously. I was from my dear old friend, Jack MacDonald. As the house was full of people at the time, I had only a moment to glance through it. I was amazed at the contents.

When all my work was finished, I went out by my river to read it over carefully. No schoolboy could have written his sweetheart a more loving letter. He began at the beginning. About our seventeen days on the scow when we went over the Waterways; how he had admired my brave spirit, facing everything that happened.

His horror of seeing me almost drowned the time I fell into the river the first year we lived on Stewart Island. How fortunate he was to have been the one to save me.

The winter when Davy almost died with pneumonia, when we were alone, and he came to our rescue. How I was always laughing and standing up to every hardship, doing my duty and enjoying it. He spoke of my sense of humor and how we always laughed together. Jack forgot nothing.

All the years he had loved my friendship, I was the bravest woman he had ever known. Now that I was alone in the world, would I let him come for me and take me to his home on Peace River? "I have a nice farm and a good house all ready for you," he wrote. Then he told of this home he had built for my comfort, and how always I had been there, he thought, sharing it with him. "Now, Peggy, will you let this dream come true? Will you be my wife?" he asked. It was a long, long, loving letter. I had never known he felt this way about me.

The same day a letter came from Doctor La Chapell saying he was going to Mayo on a hunting trip and would stop on his way, and that I must be all ready to go home with him.

Later, when he arrived in his boat, he bustled into The Roadhouse. "Hello, Mother," he shouted, his ruddy face shining. "When I get back you must be all ready to go home with me. I'll get some good bear meat to take back with us."

There was a dance-hall girl at The Roadhouse waiting for the Mayo boat. She was in a big hurry as she wanted to get her business in Mayo finished and be back to Stewart in time to catch the last boat going Outside before the freeze-up. The doctor, with his usual generous spirit, offered to take her in his boat; and in that way she would save time. The girl was very grateful to get this opportunity. I was glad to see it working out so well for her.

She ran down the trail following the kind doctor, skipping like a schoolgirl. Turning around, she waved her hand to me. The doctor shouted, "I'll be back soon." I stood watching them out of sight.

I thought of the story the girl had told me. Poor girl. I did so hope she could make the boat for Outside. She wanted to get back to the States to be with her mother and little daughter. She cried as she told me about her mother.

"Poor Maw," she said, "how good she always was to me. When my husband was sick and later died, she took us in and cared for baby Hazel while I worked. I got the crazy idea of going to the Klondike. She didn't say much against it. I could see she did not want me to go, but she gave me all her life's savings, and promised to care for Hazel. She was that kind of mother. I never realized how good she was until I got up here and was all alone. Dear Maw, if I can only get home I'll make it all up to her. I came up North thinking gold could be picked up anyplace, just picked up. What an awakening I got!

"At first I did the simple things I knew, cooking, making beds, and waiting tables. It was all so cold and lonely. I kept thinking of poor Maw and little Hazel. I must send them money and I couldn't make enough, everything cost so much just to live.

"It was then I met a girl who worked in a dance hall. She was getting rich and saving all she could. I went with her to get a job. Then it was all over. I didn't dare let myself think of what Maw would say. I sent home all the money as fast as I made it.

"I'm glad they'll never know. Sometimes I almost go mad remembering. Do you think when I get back home I can ever forget and begin over again, a new life with Maw and little Hazel?"

"To be sure you can," I told her. "Your life here is ended, just as if a door closed, shutting it all away. Life is like the Yukon River. Rushing on and on, flowing, flowing — that is life. Everything passes. Nothing stays. There is nothing made by regrets; let them go like the river. Build a new life, new and clean. You can do this. You have the present. That is all there is. You must be happy for your Maw and little girl."

"I'll never forget what you have told me," she cried. All at once she threw her arms about me.

"Oh, you do believe I can do it! I was afraid. You tell me what I have tried to believe. Now I know I can do it. Thank you! God bless you! I never was so happy in all my life. I'll never forget about the river."

When, in a few days, the boat arrived from Mayo, I expected the young woman who had gone away with the doctor. I worried, for I was afraid she would miss the last boat going Outside. After all her happiness and anticipation, I did not want her to miss her chance. I had the operator telegraph to Mayo. There was no word about her. Up to the last moment before the boat sailed, I hoped she might appear in the doctor's boat in time to catch the last boat before the freeze-up. But the boat pulled out and the girl had not come. I knew something had happened.

Fear struck me when, later in the day, Rufus, the doctor's little cocker spaniel, scratched at the kitchen door, crying to get in. I opened the door. He ran about in circles, crying and acting unlike the usually quiet little dog he was. He was almost starved, and gulped a few mouthfuls, then ran all over the room, whining and looking for his master. Finally he jumped up on the couch in the Public Room, still crying.

I hurried to the Police Barracks. A search was started. They found the doctor's boat upside down. But the bodies of the young woman and the doctor were never recovered. What had happened could only be surmised. All that was left was the doctor's faithful little dog who had been days finding his way back to his master's friends.

For weeks, until the freeze-up, the police continued their search for the doctor's body. As for me, I went about the house in a stupor.

The kind, generous doctor who had always been a wall of strength to me! Little Rufus followed me very close, turning his sad, soulful eyes up to my face. A long, lonely winter lay before me. I didn't have the doctor's home now, his love and kindness.

In my letter to Jack I had told him how he was as dear to me as my own brother Jack, and that I longed to see him; for the rest I could not promise. In the spring, when navigation opened, I asked him to come on a visit to Stewart. It would do us both good to talk over old times. I could not promise to marry Jack. How could I? Davy had been my husband, and always would be.

During this time I tried to fit my life into a new and different groove. Few winter travelers came in over the trail, and I had little to do. I did not understand why I felt so weak. Rheumatism was affecting my feet. There were times when I found it hard to walk. My hands were swollen, too, and very painful.

The telegraph operator was one of my best friends, and a daily visitor. Each evening he would come poking his head into the door, always with a joke and a laugh. I would beg him to come in. But no, he was going along; he must "catch up with his reading."

"Come in, I have something I want to tell you," I would say. Then he would come in and sit down, ready to go at a moment's notice. But we would start talking of what we had both been reading, and before he arose to go the clock would point to eleven or twelve o'clock. Every night there was the same procedure. This man was well read and full of information. Each month he allowed himself ten dollars' worth of books and magazines. These he shared with me. We discussed and argued the world's news, the reports of which he brought each night.

At Christmas time he made a path through the

woods to the little cemetery, and he took me there
and left me by Davy's grave. I could hardly walk,
the rheumatism was so bad in my legs. He came
for me later, and helped me home. He was a kind
man.

Hughie was kind to me, too. He had lived in The
Roadhouse for years after Walter's death, and had
carried the mail. In the winter he had a trap line
that he went over. It took him away from home
for days at a time. When he returned he would
come in, his coat, parka, mittens, all covered with
frost. "Well, how have you been keeping since I've
been gone?" he would say. He was a comfort to me.

The house was lonely and quiet most of the time.
Never a day passed that I did not go out and sit
by my river, even in the cold. The river was a beloved friend and companion! On long winter nights
I would sit until I was almost frozen, watching the
river like a silver road, a highway paved with diamonds, the distant, majestic mountains sleeping in
the Great White Stillness, and overhead a glorious
velvet sky with shining stars. I mind of how as a
child my father showed me the stars, and I thought
they were tiny peepholes into Heaven, and had wished
I could look closely and see the angels playing their
golden harps.

It was a marvelous experience there alone. I would
forget how cold it was, and stay on and on. I did
not feel lonely then, but content, just as if I were a
part of everything, even the sleeping river, the sky,
and the Great White Stillness.

I had the good fortune to witness a strange sight
that winter. In the distance, over the white, sleep-

ing mountains, hung a golden lantern in the sky, just as if a giant who had been carrying it had disappeared, leaving the golden Chinese lantern suspended in space. All at once it opened up like a big book, the pages fluttering, as on and on it sailed. I sat watching, waiting for something more to happen, but that was all. It stayed suspended, fluttering and waving. I grew so cold that at last I had to leave. But the next night I was there to watch, and again the Chinese lantern appeared. Again it opened into a book and there it stayed. This kept up for a week or longer. I wondered that there was not more excitement about such an extraordinary phenomenon. "The Northern Lights have seen queer sights," as Robert Service said.

Winter was away. Spring was in the air. I was looking forward, day to day, watching the ice go out, thinking of Jack's promise to be on the first boat. How I would enjoy seeing him. Could Jack make me laugh, as of old? I sat by the river—waiting.

The first boat arrived at last. It was bringing my dear and faithful friend. I put on the new dress that Belle had sent to me, and even a touch of powder.

As the boat tied up, I stood at the head of the trail, waiting. People were coming up. Where was Jack? A big, tall man was pushing through. No, it was not Jack. Everyone coming ashore was at The Roadhouse. He might be talking to the captain. I could not believe he had not come. Jack was not like that; he always did what he said.

The first boat of the year caused much excitement. I was putting the dinner on the table—when I saw someone laying my mail on the sideboard.

There was a letter from Peace River. It was not in Jack's handwriting. A little shiver ran through me. What had happened? I asked the captain if Jack MacDonald was on the passenger list. I did not need to listen for his answer—I knew. As soon as I was free, I took my letters and went out by the river. I stared at the letter from Peace River. Was Jack so ill he could not write? I dreaded opening it. I held it a long time in my hands. Then I read:

I am grieved to tell you that my brother Jack died just a week ago from pneumonia. His death was very sudden. He had been working hard to have things in perfect order on his farm. He was bringing a wife back, he told us. He did not say who she was, but I knew you were the only woman he loved.

I hasten to send you this sad message, as no doubt you will wonder at his not arriving on the first boat.

JACK'S BROTHER

No more could happen. I did not move. My river continued to flow on and on. All ties were cut —brother Jack, Davy, Belle, and the kind doctor, Jack—no one left! I sat by the river all night. In the morning I went in to carry on the daily duties of my life.

Mr. Lawrence came to my door and said: "Come see this." I took my hands from the dough and quickly washed them, drying them on the corner of my apron as I hurried to catch up with him. Something of importance must have happened or he would not call me like this. We stood on the bank of the river looking into a large city with tall houses, people walking, cabs drawn by high-stepping horses, trees blowing, a street full of activ-

ity; a city there by the river, up in the sky. The
illusion lasted but a short time, then gradually faded.
We looked at each other. We had beheld a miracle
of nature.

"It may be a premonition that someday there will
be a great city right here," I cried, breathlessly.

"No," said Mr. Lawrence, "it is only a mirage.
It occurs when the lower strata of air are at a very
different temperature from the higher strata so that
the sky is seen as a reflection."

"That happens once in a lifetime," said another
man who had also been watching. "The sun shining
brightly on some city reflected against the high
glaciers and is again reflected here in the clear air."

Nevertheless I liked to think that someday a city
might be born beside my river, where many people
would come to know the beauty of this beloved
land, the sweet clean air, the distant mountains, and
the power of the mighty Yukon.

The Mystery Woman first appeared out of no
place. The wires buzzed all along Telegraph Creek.
But it was a month before she arrived at The Roadhouse on Stewart. She had followed the poles via
Telegraph Creek and Atlin to Whitehorse, and to
Stewart Crossing, which was about fifty miles up
the Stewart from Stewart City. The operator on
Stewart Island had heard about the Mystery Woman
from the other operators, and her appearance was
anxiously awaited all along the telegraph line. She
must have satisfied the police, or she could not have
passed Whitehorse. However, the police do not talk.
It remained a mystery, why a young woman, un-

known, with only one dog, packing a frying pan, a tin coffeepot, a few provisions and a small roll of blankets, could be walking alone through the country, telling nothing about herself, answering all questions with a smile and a shrug of the shoulders. Where did she come from? Where was she going? No one knew. It made everyone anxious about this lone woman, sleeping out in the open whenever she could not make it to a camp.

In summer bears were to be feared, even by hunters. When coming into a camp she was offered the hospitality of the North, which she accepted, eating and sleeping, offering no money in payment, but leaving with a quiet "thank you," revealing nothing about herself. Though she talked little, she listened with a smile to the good advice about the country and the dangers that beset a lonely traveler.

She lost her dog. It was drowned in crossing a river. She seemed to become more human and less mysterious, telling everyone how she missed her companion. But absolutely nothing about herself. When she left a station, the operator sent the information along the line. She followed the poles to Stewart Crossing and stopped at the surveyors' camp near Mayo. The men told her that if she would wait, some of the men who were going to Dawson in a couple of days would take her along, since she had told them she was going that way. Smiling, she refused, without explaining why. It was aggravating to the men. She was stubborn, they thought.

Below Mayo she bought a long hunting boat from an Italian. It was a cumbersome thing, hard even for a man to manage, to say nothing of a woman.

She evidently had money for she paid him sixty dollars for the unwieldy craft. The men at the surveyors' camp told this Italian he should not have sold her such a dangerous boat.

She arrived at The Roadhouse on Stewart Island. She came in one evening, smiling and friendly. Supper was over, but I set about preparing a meal for her. I never pried into the affairs of my guests. If they wished to tell me about themselves, they could do so. I thought the woman might be Russian. She was quite good-looking, except that her teeth were badly decayed. She spoke with an accent, using gestures to make her meaning clear.

The next morning she came to the kitchen and smiled at me. "I go now, and thank you." She offered no money. I was glad. It just saved a lot of talk, as I would not have taken it.

"I go on to Dawson. Everyone ask why I go alone. I not tell them. Someday I come back! Then I tell *you*, but now I do not talk. You were kind to me. Thank you." She moved with a gentle grace and spoke in a soft, foreign way.

When she left I went with her down to the river. She got into her boat. It was during the equinoctial storms and I have never seen the river wilder or more on a rampage. I was worried about the poor young thing. Around and around she whirled in that crazy boat. I was badly frightened. It was a job for a strong man, and few would have undertaken it. But she seemed utterly devoid of fear. About an hour she struggled to get into the main stream and on her way. I was worn out from watching her. At last she won out and went whirling along. A wave of her little thin hand, and she was out of sight around the bend of the river. I worried about the girl for days, until word came that she had reached Dawson in safety.

The police at Dawson would not permit her to go on at the time. She spent the winter, working in one of the hotels as a chambermaid. Still no one got her story. She never told anything of her past. She remained a mystery woman.

In the spring she was off. The police could not detain her. She knew her rights. She said she was going to Alaska, nothing more. No word was heard from her. Someone found an old sweater she had started away in, and that is all we ever heard about her. Even the police were helpless to find the Mystery Woman.

CHAPTER SIXTEEN

I Go Outside

Now THAT I WAS alone much of the time I took great pleasure in my pets. They were good company. When Davy and I had first come to the island years ago, there were many squirrels. A family of them ran about on the roof and played in the trees. Davy enjoyed feeding them. When he went out to the woodpile, they ran over his back and shoulders while he was working.

There are always enemies for the little folk of the forest. The squirrels had been able to outwit the dogs, but one day along came a "smart-aleck old fool," and unknown to us, he shot all the little squirrels for amusement and laid their warm little bodies on the floor at my feet, saying, "Here, now, we can have fried squirrel for supper." One could imagine how I welcomed this. I felt like shooting him.

There had been few squirrels about for years. A family of them came scampering over the roof and played about. I welcomed anything that asked for my attention. It was a cold winter, and I was afraid that they might not have enough to eat. Every morning I fed them their favorite food. The little fellows would come to the kitchen door, climbing to the very top, and feeling about the crack with their little paws, "peepin" in at the windows, watching anxiously until I came with their breakfast of grain or prunes. I had a hard time keeping them out of the house. They were afraid of strangers but, when

I was alone, in they would scamper, if I left a door ajar. They would run over the room, dashing about, getting into anything, even lifting lids of pots and pans. When I fed them they sat up, blowing on their little paws to warm them, turning the prune and nibbling all about it. They seemed to laugh and chatter, their bright eyes sparkling. They afforded me a great deal of entertainment.

The same winter that the squirrels appeared, a flock of birds were late in getting away. They had been about the door eating some of the grain with the squirrels. They put off their departure from day to day, until at last it was cold, and I was afraid they were waiting too long to fly South. I was grieved when I knew they could not possibly get away. Each day when I fed them with the squirrels, they sat close to the windows, on the window shelf, for a bit of warmth, "The pity of the poor, doomed things!" I grieved. One deadly cold spell they all froze. The yard was sprinkled with their dear little bodies. It was too much for me. I was sick to see such a sorry sight.

It was now the fourth spring since Davy left me. I was never the same, for he had taken a part of me with him. I need not dwell on it; it is an experience every woman knows who has lost a lifetime mate. And yet, when one is self-supporting and alone, there is nothing to do but to go on from day to day, keeping things moving, without too much time spent in self-pity. I had to learn this lesson as all do. Others counted on me for encouragement and cheer. Was I to let them down? Could I laugh a happy laugh no more?

The winter had been very quiet. There was not much gold mining, though the silver mines at Mayo were still operating, and there was always wood to be cut. But few people were traveling over the ice trails now during the winter, although after the breakup the summers were as busy as usual. Busier, in fact, since more tourists were coming each year. The old sourdoughs were not fond of them. "They ask such fool questions, and are a lot of trouble," they would say. But for my part I was glad to have them, and I saw it in a coming rebirth of activity for this area.

My eyes were troubling me. I could not read with the poor glasses I had, and I planned to go to Dawson to have new ones made. My teeth, too, were giving me trouble; many long winter nights I had the toothache for unwelcome company. On one of the boats in the early spring, a young doctor came ashore saying, "My wife told me not to come back if I had not pulled your teeth, so let us get at it." The doctor and his wife had visited on the island the summer before. The young woman had taken a fancy to me, and had wanted me to come to Dawson to have my teeth attended to.

The doctor pulled eighteen teeth for me. He was not a dentist, but he made a good job of it. I wished to pay him.

"If I took money from you, that wife of mine would have me scalped," he exclaimed.

The captain of the boat had tied up on purpose so the doctor could pull my teeth. A year later, when this young couple went abroad, they sent word to me that they would pay my expenses to Scotland. However, I could not accept their kindness.

In the fall I was taken ill and had to hire an old man on the island to help with the cooking. At last I was forced to give up and go to bed. It was discouraging not to be able to rise and attend to my duties. I had always felt they could not go on without me. All winter I was sick and suffering. I tried not to let anyone know how badly my feet and hands hurt me. It was misery even to get out of bed and wait on myself.

I began to wonder what would become of me. It was the first time in my life I could not throw off sickness.

"Ah, the troubles that affect the just," I thought. I never knew one could have so many things the matter. I felt ashamed not to be about taking care of the travelers who came to The Roadhouse.

For the first time since I lived by the river I was glad to welcome the freeze-up and dreading to see the breakup in the spring. I had no interest in anything. The days that had been so colorful now seemed drab and dreary.

In the spring as I watched my river flowing, flowing, changing, changing, I remembered what I had told the young woman about life's being like the river. All at once I was thankful. "I still have my river," I thought. "I could not live without my river. It is all I have left."

After one particularly hard night of suffering and wakefulness, I realized that the time had come for action. No longer could I go on this way. I could not run the hotel. I was sick and miserable. But what to do? I had no one to turn to. My little prayer prayed itself over and over, "Show me what to do, and give me strength to do it."

It was only a short time after this lonely night that Hughie said, as he came in with the mail, "Here is a big fat letter for you from California! It may be from that long-lost nephew Dave was always wishing he could find." He laid the letter in my lap.

I opened it. What a surprise! Like a dream, Hughie's joke about the nephew had come true, just like a fairy tale. Here was a long letter, full of news from the nephew about himself and his wife, and questions about his favorite uncle. He recalled how his Uncle Davy and Aunt Peggy had come to see his father's family in Chicago when he was a little lad, bringing him a beautiful red setter dog, Bruce, as well as a little steam engine. This dog had been one of the high spots in his childhood, and he had never forgotten his uncle. He had lost track of him while he was at college, when his father had died and the home was broken up.

For years, he said, he had tried to contact his uncle, and at last relatives in Scotland had sent him this address. He hoped to hear all about us. It was a kind, friendly letter, and it put new life into me. I answered it at once, telling him of Davy's death, and of my illness.

Back came a letter as soon as possible, with a kind invitation to come and make my home in Southern California. My nephew had plenty of room in his home. His wife, who had just lost her mother, put in a kind letter, wanting me to come. Captain Hogan and his wife, who lived on the island, would gladly pay my price for The Roadhouse. It was all easy.

Only—I could not make up my own mind! How could I leave my home on the island? Davy's grave and my river?

Hughie thought I was foolish.

"Don't you remember those poor birds that froze to death because they didn't go when they had the chance? You often talked about how foolish they were, not to get out, go south. Well, it looks to me you might be like them."

I lay awake all night for many nights, wondering what to do. Before, my prayers were always answered. Now I must wait and wait. Many friends gave advice, yet, I, myself, did not know what I wanted to do.

I knew I could sell The Roadhouse if I wished. In fact, I had a family who wanted it and were waiting for me to make up my mind. But what is this thing within us which refuses to yield? This stubborn something which clings to the dead past, to old things?

Deep within me, I found the answer. I couldn't give it up until I had something else to take its place. That was what I had to find. Something to take hold of, something to carry me on, not just to sit and be a has-been. As time passed, it came to me that I needed first of all a change of heart, a newness of spirit, that eternal something which makes all things new. When everything else is taken away, when one starts losing one's sight and cannot read, when one loses one's health and cannot work, then the time has come. "Man's extremity is God's oppor-

tunity." I had let my life become stale, with grief
and the self-pity habit. Daily I prayed my little
prayer over and over, "Oh, God, show me what to
do, and give me strength to do it." Sometimes it
was just words, then again there was great illumi-
nation.

Then, in time, a change began to come. Too long,
now, Peggy had done it all, Peggy, with her determination and drive, Peggy, who always had the feeling there was nothing she could not do and that
she would always be equal to anything. But time
had beaten the old Peggy down, it seemed, and now
she had to be really willing to leave it to God to
lead her on, to take her there, all the way, and not
to leave her useless, too late, helpless like the birds.

It was not at all what one might have expected.
The way it worked out, it was quite plainly and
simply what one might call a beautiful ending to
a long journey, and quite in line, I think, with
everything else that has happened in this wonderful
life of mine. It was to take me on, on, and on, for
many new years of health, happiness and love, sunshine, warmth and freedom. The dim, dark winter
of my life, of which I have told in this chapter,
was to pass away as a dream.

The real thing that decided it, however, that
seemed to be the answer, came one morning in the
mail. It was a letter from Belle, telling of her husband's illness, and that now she could never come
back to the Yukon, how she wished I was near her.
So once more someone needed me. I gave in and
wrote to my nephew that I was coming Outside.

The main reason was to be close to Belle—to be of use once more.

Now that I had made up my mind, my time was taken up in preparation. I had sold my Roadhouse, in which I had spent so many happy years. It was hard to give it up, but I did not hesitate. Determined to leave everything in perfect order in the garden as well as in the house, I toiled early and late.

I gathered papers, old clothes, and personal things into a pile and set fire to them. The flames liked the dry grass, the fire blazed high. All at once I realized I was surrounded by flames, like greedy hands, catching the grass all about, reaching for my clothes. The dry grass came up to the very door. I cried out, not knowing which way to run. A young man who had been working for me came to my rescue, and with wet blankets and brooms beat out the flames. He saved The Roadhouse. I was worn out by the battle with the fire, knowing the whole island might have burned.

Now I must leave my river, and I might never see it again. Toward midnight I crept away to the little graveyard among the pines to say good-by to Davy's grave.

For hours I sat where Davy's voice whispered to me in the breeze through the pines overhead. Once I reached out to touch the mound of earth, and with the contact of my fingers on the pine needles, I could feel a steady flow of warmth. Somehow, it came to me then that he had not gone, that he had not died, but that he would sing forever in the soft wind that breathed through the pines above me.

The next day I was ready to go with my friend,

Jim McLaughlin, who had offered to take me in his boat to Dawson. He knew I would enjoy the trip, and I could rest before the journey Outside.

My worldly possessions were in a small basket at my feet in Jim's boat when we started our journey. It was June, springtime in the Yukon. In the trees along the bank of the river the birds were singing, and gay flowers decked the woods in a riot of color. The river was swift, full of strength and power, but I found Jim to be a splendid boatman. There was nothing to be anxious about; it was all beautiful! I lived in the present and enjoyed the trip to the utmost, letting go the thought that this would be my last boat ride upon my river. All too soon the hundred miles slipped past and we were in Dawson.

I went to a hotel, as I did not want to go to my friend's home until I had completed my plans and had bought a trunk and suitcase and packed my new things into them. I had to have a dignified appearance among my old friends. Also, I wanted to do something I had longed to do, ever since I had come to the Yukon. I wanted to see the Klondike district. Now that I was leaving the North, I must view it, even from a distance!

Later I stood, in an unforgettable moment, on Midnight Dome, or King Solomon's Dome as it is also called, where one can have a splendid panoramic view of the whole Klondike. To this prominence, 4,220 feet above sea level, I had longed to come, ever since I had entered the Yukon over thirty years before.

I was saying my good-by to the North, and I was now on my way to that long-lost land, called among us up here the "Outside." Events happen rapidly when one's mind is made up. For the moment, however, I was lost in reverie. When Davy and I had started North, the Klondike was to be the promised land to us but, like Moses, we had never been permitted to enter it. We had never put our hands on the gold of the earth, for which we and all the others had come . . . and we lived the whole time on the edge of this promised land, where our lives were spent in taking care of those others who came in or went out.

Now I must have this view, even from a distance. I paid a man to take me from Dawson to the Dome, and from there I saw all the famous creeks about which I had heard so many dramatic tales: Klondike, Bonanza, Hunkers, Last Chance, Goldbottom, Dominion, El Dorado, Eureka, Little Blanch, Indian, and many others. These famous creeks did not at all look as I had expected them to look, according to what I had heard from the original miners who had dug here for gold with their picks and shovels, and washed out their "pay dirt" in rockers or sluices . . . who had thawed the ever-frozen ground with wood fires and hoisted the gravel from the bottom of the shafts to the surface by hand-operated windlasses.

I was shocked now to see the great piles of "tailings," gravel, stone, and yellow dirt which had been torn up by the huge dredges which later had come into use. They were capable of mining more ground in a day than a dozen men could in a year. All was changed since the men I had known had worked these creeks. Some had gone away rich and successful, some beaten and broken. Now, even the great dredges were mostly abandoned.

The few miners I had known who had stayed on were like the birds—too late. I found myself saddened. I, too, belonged to the thrilling past of the great gold rush, days and years filled to the brim with excitement, adventure, and romance. But as I stood there, it was with deep gratitude and conviction that I realized that this was not all . . . for this little bird was poised for flight, to state it simply. Oh, yes, there would always have been a life for me here, if I had wished to remain. I knew that. I still had friends, I still had security, I still had usefulness in me, and I still had the feeling that this was home. The tourists in summer would have kept The Roadhouse alive, and I would always have welcomed them as they came in increasing numbers. But it was time for me to retire and seek more comfort and a more temperate climate where I would not have the hard winters to endure in my later years. Then, too, I would be with my own relatives and, best of all, with my dear friend Belle.

The greatest peace comes when one knows that one is not running away from anything . . . when one knows that all is well, whether he *stays* or *goes*. Then one can go happily, joyously, freely, courageously, and face the opportunity which lies ahead.

This, then, is what I knew as I said farewell to the Klondike from the heights of the Dome and went back to Dawson to prepare for my journey. Davy's nephew, Graham Shand, was to meet me at Skagway and I was going with him to Southern California. There I was going to live with Graham and his wife, and be near Belle, too, which was best of all.

I had some bills to settle in Dawson. I was moved deeply by the kindness of old friends. Of all the merchants with whom we had done business, several told me, "No bill here at this store." One druggist cut his bill in half, after I refused to let him cancel it altogether. I was leaving the Yukon not owing a cent. I was not a rich woman, but I felt I had been successful in serving and surviving, and had a little to show for it, though not a great fortune that Davy had dreamed about.

On the trip back, as the boat passed Stewart Island, I could not go out and meet my friends, even though they were gathered there to see me off. I hid in my cabin until the boat pulled away from the shore, and then I crept out to watch the world I knew slipping away from me.

The boat took me to Whitehorse, and from there across White Pass I traveled by the railroad to Skagway. My nephew met me there.

"I would ha' known you any place by that Scotch face of yours," I said to him after the first words of greeting. "I mind so well how you looked as a wee lad, when your uncle gave you the dog, Bruce." I still held his hand in mine. "Your uncle talked about you all the years and tried to find you. It is a sad thing that he is na' with me this day."

There were several friends I wanted to see in Skagway. We called on one, the agent of the Canadian Railway. He was pleased to hear about my future home in Southern California. "I certainly hope you do not encounter difficulties getting your aunt into the United States," he said to my nephew, shaking his head doubtfully.

I could see my nephew was surprised. He hadn't considered this angle when taking on this new responsibility. It had not occurred to him that there might be trouble with the United States Department of Immigration. My friend suggested that we go to the Labor Commissioner in Skagway and perhaps he would know what to do. We found the Commissioner an agreeable gentleman. He made us happy by assuring us that we would have no trouble entering the United States. He would give us a letter to the Vice-Consul at Vancouver. He had done this many times and had never heard of any trouble connected with such cases. It did not enter our minds but what he knew what he was talking about.

My nephew exchanged his ticket for a Canadian vessel that would stop at Vancouver. He bought my ticket and had all my worldly possessions shipped in bond to San Diego, my future home.

I now had the opportunity to enjoy the beautiful scenery of the Inside Passage and to live over the experience of the other trip Davy and I had made in these same waters. The boat at that time had been crowded with gold seekers. What high hopes Davy and I had had for the future. Davy was always confident he would strike it rich. Oh, well! We had had a happy life in the Yukon, whilse. Those memories shine brighter than any gold that glitters. I would na' trade them for all the lucky strikes made in the gold rush. How many thousand times I have wished Davy and I could live them all over again.

When my nephew and I arrived in Vancouver, I was startled at the change in everything. The traffic and noise confused me. I stopped stock still and looked about.

"Where is everyone going in such a hurry?" I asked. What a difference from the horse and buggy days that Davy and I had known! I longed for Davy to be with me, watching this changed world. Automobiles filled the streets. They went so fast and honked their horns so loud. I was almost afraid to get into the one my nephew hired to take us to the office of the Vice-Consul. But I wouldn't let on.

At this office my nephew presented the letter. The Vice-Consul read it, then laid it down. He looked at me a long time.

"Madam," he said, "it will be impossible for you to enter the United States at this time. There are over two thousand requests ahead of yours. It will take a year or more before your application can even come up for consideration."

I stared at him blankly. What did he mean? *I could na' understand.* I had sold my Roadhouse and accepted my nephew's kind invitation to live with him. It was all settled.

The Vice-Consul cleared his throat, took his glasses from his nose, cleaned them with his handkerchief, and put them back on. Then he looked at me kindly. He seemed to realize what a shock this was.

"I'm sorry, Madam," he said, "but these are government regulations. I can do nothing about them. I could not take my own mother into the country under these conditions. You understand how it is. It takes a long time to get through," he explained.

My nephew's face went white. I could see he realized he had made a big mistake. He was not the kind of man to get himself into embarrassing situations.

He looked at me. There was so much pity in his eyes I could hardly bear it. He realized what he had done. I was uprooted from my home and brought into all these difficulties, in a strange place, after years in the Yukon. I could see how sick he felt. Yet his intentions had been the best. He wanted to give me security and comfort in my old age.

"I'll put up a cash bond," my nephew said quickly. "That will assure you my aunt will never become a public charge. Also, I will guarantee to provide her sufficient money for all her needs."

"I'm sorry," the Consul said, "but that is impossible. However, you might take it up with the Immigration Department. Perhaps you might get in for a year's visit."

Listening intently, I tried to appear calm, but my hands trembled. Fumblingly I removed my gloves and put them into my new pocketbook.

What was happening? Why should it be so difficult for me to get back into the United States? Davy and I had lived there for years before we went to the Yukon. What did it mean?

From the time I had made up my mind to accept my nephew's offer and had sold my Roadhouse, everything had fitted into a pattern. This was the first thing to go wrong. I looked at my poor nephew. I had never seen anyone so upset, so shaken. I felt that sorry for him I almost forgot about myself.

"Come," he said, taking my arm in a protective

way, "we'll go to the Immigration Department and
see what we can do there."

The clerk at the desk gave me a visitor's application blank to fill out.

"You might make a three months' stay," he suggested.

"But by that time," I explained, "the river will
be frozen over and I could na' make the long trip
over the ice by dog team."

I thought to myself, "Where would I go if I did
go back? I have no home."

"When does the ice break up and the boats get
through?" he asked.

I told him. He set a date that he thought would
give me plenty of time. Then he picked up the papers
and ushered us into another office.

Here the man was more considerate.

"Why don't you stay a year?" he asked.

After many questions and explanations, the papers
were made out, not for a year, but this time for
permanent entry.

We were sent to still another department. We sat
in the outer office adjoining the Committee Room.
The door was closed between, and a man was peering
through the keyhole. I surmised he was trying to
hear what was going on inside. When a young couple
came out, he joined them. My nephew said that he
must be their lawyer and had advised them what
to say.

"I wish I had obtained this same coaching for you,"
he told me.

The door opened again and an officer beckoned
to me. We both rose, but my nephew was denied

admittance. I followed the man. Several officials were seated around a big table, with a stenographer taking notes. I sat all by myself in a big chair, my feet not even reaching the floor. I tried to hold my own in spite of the hard grilling. I was questioned until my head was in a whirl.

In about an hour they asked my nephew to come in. From the serious faces of the men, it was clear something was definitely wrong.

"Sir," began the chairman, "we are sorry to inform you that your aunt cannot be admitted to the United States. As far as we can ascertain, she is a British subject. She voted at the local elections and she claims to be as favorable to the Canadian government as to the United States. Her answers will not admit her. This report must be sent in. However, you have the privilege, if you so desire, of appealing our decision to Washington."

A painful silence filled the room. All eyes were upon me. I tried not to betray how upset I felt. I minded I must be like my mother used to tell me when I was a wee lass. "Never shed tears before folk," she often cautioned. "Be cool, calm, and collected."

But I was sure that if I did not get out of that big chair and away from the men staring at me, I'd disgrace myself by crying. There was a lump in my throat and my eyes burned. The strain was almost more than I could bear. I looked at the members of the committee and thought, "Now those men really want to help me if they can only find a way to do it." Then I smiled at them, and the tension was broken. They moved restlessly in their chairs.

Something must be done before this meeting was adjourned. Even I could see that.

My nephew arose and addressed the committee. He told me later a Divine Providence must have prompted him to say what he did. He remembered all at once that his uncle had enlisted in the Spanish-American War and was assigned as an engineer on the *Oregon* which was to take a trip around the Horn. However, before the ship left San Francisco, he was taken down with a recurrence of tropical fever that he had contracted in the jungles of South America. He was sent to the hospital and later discharged from the navy for physical disability.

I was proud of my nephew. He told them Davy had offered his life to serve for his adopted country —now they would not let his widow re-enter the States where there would be security for her old age. He felt his country was not fair and just under the circumstances. I could see the men were impressed. They discussed the matter in an undertone, and then the chairman spoke.

"Our advice to you is to leave your aunt in Vancouver and go to San Francisco, and if you can find where your uncle voted in the United States, send me the data and, if correct, I will start your aunt on her way to San Diego." He then gave my nephew his card and the meeting was adjourned.

Grahamie and I left the room arm in arm, but I could see that the poor man was still worried. How was he going to prove Davy had ever voted. The San Francisco earthquake had destroyed all records.

I was not sure Davy ever voted—if he had it must
have been in Novato, near our ranch in California;
the time of the Presidential election when William
Jennings Bryan was making free silver his campaign
topic. Davy was interested and talked politics a great
deal at this time. Anyway, I gave Grahamie this
information and he wrote it all down in a little book
he carried in his pocket.

I wanted him to know I felt all right about everything. He had meant so well by me. I looked up
into his face. "Dinna' you fret, Grahamie, if you
can na' get that information," I told him. "If it's
impossible for me to get into the United States,
don't grieve. You did it all for the best. You had
my good at heart, I mind this." I hesitated, then said,
"I will go back to Stewart Island and get a little
cabin. There are many empty ones on the island.
I can have a good garden and the boys will always
see that I get plenty of fresh meat. I'll get along,
whilse." I told him this in as brave a voice as I could.

But I did na' feel so brave inside. My roadhouse
was mine no more. Travelers would not be coming
and going, boats stopping and the captains always
dropping in to see how I was keeping. In the little
cabin it would be lonely. Few would find their
way through the woods to my door. Then the cold,
dark winter—that would be hard. I had always
been able to read a great deal in winter. It was my
greatest joy, but now my eyes were getting worse.
The eye doctor I went to see in Dawson about
glasses said I would be compelled to have the cata-
racts removed from my eyes. This worried me a
great deal.

Worst of all, Belle needed me. Her husband was very ill and she was looking forward to my being close to her. This had been the deciding reason for my going to California—to be near Belle. We could see one another often. This was my greatest comfort. Now, if I could na' get to California, I would never see my dear friend again. Fear tore at me. I said to myself, "This won't do!" and I prayed my little prayer. All at once I thought of the time on Chilkoot Pass, and again a wave of strength and power welled up in me. Of course I could go back! I had faced everything that had come to me in my life. I could face this, too. I would still have my beloved river. I would be near Davy. I could sit by his grave and live over the happy years. Yes, I could go back.

I stopped and looked at my nephew. But this time it was different as I patted his arm and smiled into his face. He smiled back at me.

"Don't worry, Aunt Peggy," he said. "I'm not so easily licked. I'll dig up the information. I'm going to take you back to your friends here in Vancouver. You stay there until the authorities let you know just what you can do. I will send you instructions, telling you when you can sail, and make all the arrangements. Now, don't worry."

Later he took the boat for San Francisco. It was hard parting before he left. I knew what it meant to him, and how he blamed himself. Tears were in his eyes and he looked so grieved for me I had a hard time keeping back the tears myself.

Two days later he telephoned me. "I have the information and it is all arranged."

Later his telegram arrived with full instructions as to what I should do. When to sail, and on what boat. He would wait for me in San Francisco and then we would take the steamer for San Diego.

Later, he told me the story. In San Francisco he had presented the case to the Immigration Department. There was a bit of delay. Then he was instructed to call, by long distance, the California State Librarian at Sacramento and have the records examined. The clerk said the records would show if his uncle had voted at this little town, Novato, California, at that time.

Poor Grahamie! It was a painful wait for him. He had doubts if he could get the information—he walked the streets of San Francisco—"sweating blood," as he said. What could he do next if this failed? He couldn't let me down. He said he never had a harder time in all his life. He would never forget those hours. When he went back to the hotel the clerk handed him a special delivery letter. He was afraid to open it. It said:

DEAR SIR:

I have examined the records and find that one David C. Shand did vote in the year ( ) at Novato, California. While the date on the papers did not state that he was a naturalized citizen, it was not customary to do so at that time. It is my opinion that David C. Shand was a citizen of the United States.

Signed
California State Librarian.

I followed Grahamie's instructions and, standing on the deck of the steamer, I looked far out at the blue Pacific, and my thoughts went back to that day, long ago, when I waited on Chilkoot Pass, looking up at the Summit and wondering what lay in store for us—Beyond.

It was a good life. I would live it all over if I could, every day of it. Now, a new life! Yes, and I can never lose the stars overhead.